W9-DDW-672

World Yearbook of Education 1991

Previous titles in this series

World Yearbook of Education 1982/83
Computers and Education
Edited by Jacquetta Megarry, David R. F. Walker, Stanley Nisbet and Eric Hoyle

World Yearbook of Education 1984
Women and Education
Edited by Sandra Acker, Jacquetta Megarry, Stanley Nisbet and Eric Hoyle

World Yearbook of Education 1985
Research, Policy and Practice
Edited by John Nisbet, Jacquetta Megarry and Stanley Nisbet

World Yearbook of Education 1986
The Management of Schools
Edited by Eric Hoyle and Agnes McMahon

World Yearbook of Education 1987
Vocational Education
Edited by John Twining, Stanley Nisbet and Jacquetta Megarry

World Yearbook of Education 1988
Education for the New Technologies
Edited by Duncan Harris (Series Editor)

World Yearbook of Education 1989
Health Education
Edited by Chris James, John Balding and Duncan Harris (Series Editor)

World Yearbook of Education 1990
Assessment and Evaluation
Edited by Chris Bell and Duncan Harris (Series Editor)

World Yearbook of Education 1991

INTERNATIONAL SCHOOLS AND INTERNATIONAL EDUCATION

Edited by Patricia L Jonietz
and Duncan Harris (Series Editor)

Kogan Page, London

Nichols/GP Publishing, New York

First published in 1991

Kogan Page Limited
120 Pentonville Road
London N1 9JN

British Library Cataloguing in Publication Data

A CIP record for this book is available from the British Library.

ISBN 0 7494 0296 2

Library of Congress Cataloging-in-Publication Data

Main entry under title:
World Yearbook of Education: 1991
1. Education - Periodicals

ISBN 0-89397-405-6
LC Catalog No. 32-18413

Typeset by DP Photosetting, Aylesbury, Bucks
Printed and bound in Great Britain by
Biddles Ltd, Guildford

Contents

List of contributors

Robert Blackburn	*Chapters 2 & 26*
Joseph J Blaney, UNIS, New York, USA	*Chapter 23*
James M Caccamo, Special Programs, Independence, Missouri, USA	*Chapter 21*
Maurice W Carder, Vienna International School, Austria	*Chapter 13*
Malcolm Davis, Vienna International School, Austria	*Chapters 7 & 14*
Caroline Ellwood, Vienna International School, Austria	*Chapters 7 & 14*
Joan Freeman, European Council for High Ability, UK	*Chapter 22*
Deon Glover, Atlantic College, Llantwit Major, UK	*Chapter 15*
Ole Hansen, HELIOS, Denmark	*Chapter 19*
Jan Hedvall, JAHAB, Sweden	*Chapter 20*
Robert L Henley, Superintendant Special Programs, Independence, Missouri, USA	*Chapter 21*
Alex Horsley, Atlanta International School, Georgia, USA	*Chapter 12*
Bernard Ivaldi, International School of Geneva, Switzerland	*Chapter 24*
Patricia L Jonietz, London, UK	*Introductions & Chapter 26*
James Keson, Copenhagen International School, Denmark	*Chapter 6*
Jeff Koopman, Jeanne d'Arc, College, Maastricht, The Netherlands	*Chapter 10*
W G Mattern, ECIS, UK	*Chapter 25*
David Parsons, International School of Tanganyika, Dav es Salaam, Tanzania	*Chapter 17*
John Paterson, International Education Consultancy, Somerset, UK	*Chapter 4*
Richard Pearce, International School of London, UK	*Chapter 16*
Gerard Renaud, IBO and ISA, France	*Chapter 1*
John Sadler, UCLES, Cambridge, UK	*Chapter 5*
David Brooke Sutcliffe, United World College of the Adriatic, Duino, Italy	*Chapter 3*
Arturo Tosi, Royal Holloway and Bedford New College, Surrey, UK	*Chapter 11*
John Turner, East Midlands Exam Board, Nottingham, UK	*Chapter 18*
Michael Waldron, Brussels, Belgium	*Chapter 9*

Preface

The *1964 Yearbook of Education* focused on 'Education and International Life'. It was a weighty volume in which individuals from South African, French, Australian, Ceylonese, Russian, British, and American universities, British secondary schools, UNESCO, the Council of Europe, the US Peace Corps, NATO, and a variety of smaller national and international organizations reviewed the 20 years since the end of the Second World War. Just one of the 1964 volume's four aims actually related to schools, organizations, and institutions supplying international education. The contents of the volume imply that only politicians, diplomats, missionaries, and volunteer social welfare organizations really go overseas. In that period of time when the borders to China were closed, the Iron Curtain stretched across Europe, and nations chose sides in the Cold War, the notion of a flourishing global community seemed out of place. The idea of education with an international perspective appeared to be difficult to implement when everyone's map omitted different areas or nations.

One of the final chapters in the 1964 volume proposes the existence of a new concept – international schools founded with the specific purpose of furthering international education. This article identifies about 50 international schools and a new organization, the International Schools Association. However, the editors of the 1964 volume conclude that:

> International education at present is thus not only short on means and not far-reaching enough in its spread, but uncertain of its aims and fundamental premises.

Is that statement still true? More than 25 years later, has the picture altered? Why should we return to the topic?

We return because we know from looking at our own lives how much the world has changed. Twenty-five years ago, men did not fly into space and return by landing their craft at an airfield. Twenty-five years ago, the countries of Belize, Mozambique, and Papua New Guinea did not exist on our maps. Twenty-five years ago, our political enemies were easier to identify. Twenty-five years ago, universities did not offer courses in design technology, biogenetic engineering, and women's studies. Twenty-five years ago, we were not concerned with animal exploitation, environmental pollution, and global warming, and we believed oil, air, and water were limitless. Twenty-five years ago, we devoted little time to worrying about drugs, alcohol, or Aids. Twenty-five years ago, only diplomats, foreign correspondents, and the military lived overseas. Twenty-five years ago, international education was a post-war philosophic topic discussed by a small, but devoted, band of academics, and those 50 international schools were insignificant in number.

Twenty-five years ago, many of the contributors to this current volume were still at school or university, and the generation presently enrolled in international schools was not born. These students have never known a world without satellite television, home computers, microwave ovens, and supersonic jet travel. Their world geography, their university studies, their political realities, and their social concerns are different.

Many of these students live outside the country of their nationality because one or both of their parents have chosen work in that location. Perhaps, they were even born outside their national land. One of their parents may have a passport of a different nation from their own. They may speak more than one language, and they may understand more than one culture. For them, international education in international schools is reality. They and their schools are no longer an insignificant number, and the number has been growing steadily for two decades.

We must ask ourselves if in the past 20 years, we could have unknowingly fostered the growth of an educational system for a generation of students whose experience now allows them to perceive the world differently? If so, then we must investigate the elements which compose this educational system and identify the areas of expertise within it. To do this, the following series of questions is posed to describe the implementation of contemporary international education in today's international schools:

- ☐ Who is involved in international education and international schools?
- ☐ What are the benefits and disadvantages of international education in international schools?
- ☐ What is the content of international education and the curriculum of an international school?
- ☐ Are there links present or developing between or among national and international schools?
- ☐ What does the present suggest for the future of international education and international schools?

These questions have relevance for a broad audience. Pick up any current magazine or newspaper and you will find many people (philosophers, financiers, consultants, politicians, businessmen, educators, environmentalists, and performers) who tell us that our planet is very small, and that we have much in common with others around the world. They suggest that we must open our national boundaries in education and other areas not to destroy them but so that we can grow and profit from the knowledge and experience of others. It is possible that international schools and international education may have something to share with all of us which may help to improve the quality of our individual or national lives.

In 1991, internationalism is no longer a dream or an idealistic goal; it is *now*. We can see an example of that by reviewing the biographies of the authors included in this work. They are not diplomats, journalists, or military personnel, but they travel, live, or work overseas. Many were born in countries other than their national ones. Many work and have worked more than once in countries other than their original ones. For some, an interest in international education came from their personal experiences with international life; for others, international education holds possible solutions to national problems in which they are actively involved. They understand that today's young people have futures which do not always depend on national boundaries. Rather, their future universities, their future employers, their future families, and their national interest may be only part of their larger global picture. International schools and international education may teach them to tolerate difference and to seek multinational solutions to problems. This yearbook will investigate the creation of their broader perspective to speculate if its adoption by more of us would help ensure our mutually dependent futures.

Patricia L Jonietz
Editor

Part 1: Current participants in international education

Introduction

Patricia L Jonietz

On first encountering the European Council of International Schools (ECIS), newcomers to international education may be surprised at the far-reaching extent of its membership. In 1990, over 290 primary and secondary schools serving over 60,000 students in more than 70 countries sought to join the organization along with colleges, universities, publishers, educational equipment manufacturers, and educational organizations. To these 60,000 students, the seven United World Colleges (UWC) add over 1,500 students a year. In both ECIS-affiliated and non-ECIS affiliated schools offering the International Baccalaureate (IB), about 10,000 students sit exams yearly. These numbers could not have been gathered in 1964 because the means for international education did not exist.

One recent research study (Matthews 1989) suggests that ECIS and UWC are only the 'tip of the iceberg' of existing international education. It goes on to propose that a system of international schools of various descriptions (international schools, national schools abroad, national government schools with international sections, independent schools offering national education, restricted enrolment multinational schools like the EC, and company/religious affiliated schools) enroll students in number equal to a nation with a population of three to four million. The significance of this number is seen when about 90 per cent of the students leaving the system each year enter higher education, and this number increased about 70 per cent between 1980–1986 (Belcher 1989). Matthews offers the following data to support his conclusions:

Type of school	*Total students*	*Students aged 16–19*	*College entrants*
International (1)	500,000	100,000	40,000
UK Independent (2)	500,000	67,000	15,000
Scottish Maintained (3)	950,000	85,000	8,000
English Maintained	7,500,000	305,000	43,000

1. These figures are approximations based on:
   (i) The figure of 314,000 students at member schools of ECIS (1988) extrapolated to include all other categories of international schools.

(ii) The observed even distribution of students throughout the age range in international schools.
(iii) The value of 89 per cent university entry which emerged from the research.

2. *Statistics of Education – Schools*, DES 1987
3. *Scottish Statistics of Education*, HMSO 1987

Belcher's research, completed on behalf of the British Council, projects this growth to continue in 'response to higher levels of international population mobility'.

Although in 1964, the aims of international education were described as 'unclear', the aims of international education in the 1990s are reflected in the goals of the various organizations involved. They seem to see their mission as: offering to the international community a high calibre academic program which focuses on education for global understanding and ends in an internationally recognized diploma.

The purpose of this section is to clarify for the reader a picture of contemporary international education by identifying some of the active participants and describing their work.

Renaud presents the International Schools Association (ISA) developed to meet the needs of the internationally mobile community by enhancing cooperation among member schools and developing experimental programmes and examinations. After launching the development of the International Baccalaureate Organization, ISA is now engaged in pilot studies for a curriculum for the 11–16 year age group. This academic programme is introducing the concepts of international humanism and global education in a rapidly expanding group of national and international schools.

Blackburn reviews the original aims, purposes, and educational philosophy of the International Baccalaureate Office and the extent to which these have changed with international growth. Making the IB more international meant re-evaluation of the methods of assessment as well as curriculum development. There is growing international interest in the IB which may lead to extensions of the current recognition agreements for entry into higher education worldwide.

Sutcliffe presents the United World Colleges and their relationship with the International Baccalaureate Office, both born in the 1960s as idealistic and practical responses to the challenges of the Cold War and of the emerging needs of internationally mobile families. He asks 'What have been UWC's achievements and what lies in the future?'

Paterson's summary of the foundation and the growth of the European Council of International Schools is condensed from the account written for the 25th anniversary of the organization. His particular emphasis is on the growth of support activities (accreditation, personnel, college recruitment, publications, and research grants) developed by ECIS for members around the world.

Sadler is involved with another international curriculum for students aged 14–16, the International General Certificate of Secondary Education (IGCSE) developed by the University of Cambridge Local Examination Syndicate in cooperation with the European Council of International Schools. Students can sit single exams or a set of exams leading to the International Certificate of Education. The programme encourages preparation for further study at GCE Advanced or IB level and offers students a base from which to enter vocational training or employment. Forty-seven countries around the world offer IGCSE exams.

1. The International Schools Association (ISA): historical and philosophical background

Gerard Renaud

Meeting the needs of the international mobile community

In the fifties when the International Schools Association (ISA) was considering the development of a genuine international system of education, it was essentially to meet the needs of the increasing number of mobile families.

This phenomenon of mobility had developed considerably since the Second World War, not only numerically but also in terms of social classes. In the past, two main categories of internationally mobile groups existed: one at either end of the socioeconomic scale. On one hand were diplomats, servicemen, and senior level commercial or business executives. On the other hand were the migrant workers, but in a proportion considerably less than that of today. In the fifties, not only were these two sections of the mobile population growing year after year but also the mobility was moving towards the centre of the social scale, especially at the level of middle grade technicians.

In most countries facing the problem of immigration, the only aim of their educational authorities was the best possible integration of foreign pupils into the local national system by means of 'remedial classes' and adjustment programmes. In actual fact, syllabuses and methods designed for a national community are ill-suited to the socioeducational needs of an international community. This is especially true in the case of multilateral or successive mobility, where a family is obliged to stay for only a limited time in one country and then moves on to a further posting.

This explains the rapid development of international schools in the post-war period. Most of these were founded by parents who had failed to find in the host country conditions of schooling corresponding to their children's needs, or at least not without considerable disadvantage. But what is – or what was – an 'international school'? Frequently, it was an institution offering several national streams in a kind of educational department store. The result was the coexistence of different communities, these being juxtaposed more than integrated.

Such a situation derived mainly from the need to prepare students for national school-leaving examinations, each with very different requirements. If ISA, after having developed pre-school and primary curricula, jumped to the final stage of secondary education, it was not because this phase was more important pedagogically than earlier stages but because the first need was to eliminate the constraint of variegated examinations.

Fostering international understanding

It is important to underline that the objective of serving the mobile community has constantly been supported by a more general educational aim: to foster international understanding especially through a new perspective in social science teaching.

ISA was given three successive contracts by UNESCO to study practical ways of harmonizing curricula and methods for the development of international understanding.

The first experiment involved the drafting of a modern history syllabus leading up to an experimental examination, first held in 1964. Several major universities and a number of Ministries of Education expressed interest in this initiative. This encouraged the promoters to extend their investigation to other subjects, with the ultimate aim of producing a comprehensive secondary curriculum which would meet the needs outlined above.

The project of an international baccalaureate

In 1963, to support these combined objectives, the United States-based Twentieth Century Fund gave ISA a grant spread over three years to establish machinery to develop for international schools a common curriculum and examination programme which would facilitate student admission to the university of individual choice. Such a project obviously needed a specific infrastructure. In 1965, the International Schools Examination Syndicate (ISES) was set up for that purpose. In 1967, the syndicate was renamed the International Baccalaureate Office (IBO), with the status of a foundation under Swiss law and having its headquarters in Geneva.

The development and the success of the new organization is well known. After a preparation period (1965–69) when the syllabuses in the various subjects were intensively elaborated and tested in a limited number of schools, an introductory period (1970–76) took place under the eminent leadership of Alex Peterson. All investigations carried out during the last two years of the experimental period among participating schools, governments, universities, and educational experts demonstrated that it was worth establishing the International Baccalaureate as a permanent institution. By 1976, the number of schools offering the IB had grown to 55. In 1990, it is in the region of 400 spread over 50 countries on five continents.

Further development of ISA

Throughout the period of successful elaboration and consolidation of the IB, the ISA has constantly maintained its fundamental vocation, which is to help international schools to exchange their experience, their problems, and their views with the aim of better preparing students for a world of mobility and intercultural exchanges, along the lines so well illustrated by the IB experience.

Each year, the major event of ISA is the General Conference, usually held in July, which allows heads of schools, teachers, and experts to exchange views in workshops and seminars. It is during these meetings that the development of a curriculum for the crucial phase of the middle years of schooling progressively took shape.

An international curriculum for the middle school

The following is an extract of the general statement adopted by the 1982 ISA Conference held in London:

> The programme is designed for the 11–16 age range. This period encompassing as it does early puberty to mid-adolescent is a particularly critical phase of personal and intellectual development. Such a time of uncertainty, sensitivity, susceptibility, resistance, and questioning requires an educational programme that will provide disciplines, skills, creativity, challenging standards, and flexibility to help the growth towards responsible self-reliance and interdependence.
>
> Learning how to learn and the development of the whole person are the guiding principles of this programme. The overall curriculum is designed to encourage moral development in our children and a sense of responsibility to the world community and its environment.

The subsequent annual conferences of ISA have been mainly devoted to the elaboration of the new curriculum in an atmosphere of active and intense cooperation. These conferences took place successively in Cyprus (1983), the Netherlands (1984), the United States (1985), France (1986), Denmark (1987), Singapore (1988), and Spain (1989). Between the annual meetings, subject programmes have been steadily developed in a number of workshops held in various schools in France, the Netherlands, Switzerland, Canada, Singapore, Austria, and the United States.

In 1988, the curriculum was advanced enough to be introduced in a group of pilot institutions, both state and independent, in Europe, North America, and Latin America. Many other schools, national and international, have let it be known that they intend to adopt the programme in the near future.

An international philosophy of education

If more and more state schools, while being well equipped in their national system in terms of academic material, show their interest in the ISA programme, it is for its international and intercultural perspective. The responsibility of educators is no longer just to prepare good mathematicians, good biologists, or good historians. The mission of schools is to prepare young people – the decision makers of tomorrow – to live in a complex multicultural society undergoing a process of rapid change and opening up a new world.

Of course, the cognitive component of an educational system is fundamental for the acquisition of intellectual and professional skills. Even more important is the acquisition of attitudes in the learning process in a context of cultural exchanges.

At the IB level (16–18 years), the constraints of the forthcoming examination, depending in turn on university requirements, impose serious limitations on the implementation of the curriculum which would really correspond to the philosophy of an international system of education. The age group for which the ISA middle years curriculum (ISAC) has been developed is certainly more appropriate to that purpose since the perspective of an examination is remote enough to allow more freedom to schools and teachers.

The spirit of ISAC has been defined as 'an international humanism' by Robert Belle-Isle, former chairman of ISA who regrettably died in office in 1988. That spirit is based on three guiding principles.

Globality

The adolescent is faced with the complexity of the world. School should give a global view of situations and problems, and should make the pupil aware of the interactions and complementarity of various fields of study.

Yet, this must not be to the detriment of the disciplines, for each area of study demands a specific methodology, otherwise the so-called 'interdisciplinarity' might just result in a mental confusion and a superficial grasp of realities. This is why the ISAC school subjects, while strongly maintained in their identity and their integrity, are interconnected in 'areas of instruction'.

Communication

A basic need of any child is to express him or herself and to give something from inside. The learner, formerly regarded as a receiver of *knowledge*, is becoming more and more an *actor*. Thus ISAC gives particular importance to communication skills, especially in the form of oral and written language as the basic tool of communication:

- ☐ In the immediate context of the school for the efficient learning of the various subjects;
- ☐ more generally and permanently, for the development of social contacts;
- ☐ thus, for the cohesion of personality, 'the means of self-identification'.

All other forms of expression and communication, particularly the arts, should of course be involved in this process.

Intercultural awareness

This is the most specific aspect of the curriculum. The history of ISA has clearly shown that its basic mission is to promote international understanding among young people – those who will have to play a vital part in the society of the future.

Along the same lines as what has been said about communication, intercultural awareness is not merely a receptive attitude in the sense of showing interest in manifestations of other cultures. It must be of mutual enrichment by the discovery of ways of feeling and thinking that are different from our own. The international character of ISAC is therefore reflected not only in the *content* of certain syllabuses – in particular those of languages, humanities, and the arts – but also in the *methodology*, by making pupils aware of the different ways of approaching the same problem or topic. The sense of common values means also the acceptance of differences.

Thus, the pupils will have gained a substantial advantage, for they will be able to adapt more easily to different sociocultural environments in their further studies as well as in their future professional life. The world in which young people will have to live and work *must* be a world of mutual understanding and cooperation. The education given by the school will influence them for life. One of the most important factors in their training is the vision underlying the various programmes distilled over the years in their minds. Every effort has been made by the working groups of ISA to embody the basic guiding principles in a consistent framework.

ISAC outline

The curriculum initially known as ICMYS (International Curriculum for the Middle Years of Schooling) and recently given the more simple and understandable acronym ISAC (ISA Curriculum) is illustrated by Figure 1.1, which shows the following points.

- ☐ The *child* schematically represented at the centre recalls that his or her own personality is and should constantly remain the focus of the whole teaching/learning process.
- ☐ The distribution of the components of the curriculum around and inside a polygon illustrates the concept of *global education*.
- ☐ The two-way arrows underline the concept of *interaction* between the components of the curriculum.

A two-fold curriculum

The school subjects distributed on the outside polygon, while being the traditional basic components of any curriculum for the middle years of schooling, have not been considered as the first priority in the overall teaching/learning process. The following explains the sequence in the presentation of the two major sections of ISAC:

The areas of interaction

The concentric circles surrounding the child in Figure 1.1 should not be interpreted as additional subjects. They are intended to develop the personality of the child and to put the school subjects *into their right perspective*. They include, of course, a content but this content has to be shared by teachers of various disciplines *in their own programme*.

There are five 'areas of interaction' distributed in three concentric circles.

Représentation schématique du plan d'études

Schematic Study Plan

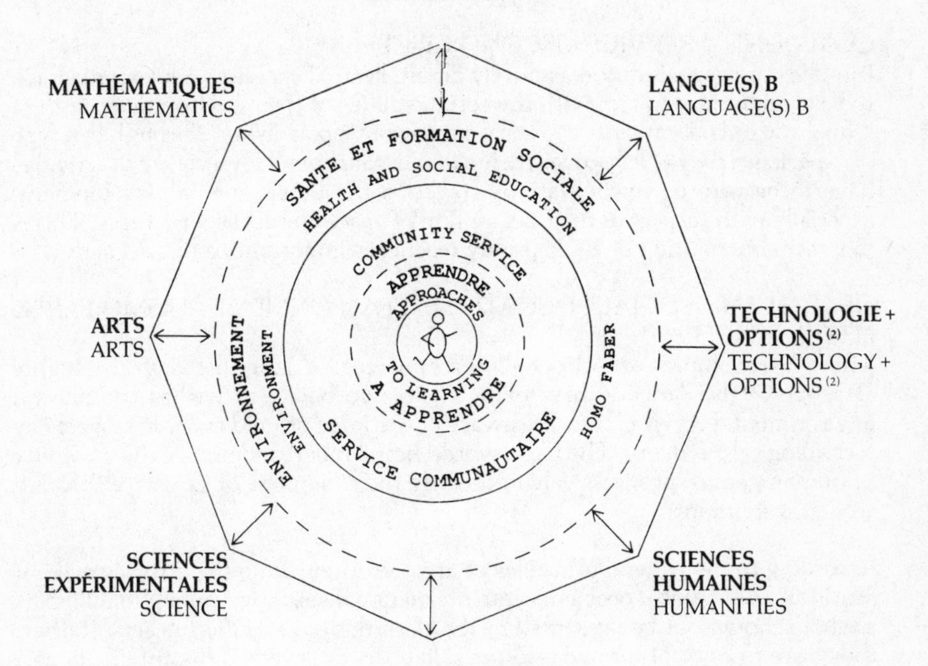

Figure 1.1

(1) La langue A est la langue dans laquelle l'élève reçoit son enseignement; dans de nombreux cas elle est également sa langue maternelle, sinon on dénomme:
- A1 la langue d'enseignement;
- A2 la langue maternelle.

Toutes les autres langues sont considérées comme des langues B.
Technologie: obligatoire pendant au moins deux annees au cours du eycie.

The language A is the language in which the student is taught. In many cases. It is also his (her) mother tongue, if not:
- the Language A1 is the language of instruction:
- the Language A2 is the mother tongue.

All the other languages are considered as Languages B.

(2) Technology: compulsory during at least two years during the course of studies.

APPROACHES TO LEARNING (FIRST CIRCLE)
This is the key to the whole method, the condition on which the effectiveness of the whole teaching process depends. The teachers, working together, instruct the pupils in a method of approaching school work (note taking, using library resources etc) and this leads gradually up to more conceptual aspects, such as inculcating a spirit of analysis and synthesis and a taste for working independently. Finally, for those intending to go on to the IB, this will constitute an introduction to the Theory of Knowledge.

COMMUNITY SERVICE (SECOND CIRCLE)
ISA does not see education as purely an intellectual exercise. Adolescents have to be brought face to face with the social realities of their environment, both at school and outside, and have to learn a sense of responsibility. Through this type of experience they will discover their own personalities. However, such activities have to be tailored to the various stages in the pupils' mental development, especially with respect to their perception of space and social structures. This is why the contribution of a geography teacher is important to this domain.

HEALTH AND SOCIAL EDUCATION – ENVIRONMENT – HOMO FABER (THIRD CIRCLE)
These three topics are closely interconnected. Young persons are highly sensitive to the dangers threatening their own bodies as well as the natural environment. Likewise, they are aware of the hope offered in these respects by technological discovery. The Latin words 'homo faber' underscore the creativity of human genius, progressively improving the conditions of existence through technical solutions.

According to the general principles of areas of interaction, these topics making pupils aware of global problems and international solidarity among mankind as a whole should not be presented in the classroom as specific subjects. Rather, they have to be incorporated into the syllabuses of several different disciplines. For example, 'the environment' might form part of geography, biology, and language A or B (through the choice of appropriate texts). There is never any hard and fast breakdown. The way the topic is shared by various disciplines will generally depend on the particular conditions in a given school and the teaching staff available.

The disciplines

Figure 1.1 shows eight subjects, each of them possibly generating several subjects. This is the case with:

- ☐ Science which, after a common core in the first two years, will break down into biology, chemistry, and physics.
- ☐ Humanities including history and geography.
- ☐ Languages, the number of which depends on the needs of the pupil in terms of Language(s) A and B as indicated in the figure.
- ☐ Technology is compulsory for at least two years during the five-year cycle. Depending on local conditions, constraints and resources, a number of options can be integrated into the curriculum.

In general terms, all subjects are based on *concepts* in order to develop understanding and not just memorization of facts. At the same time, in an international context, these concepts can be applied to different situations and different examples. Thus, the curriculum, while being basically the same in all schools, allows for individual flexibility.

Interdisciplinarity in the classroom

The concept of interdisciplinarity is now common but *dangerous* as it has been stated above. Interdisciplinarity should mean that all subjects, while keeping their respective methodology, contribute to the perception of the real problems of the world and to their solutions. These problems are complex and call for the contribution of a number of interactive disciplines. The combination of school subjects and areas of interaction, associating knowledge, experience, and critical observation, is probably the best way to avoid the separation – as frequently happens – between the world of the school and the 'real world'. The vocation of the school is to prepare young people for life.

Evaluation procedures

Any educational process, to be efficient, needs to be 'measured', first, during the training itself, and, secondly, at the end of the training in order to provide the teachers, parents, and students themselves with an instrument of orientation for the next stage of education. In that respect ISA does not consider assessment to be an end in itself, avoiding in particular the use of the term 'examination'. The evaluation system is based on the following elements:

1. *Accreditation* of the school applying to adopt the ISA curriculum (ISAC), according to defined criteria.
2. *Internal assessment* conducted by the staff of the school on all components of the curriculum according to the rules established by ISA, and *moderated* at the end of the cycle by experts appointed by ISA.
3. *A personal project* worked out by the pupil and relating to one of the areas of interaction; such a project may, *inter alia*, take the form of a 'mini-essay' or a work of art, accompanied in all cases by a document explaining the methodological approach adopted by the pupil who will 'defend' the project in an interview with the panel.

All of the elements of the above-mentioned evaluation will be set down in a *school report* which will also contain information on the type of community service undertaken by the pupil. The report will be checked by ISA for approval. On recommendation by the accredited school, a pupil whose school report is up to certificate standard will be awarded the *ISA Diploma of International Secondary Education*.

Looking ahead

Such a programme designed to meet the needs of schools – national or international – who are eager to promote the sense of responsibility gained through fostering intercultural understanding among their students, calls for strong cooperation between teachers and administrators. The work presently being conducted shows that this cooperation, far from being resented as an additional burden, generates faith and enthusiasm. All partners see it as a new form of education, open to social and international realities.

International schools, in particular, enjoy a privileged position because of the presence of many cultures; they are pre-eminently the fields where the seeds of international understanding can germinate. 'International humanism' is an attitude at the root of which lies understanding and respect for other people's cultural backgrounds. This kind of attitude will be the only way that will lead to the progressive disappearance of prejudices and mistaken ideas about 'foreigners', prejudices which underlie intolerance and isolation.

The International Schools Association is now approaching its 40th year of existence. Life begins at 40! The comprehensive set of purposes of those who created ISA is still as real as it was at the beginning of the fifties. ISA is now faced with a new challenge – to implement an innovative curriculum. The rapid development of international education over the last decades calls for the conjunction of all forces involved in this field. There is no doubt that the concept of 'interaction' on which ISA has been based will *a fortiori* apply to organizations and institutions working for common ideals.

2. The International Baccalaureate: a curriculum at upper secondary level and a university entrance examination

Robert Blackburn

Introduction

The International Baccalaureate provides an international pre-university curriculum and an international university entry qualification. It is gained by examination following two years of study at the end of upper secondary education and now gives access to higher education on a worldwide basis - an 'international passport' to higher education - in more than 30 countries.

But the IB is more than an examination; it is also a curriculum and a growing movement in international education. In fact, the founders of the IB were less concerned with establishing an examination than helping to extend and improve the quality of international education. They were idealists. They believed international education was not a luxury but a necessity in an increasingly interdependent and multicultural world.

However, the IB was also created to meet several practical needs:

1. To provide international schools with an appropriate common curriculum at upper secondary level and a matriculation examination which had wide acceptability.
2. To assist such schools to help solve the problems of the growing internationally mobile community - parents who had to find secondary education for their children overseas but who wished to return them to higher education in their own countries.

The aims are still the same: to promote international understanding and to promote student mobility. However, the International Baccalaureate Organization (IBO) has now begun to meet other requirements which were not foreseen at the start. Most significantly, the IB is being used by Ministries of National Education on a limited scale in state schools in some countries. The relevance and potential of this development within national systems, especially in the Europe of post-1992, is now becoming recognized.

The organization of the IB

The IBO is based in Geneva with other offices in Buenos Aires, London, New

York, Singapore, and Cardiff (the examination office). There are representatives in India, Mexico, the Caribbean, and the Middle East (Sultanate of Oman). The IBO is a non-governmental organization holding consultative status with UNESCO and the Council of Europe. It is registered as an educational charitable foundation under Swiss law, and as such is governed by an International Council of Foundation supported by a Standing Conference of Governments and Heads of IB schools.

The Council meets annually, usually in Geneva, and is the supreme governing body of the organization. The current president is Dr Piet Gathier, formerly Director General of Secondary Education in the Netherlands. The Council elects one-third of its membership from participating schools; one-third from participating governments, and one-third are *ad personam* members distinguished in the fields of international affairs, education, and business. Recently elected *ad personam* members included: HRH Princess Sarvath El-Hassan of Jordan; Signora Susanna Agnelli, Under-Secretary of State for Foreign Affairs in Italy; and leading international businessmen such as Dr Curt Nicolin (Sweden) and Dr V Krishnamurthy (India). The Standing Conference of Governments arrangement ensures essential governmental participation in the project, for example in the field of recognition and equivalence, but also in the academic independence of the organization.

Participating schools play an essential role. The IB arose out of the needs of international schools and was largely created by them. Representatives of schools are actively involved in the governance of IBO and in the continuing process of IB curriculum review and development on the Curriculum Board and Subject Committees. As a result, the schools influence the programmes they teach. It is this partnership between schools, administration, and examiners which makes IBO different from many national examination systems.

A Board of Chief Examiners, largely independent of the main administration structure, is ultimately responsible for the setting of question papers, assessment, and the award of grades. Chief Examiners are usually university professors who are distinguished in their own field and of many nationalities. A team of 1,100 assistant examiners worldwide assists the Board of Chief Examiners, and the examination administration is handled by the Examination Office in Cardiff.

Only students in affiliated IB schools can take the IB examinations, and all students take the same IB examinations irrespective of where they are taken. There are currently some 400 such schools in 58 countries in every continent. The variety is enormous: national and international; state and private; large and small; rich and poor. However, all schools are accepted on common worldwide criteria and by common procedures. Growth has been rapid over the last few years, and the controlled expansion of the project is some 10 per cent annually.

The curriculum and examination

To some extent the IB curriculum represents a common denominator of the educational traditions of continental Europe, Britain, and North America, but it is becoming increasingly international as other continents and cultures become involved. The IB is a group diploma examination in which each student must choose six subjects – normally three at Higher and three at Subsidiary level – with definite distribution requirements. The curriculum is shown in Table 2.1

Table 2.1 *Curriculum and examination*

The curriculum consists of six subject groups:

Group 1 *Language A* (first language) including the study of selections from World Literature

Group 2 *Language B* (second language) or a second language A

Group 3 *Study of Man in Society*: History, Geography, Economics, Philosophy, Psychology, Social Anthropology, Organisation and Management Studies

Group 4 *Experimental Sciences*: Biology, Chemistry, Applied Chemistry, Physics, Physical Science, Environmental Systems

Group 5 *Mathematics*: Mathematics, Mathematical Studies, Mathematics with Further Mathematics

Group 6 *One of the following options*:
(a) Art/Design, Music, Latin, Classical Greek, Computing Studies
(b) A school-based syllabus approved by IBO.

Alternatively, a candidate may offer instead of a Group 6 subject: a third modern language, a second subject from the Study of Man in Society, a second subject from Experimental Sciences.

IB GRADES
At both Higher and Subsidiary level, each examined subject is graded on a scale of one (minimum) to seven (maximum). The award of the Diploma requires a minimum total of 24 points.

This pattern ensures that every IB student will continue to study a combination of the social sciences and languages, together with the natural sciences and mathematics. This is a proscribed pattern, unlike the British A and AS level arrangements or the American College Board examinations, but candidates may also offer single subjects for which they receive a certificate. In addition, the balance of higher and subsidiary level subjects meets the needs of the specialist university systems and the needs of a broad general education.

There are several other distinctive features in the IB pattern. Every diploma student must write an extended essay – a piece of personal research work of some 4,000 words; follow a course in the Theory of Knowledge; and spend the equivalent of one half-day a week on some form of creative activity or social service (CASS). These are essential requirements for the diploma. IBO has three working languages – English, French, and Spanish – and all subjects are examined in these languages. Languages play a central and fundamental role in any international examination system, and all students must take:

- *Language A* – This is the language students choose as their best language and is usually their mother tongue or the language of the school. This is

Figure 2.1 *International Baccalaureate: registration by schools 1987–1989 May and November (by working language)*

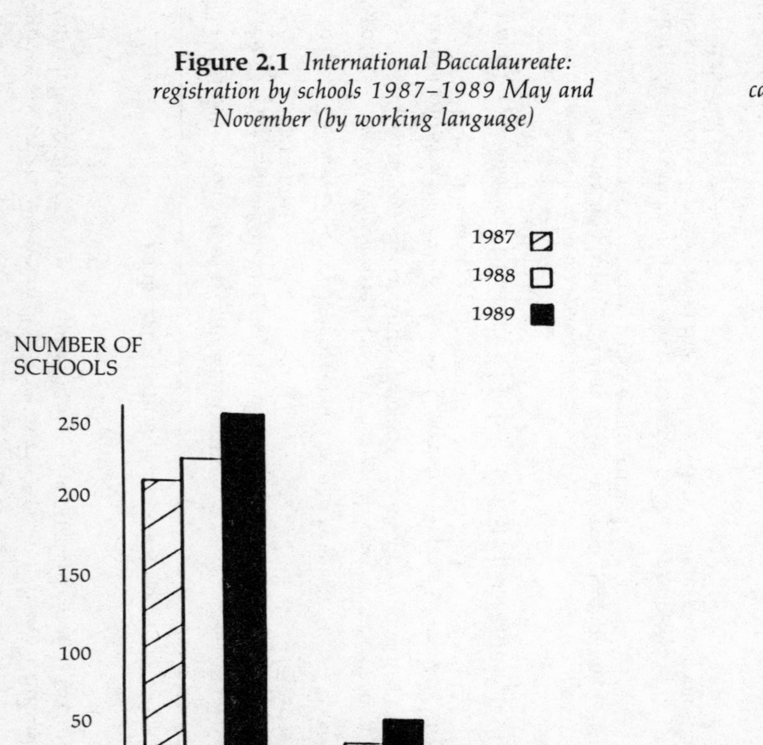

Figure 2.2 *International Baccalaureate: candidate registration 1987–1989 May and November (by working language)*

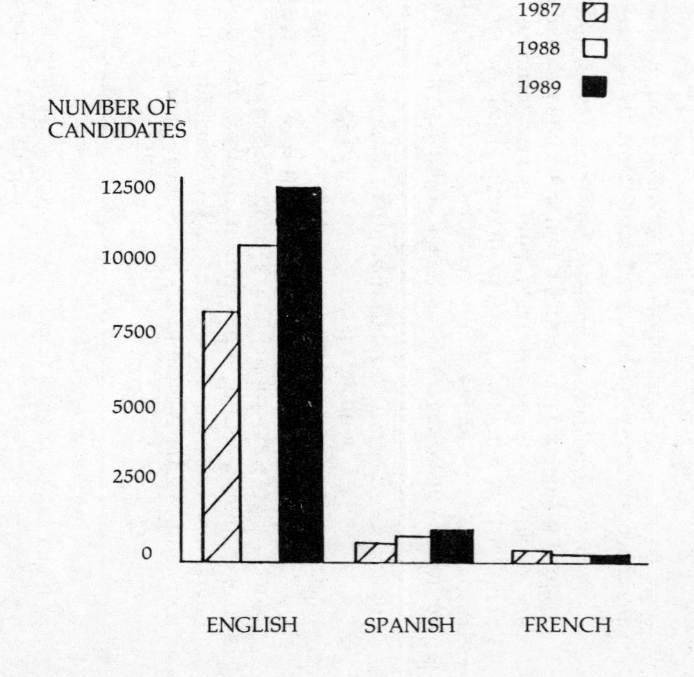

taken with a course in World Literature which accounts for 30 per cent of Language A marks. Many students are being educated outside their own country. It is essential that these students do not lose touch with their own language, literature, and culture. This is the essential basis on which to add an international dimension. It is also necessary if they wish to return to higher education in their own country.

☐ *Language B* – This is the language the students choose as their second examination language – usually for them, a foreign language. This is also obligatory.

A wide range of languages are offered and examined on a 'regular' basis, and other languages may be offered on special request from schools. Figures 2.1 and 2.2 illustrate the distribution of the IB working languages of schools and candidates.

Examination growth

Examination growth has been rapid over the last few years. There was a 25 per cent increase in the number of schools entering candidates from May 1987 (246) to May 1990 (301). Over the same period, there was a 40 per cent increase in the number of candidates taking IB examinations, from 9,000 in 1987 to 14,000 in 1990. Although the IB is still a small entry examination by many national standards, there is considerable evidence that this recent growth rate can be maintained or increased in the future. Currently, there are 25,000 individuals worldwide who have obtained an IB diploma since 1971. It is interesting to note that it took all the years up to 1985 to reach 10,000 but only four more years to double this number in 1989.

Curriculum development: an international curriculum

Within the IB, curriculum development is arranged primarily through Subject Committees, usually chaired by the Chief Examiner in that particular subject. In addition to examiner representatives, each Subject Committee also involves selected schools representatives and outside experts in the particular field or discipline. The Subject Committees are responsible for the general oversight and review of all existing programmes on a continuing basis to ensure that IB programmes are as well developed as any comparable national programmes. A Curriculum Board, chaired by the Director General, coordinates overall curriculum development within the project.

During the last few years, the highest IBO priority has been to improve the quality of the method of assessment used. Real progress has been made in 1990 with the setting up of a new Examinations Office in Cardiff, with appropriate professional staff, a state-of-the-art computer, and space for expansion and development.

The highest priority now is to revise the curriculum and to make it more fully international and more representative of the growing variety of cultures and educational traditions represented within the programme. A justified criticism of the IB in the past has been that the programme has been too Euro-centred and not sufficiently sensitive to the requirements and educational susceptibilities of other regions and civilizations. Action is now being taken to improve this situation and make the curriculum more genuinely international.

The IB curriculum certainly has international features – probably to a unique degree. There is World Literature in Language A; a foreign language requirement for all students; themes in world history and regional options in the modern history programme; three working languages and some 40 mother-tongue examinations; the inclusion of global issues such as Environmental Systems in Group 4; and new programmes in Group 6 to promote internationalism, such as Art/Design and Ethno-musicology (pioneered at an IB school in Swaziland).

But how really international is the curriculum? In an international school where students from many countries study, work, and live together, the IB is obviously an appropriate programme and it is easy in this context to conclude that the IB is more international than it really is. But what element of internationalism does the IB curriculum bring to a gymnasia in Trondheim or to a MARA College in Kuala Lumpur? The growth of monolingual and monocultural schools within the IB has forced the organization to look at this fundamental question.

There are easy cosmetic answers and certainly organizations such as IBO can spend inordinate amounts of time debating the real meaning of international education and examining their own collective consciences. However, for IBO the blunt reality is that the organization must continue to do what already has been started on the basis of the present diploma structure which no one in IBO wishes to change. Maybe this is 'doing the unusual and doing the usual in an unusual way', but certain important changes are planned and are taking place:

1. The Curriculum Board (which has overall supervision of the IB programmes) will be strengthened and bring in more international experts in their own field.
2. The Subject Committees will be asked to examine their own academic subjects for cultural bias and opportunities to be more international, for example the introduction of global issues.
3. Regional meetings of experts must look at the IB curriculum from the point of view of a particular culture and region to see what improvements can be made or what cultural bias can be eliminated. Such regional meetings have been successfully held in Nairobi; in Japan hosted by the National Ministry of Education when IB and Japanese science and mathematics programmes were comparatively reviewed; and in March 1990 at a meeting convened by the Minister of Education in Jordan and attended by experts from the national systems in Bahrain, Egypt, Kuwait and the Sultanate of Oman.
4. New CASS (Community Action Service) guidelines for all IB schools have recently been agreed. These emphasize and provide a framework for a wide range of environmental and international projects and CASS now is an integral part of the diploma and a requirement for each student.
5. IBO teams of Chief Examiners and Assistant Examiners must continue to be made more international and, similarly, so must the administration.

These plans may seem a little prosaic, but IBO does not have the luxury of complete independence, and the organization can only move so far so quickly.

However, these – and other – developments are well underway with enthusiastic support from IB schools worldwide, and it is hoped, will produce an IB which is more genuinely international, more sensitive to other cultures, and more involved in the major issues of the time. That is the objective.

Current international developments

As has been mentioned earlier, IBO has now begun to meet requirements which were not foreseen at the start of the project. Most significantly, the IB is now being used by national systems of education in Europe, in some Latin American countries, and in North America, where more than 150 public high schools currently teach IB programmes and take IB examinations.

Western Europe

Developments in Western Europe are of particular interest with 1992 and the creation of a single common market just over the horizon. In Norway, four of the leading gymnasia (Oslo, Trondheim, Bergen, and Stavanger) have been nominated by the Ministry of Education as IB centres – and these are probably the most prestigious schools in Norway. In Sweden, there are three IB state schools, and two in both Denmark and Finland. In the Netherlands, out of 11 IB schools, seven are authorized by the government to introduce international English language sections based on the IB. IBO is currently negotiating with the Spanish Minister of Education for the IB to be used in 40 schools – 20 in the state sector and 20 private sector schools. In all these cases, the IB is used as a complement to national systems – never intentionally as a rival or competitor.

It is difficult to predict the future extent of this development, but the European Commission (EC) and the Council of Europe are now taking a positive interest. In May 1990, they jointly sponsored a conference together with IBO and the European Schools on the educational implications of 1992. Important topics included the introduction of more international elements into the secondary school curriculum and the improvement of student mobility at the level of transfer from the secondary school system of one European country to the higher examination system of another.

The conference was attended by experts in bilingual and international education from a wide range of European countries. An agreed report and recommendations will now be presented to the European Committee of the European Community and then, it is hoped, to the European Council of Ministers of Education. Several of these resolutions specifically concern the IB and propose that:

1. Consideration should be given to the extended use of the IB within state education systems in Europe.
2. A new European convention on recognition agreements should be negotiated which would place international qualifications on the same basis as recognized national qualifications and which would provide a legal framework within which detailed IB recognition agreements could be arranged.

3. There should be closer cooperation between the various schools and institutions involved and in particular between IBO, the European schools, and ECIS. It was felt that there was a need to establish meetings of this group on a more formal basis.

Eastern Europe

The avalanche of change in Eastern Europe is opening up new opportunities and challenges for IBO. The first IB schools in Yugoslavia (in Slovenia) have been accepted. In Hungary, the Minister of Education is interested in incorporating the IB into several existing bilingual schools. In 1989, IBO's Director General visited Bulgaria where plans for a sixth form international college are going ahead. The authorities wish to use the IB from September 1992 and, in the meantime, IBO has been invited to act as a consultant in the planning of the college and to advise on the curriculum. Earlier in 1990, the IBO Regional Director for Europe was invited to visit Moscow and a comparative study of IB and Soviet national curricula is underway. In May 1990, a meeting was convened in Trieste by the Italian Ministries of Foreign Affairs and Public Instruction with government representatives from Austria, Hungary, Czechoslovakia, and Yugoslavia together with observers from Poland and Bulgaria to consider possible IB developments in Eastern Europe and how the Italian government might assist such developments as part of the government's foreign policy aid programme.

Australia and South East Asia

Before the IBO team visited Australia in 1988, the IB programme was known in only two schools. There are now nine IB schools (both state and private) and given the growing interest at state government level this number could possibly double over the next few years. It is typical of change in IBO that these Australian schools are interested in the opportunity to focus on Asian languages, especially Chinese and Japanese, as part of their new programme of studies.

United Kingdom

The last year has seen a considerably increased level of interest in the IB in the United Kingdom – particularly in the further education (FE) sector, and probably due to two factors:

1. Disillusion in schools and colleges, after the recent rejection of the Higginson Committee report, that government policy will produce a broader and more relevant sixth form curriculum.
2. Growing awareness of the educational implications of 1992 and a wish to create new European/international links and awareness.

Southern Africa

IB schools exist in Swaziland and Lesotho (where an EC Lomé Convention scholarship programme finances local Basutho students to take the IB). A conference on non-racial schools in Southern Africa – including the Republic of South Africa – will be held in Lesotho in October 1990 to consider the extended use of the IB in the region.

These and similar developments in the United States, Latin America, the other regions as well as the rate of expansion have raised some problems:

1. Should IBO concentrate on those areas where a sound basis for expansion has been established, for example Europe and North America, or continue to investigate important possibilities in areas of conflict – for example, Southern Africa or Northern Ireland where Lagan College, the first interdenominational school, has joined the IB?
2. Should IBO develop internationally on the basis of the present regional office structure or is a much strengthened format needed to promote expansion and deal with its results?
3. Should IBO introduce new working languages – for example Arabic and Chinese – to facilitate expansion?

However, if these are problems, they are problems of success and diversity.

Recognition of the IB diploma and university entrance

Negotiation for the recognition of the IB diploma worldwide remains one of the most important, complex, and continuing tasks of the IBO. The IB was created as 'an international passport to higher education' and it is clearly important that possession of an IB diploma should secure consideration by the university of a student's choice – irrespective of the country, institution, or faculty. It would clearly be intolerable (and unworkable) to offer IB students an excellent international curriculum and a sophisticated system of assessment if this was done at the expense of their university entry ambitions. In fact, the worldwide recognition of the diploma is essential to the international credibility of the project and rightly so.

Secondly, this is a complex task. To a large extent, IBO has independent control of the curriculum and methods of assessment used. However, recognition of the diploma is a matter of detailed, direct negotiations between IBO and individual governments and institutions. To negotiate the acceptability of a qualification issued by a quasi-independent institution on a basis of parity with national matriculation qualifications is not easy. There are real problems. This is often an area of intense national pride, and sometimes countries are fierce in protecting academic standards and ensuring that there is no international backdoor behind national qualifications. IBO must also distinguish between the requirements of countries with centralized and decentralized systems of entry to higher education.

The task is also a continuing one. Ministers of Education come and go; admissions policies to higher education change; institutions rise and fall in popularity and competitiveness; and new countries are involved as the IB extends internationally. However, in spite of these problems the IB diploma is increasingly recognized and welcomed, and the current *IB Handbook of University*

Recognition and Entry gives details of recognition arrangements and policies in 75 countries.

Conclusion

In brief, most mainland European countries now accept the diploma as a valid university entry qualification. The diploma fulfils the general matriculation requirements of all British universities and in present-day Britain, it is no disadvantage for a British student and a considerable advantage for a non-British student to hold an IB diploma. In North America, IB students use their diploma or groups of certificate subjects to gain credit, and many leading universities give up to one year's earned academic credit on this basis.

IB students have now entered more than 800 universities throughout the world. However, simply possessing the diploma is no magic key to university entry. High grades will still be required by top universities. Strict faculty and department requirements will often have to be met. But, it does work - and better than anyone could have imagined ten years ago.

3. The United World Colleges

David Brooke Sutcliffe

Introduction

The idea for the United World Colleges was born in 1957, and the first college opened in 1962. There are now seven - in Britain, Singapore, Canada, Swaziland, the United States, Italy, and Venezuela. Worldwide scholarship programmes support the entry each year of some 500 adolescents to the UWC experience. Secondary education is a famously sensitive area for national Ministries of Education and universities, but academic and other agreements have made possible the participation of almost every country; UWC students come from the whole of Western Europe, Poland, Hungary, Yugoslovia, Czechoslovakia, Bulgaria, Romania, the USSR, North, Central and Latin America, the Middle East and Africa, Australia, New Zealand, Japan, China, Taiwan, and most of the other countries of Asia as well. A prestigious International Council, a powerful Board of Directors, an International Office in London, and some 70 National Committees worldwide administer the organization. To the outsider, and one tends to be 'inside' or 'outside', UWC must appear self-confident, clear in its aims, articulate, fortunate, and ever on the move.

How have the United World Colleges come this far? Is it the idea? Their philosophy? The people they have attracted? Or just a fortunate combination of time and circumstances?

Kurt Hahn

The UWC founder is better remembered for other achievements: Gordonstoun, Outward Bound, the Duke of Edinburgh's Award Scheme, and the promotion of tough, self-reliant approach to education which had much to do with almost physical victory over one's hesitations and limitations. Kurt Hahn continues to be imperfectly understood and misinterpreted. It is probably his own fault. He never wrote a complete statement of his educational principles, relying on the combined forces of his personality, anecdotes, a lifelong habit of addressing persuasive memoranda to well-placed 'allies in the cause' (and of leaking them 'confidentially' and even more skilfully to others whose help behind the scenes won many a battle), and the flattering habit of referring to himself on every occasion as 'just the midwife'. 'Puppeteer' would have been more appropriate. He was a great manipulator, but always transparently so, and his allies and victims joined in with enthusiasm and dedication.

Kurt Hahn, of Polish origins, was born and brought up in Berlin. While still a schoolboy, he dreamed of founding schools and studied the classics, at Oxford among other places. His educational models were Plato's *Republic* and the British public and progressive schools, especially Reddie's Abbotsholme. He became one of the foreigners for whom the British way is the example in almost everything, and he fell in love with the temperate climate of Scotland. Having suffered heatstroke as a young man he was unfit for service in the First World War, so he became a reader in the English Department of the German Foreign Office and an expert on interpreting the British scene through analysis of the British press. He achieved astonishing influence behind the scenes with his eloquent memoranda which are so difficult to identify in the archives because he had them signed by other, more significant figures.

For him, morality was an essential part of politics and justified itself on practical grounds: 'Macht ohne Moral zerstort sich selbst.' (Power without morality destroys itself.) He wrote vigorous papers urging the political unwisdom of German behaviour in and towards Belgium, and the fateful consequences of intensifying the U-boat warfare. By the end of the war, he was the Personal Secretary of the last Chancellor of Germany, Margrave Max of Baden. Even the cautious Professor Golo Mann believes that it was Hahn who not only had the idea of proposing that this nobleman – well known to the Allies for his work on behalf of prisoners of war on both sides – lead the government for the vital Armistice negotiations, but that it was he who actually conducted all the manoeuvres to get the Chancellor into this position. Again in character, he accompanied the German delegation to Versailles as a minor secretary but wrote most of their papers and speeches. No understanding is possible either of Hahn's educational objectives or of his methods without an appreciation of his way of working during the activities of this period.

Hahn was clear from the outset that Versailles would be the seed-bed for extremism and revenge. More morality, more justice, and more compassion would have brought their political rewards too. His first school, Salem, set up on the Margrave's estate near Lake Constance, had an unconcealed political aim – to provide leadership for a reborn Germany such as that given to Britain over the centuries by the public schools. It was not an uncritical copy, but it rapidly achieved prestige and success, not the least in Britain itself – partly because of the success of its pupils in the annual Public School Athletics Championship at the White City. By the 1930s, it was too valuable even for the Nazis to harm. After early hesitations, Hahn declared his own war on Hitler in a series of speeches and leaflets, was imprisoned briefly, then forced to leave both Salem and Germany in 1933; but Hess himself gave instructions that no harm was to come to the school. It survived until 1944; its integrity courageously intact.

It must have been difficult to teach or to be a pupil under Hahn. One is reminded of Harold Nicholson's comment on Thomas Arnold: 'His strength of character, his very ferocity, were so compulsive that he acquired far too much influence over his favourite boys . . . . His dominance was that of an upper tree which casts a blight over those who linger too long beneath its branches.' Within months of his arrival in exile in Britain, he had launched Gordonstoun in his beloved Morayshire, in Scotland. But Gordonstoun alone did not absorb his energies. In 1940, came the first experimental courses in Outward Bound, fashioned after earlier trials in both Scotland and Germany; and the post-war years brought forth the Duke of Edinburgh's Award Scheme, the Trevelyan Scholarships to Oxford and Cambridge, the Medical Convention of Accident Prevention, and the Atlantic College in Wales.

Those who knew Kurt Hahn recall his hypnotic personality, his cultivated eccentricities, his love of drama and mystery, his almost intrusive concern for other people's welfare, his anecdotes, his sense of humour, and his strangely compulsive laughter. There was also his courage. He did not hesitate to speak out. In two sermons in Liverpool Cathedral during the war, he spoke against the pursuit of a war of revenge against the German nation; the use of the atomic bomb (which was for him, and he said so and wrote so publicly, an immoral and illegitimate act); and the Polish maltreatment and expulsion of the German population from Eastern territories in the months immediately after May 1945. Remember his Polish ancestry. Remember too that he had educated boys in Salem and boys in Gordonstoun who had fought against one another for five years. European civilization, with all its faults and bloodletting, was a reality for him, and he believed that only within it could the European nations work out their future together. 'The would-be Fuhrer of tomorrow will be nothing if we make the German young loyal to Mother Europe.' He tried hard, in the early 1950s, to create a European role for Gordonstoun, but few were convinced. It was not until 1957, when he was a guest speaker at the NATO Defence College in Paris, that he found the key.

The NATO model

At the NATO Defence College was born the concept of the Atlantic College. If middle-aged officers, who until recently had been fighting one another, could so convincingly bury their differences once engaged on a common task, then why not, he asked, attempt a non-military staff college for teenagers from the countries of the Atlantic Alliance? 'We would aim to make the boys attending this [the college] feel loyal to the common cause of the free world. Are our ideals in safe-keeping? Are our young as much in earnest about their faith as their contemporaries who live under Communist rule? These colleges could become the source of a movement which would help restore morale throughout the NATO nations.' Missionary language for an educational project which was a child of its time! The Cuban missile crisis, a few weeks after the Atlantic College opened, sharpened the message.

The concept of fighting the Cold War by other means was beguiling. With his persuasive credentials, Hahn sought out his powerful friends and disciples in Germany and Britain and in the United States too. His supporters in Britain, pleased and excited by the success of Outward Bound and the Duke of Edinburgh's Award Scheme in the Commonwealth as well as at home, did not hesitate too long about putting up the early funding. But the old Hahn ideas overlaid and concealed what was genuinely new, the formula which was to make the Atlantic College a venture of new significance in education.

The plan

A sixth form college (the first in Britain); a two-year course of residential education open only to winners of scholarships, recruited internationally (initially from the Atlantic Alliance countries); an academic programme which, once the details had been worked out, would lead to university entrance in different countries; non-academic activities and especially community service to play a key role in the programme; a statement of aims which did not go further than offering to provide a 'form of education adapted to meet the needs of our time' – these were the framework. The age of 16–19 was recognized as being especially significant for the formation of attitudes; young people would be mature enough to be knowledgeable about their roots and loyal to them, and yet open to the influence of new ones; old enough to leave home and country, probably for the first time, and yet young enough to live together in a close and disciplined residential community; old enough to have identified their principal academic interests and strengths, and yet young enough not to be under the intense pressures of university and vocational education. Above all, it is the age when idealism is strong, and attitudes take root for life. It was to be for boys only, a recognition that not only in political terms was it a child of its time!

Headmaster Throng of Uppingham always wanted 'the wall' on his side. The 'wall' at Atlantic College was St Donat's Castle in South Glamorgan. It was a romantic, beautiful, partly maintained, partly neglected Elizabethan castle and estate bordering on the wild Bristol Channel. The valley of St Donat's had been the landing place of early Christian missionaries, and in the fifth century in nearby Llantwit Major, Europe's first theological college had reputedly found its home. The first grammar of the Welsh language had been sponsored by one of the Stradling family, owners of St Donat's for centuries, and whose family motto was 'Virtue's whole praise lies in doing.'

But the castle had 20th century history too. Bought in the 1930s by Randolph Hearst to please Marion Davies (who did not like the local fog horn and preferred San Simeon), it had acquired an 11th century hall from Wiltshire, antique furnishings and fittings from all over the world, the censure as a result of the British House of Commons, 32 marble bathrooms, a 25-metre Hollywood-style swimming pool, telephones in the rose garden to keep Hearst in touch with his empire, and guests such as Lloyd George for the Eisteddford and John Kennedy when a boy. Small wonder that it has excited every succeeding generation of staff and students! Not the least unusual feature when it opened was the presence of a Rear-Admiral from Ireland as the Headmaster.

Desmond Hoare had been persuaded by Kurt Hahn to give up his naval career to found the college. His educational experience lay in the training of naval engineering apprentices. His was a dominant personality, but with his engineering background he was always ready to change his mind in the face of new evidence. His strength of personality, his lack of dismay over the dismal financial figures of the early years, his seagoing expertise in making the very most of the challenge of the Bristol Channel, and most significant of all, his readiness and ability to tackle the dynamics of a 16–19 year old community without any of the prejudgments of a professional schoolmaster, saw the college through the early crises.

The challenge of growing up

The years 1962 to 1969 were the decisive period. In that time, and with the support of the West German government, the British government, the Ford Foundation, and notable private sponsors, foundations, and trusts, the College had made sure that it was there to stay. The students, now 240, were entering universities in their home countries on agreed combinations of British 'A' level examinations and supporting subsidiary level courses. The countries of student origin extended well beyond the Atlantic Alliance and included Poland and Czechoslovakia. College teachers were taking an ever-increasing part in the creation of the syllabuses and examinations of what was shortly to become the International Baccalaureate. National committees which selected and sponsored students were working well in 20 or more countries. College students were being trained each year as crews of inshore lifeboats of the British National Lifeboat Institution, and as Surf Life Saving Association and Her Majesty's Coastguard teams, for the College had been formally entrusted with life saving duties over a 20 mile stretch of the British Channel coastline, and had already saved over 50 people. Within two years, the Atlantic Class semi-rigid inflatable craft was to enter into service with the British RNLI and with navies, coastguard services, offshore oil companies, and leisure organizations all over the world – the name was taken from the College because it had been the College headmaster who, with the daily assistance of the students, had conceived, designed, and tested this new craft until it was ready for adoption elsewhere. For a school, it was a magnificent technological achievement, and an inspiring focal point for skill of mind, hand, and body.

In 1967, the first girls had been admitted to the College 'on a strictly experimental basis'. They owed their entry to Desmond Hoare's conviction, vigorously expressed, that the College was at best half complete without them. They would have arrived earlier had the governmental body been more courageous. By 1969, they had been fully accepted by all. In 1971, the College decided that it would abandon the British system of examination in favour of the still largely unproven International Baccalaureate. Thus was the stage set for larger things.

The United World Colleges

It had all been called the Atlantic College Project up to this point. Of course, the name was no longer appropriate for worldwide expansion. When Lord Mountbatten became the President of the International Council in 1969, he insisted on an immediate change. The United World Colleges saw the light of day.

The first assumption was that the Atlantic College model was ideal and untouchable. The extraordinary success of the rescue service in the Bristol Channel imposed a straitjacket on all other proposals. Without something similar, no school could be a UWC. Cuxhaven in Germany offered a site, and a modest number of annual accidents and fatalities in the mouth of the Elbe as bait. Indecision won the day, and the site was used for other things. A second

German attempt was made at Edenkobenm in Rheinland-Pfalz, but became lost in the local bureaucracy, and a strange attempt was made to organize rescue services for emergencies in the 40-kilometre distant Rhine. Other proposals came under study, often detailed study, and at different times Iran, the Philippines, Australia, and India might have had their own colleges. Frustration over the lack of involvement of the United States in the enterprise led to an impetuously warm welcome for a college in Vermont which would, as its characteristic feature, rotate its students around several campuses in the US. A study of the likely costs sent this proposal the way of its predecessors. Happily, things were going on in Canada and South East Asia.

The Lester B Pearson United World College of the Pacific

Lester Pearson, the Nobel Prize winner and recently retired Canadian Premier, had been approached on behalf of the Atlantic College both by Sir Lawrence Darvall, Commandant of the NATO Defence College at the time of Kurt Hahn's visit, and by Lord Mountbatten. Pearson had been loosely involved in a determined but unfruitful effort to set up a Canadian version of the Atlantic College in the Banff National Park in Alberta. Then, he visited St Donat's and was enthralled. He brought his wife on a second and longer visit. When he died, his family chose a Canadian United World College as his memorial in preference over the then nascent United Nations University which found a home in Tokyo. The informal Canadian-style, village atmosphere of the timber buildings on the spectacular site on the south coast of Vancouver Island and the welcoming and warm personality of its first director Jack Matthews, enabled the Lester Pearson UWC of the Pacific to provide a loyal but fresh interpretation of the Atlantic College model and, in one bound, to surmount the difficulties of 1968 which, with some time lag, were still affecting the mother college. Pearson College was a timely shot in the arm. Its immediate success spread new confidence throughout the movement. By limiting student numbers to 200, it highlighted the importance of personal relationships, relationships between students themselves and, with almost dramatic effect, between students and teaching staff. The scholarship policy was firm – no entry without a full scholarship which covered all costs; and the Canadian federal government and the Canadian International Development Agency (CIDA) backed the college with both capital and scholarship funding.

Armand Hammer UWC and the UWC of the Adriatic

Two further colleges have been founded on the Atlantic/Pearson model: in September 1982, the Armand Hammer UWC of the American West in New Mexico and the UWC of the Adriatic in Duino, near Trieste in Italy. The American College was set up in fine American style in less than 12 months by Armand Hammer, who had been captured for the idea first by Lord Mountbatten and then by the Prince of Wales. Its extensive wilderness and rescue programme is the nearest equivalent in any other college to the rescue service of St Donat's. The Italian College, ten years in the making, is unique in the movement in having been created and funded by government – by the Regional Government of Friuli-Venezia Giulia with help from the central authorities in Rome. Like the North American colleges, it has 200 scholarship students. Unlike them, it lives, not an isolated existence, but in the middle of a village – its campus is the village of Duine. It is now playing an important part in educational cooperation between the Italian Ministry of Foreign Affairs and the governments of the countries of Central and Eastern Europe.

The United World College of South East Asia

From Singapore, UWC events had been taking a different course. Desmond Hoare had given up the Atlantic College headship in 1969. Now, he was travelling in South East Asia to drum up scholarship support. He discovered another world. Harshly, or so it seemed to his previous colleagues, he turned on his own creation. 'What have we to do with the real world problems of poverty, repression, and strife? The shift in thinking on how and why and in what to educate, the development of human instruments controlling human change, social and personal?' (1971); and 'If his (Hahn's) strength had lasted another ten years, he would, I am sure, be pushing the Atlantic College Project into the problems of 1980, especially the problems of hunger in the Third World. His passion for rescue as an educational force could not have led him elsewhere.' (1976)

From Singapore, Hoare attempted the impossible – a two-year college on a tripod, in which each student would spend one-third of the course each in Singapore, Malaysia, and Indonesia. It failed. He attempted an 'Atlantic College' on the island of Singapore, but his preferred and only site was refused him. He finally compromised with the new International School of Singapore, which was being set up by the Chamber of Commerce at the urging of the government, to provide for the expatriate business community of Singapore and with its boarding section for the many similar families scattered throughout South East Asia.

The new Third World commitment, the service element, and the outdoor physical pursuits were all catered for, after laborious negotiations between the International School and the UWC, and with a 'jungle centre' being built across the Straits in Johore. Scholarship students were to be entered into the final two years of the school by the existing and new Asian Committees; they should give leadership to the others. After a period of associate membership, the whole school was declared to be a United World College, and thus all its pupils for all ages, whatever their precise reasons for being in the school, were students of UWC. The selection and scholarship principle had been abandoned. In its place was the belief that UWC should no longer be exclusive, that it had an important but unexplored role to play in helping existing international schools to raise their sights, that such schools were a more realistic reflection of the life of the world of the international communities, and that, in this way, the UWC doctrine could be shared much more widely and at a much lower cost.

The Waterford Kamhlaba United World College of Southern Africa

The acceptance of the Singapore UWC of South East Asia was controversial. Its admission was guided largely by Lord Mountbatten, the UWC International President, who was avid for expansion. The precedent made it much easier to welcome, a few years later, the school of Waterford Kamhlaba in Swaziland. Waterford had been an intensely idealistic centre, begun in 1963 in native huts in Swaziland because the South African regime could not tolerate such a school. Entry is not by scholarship alone, but no pupil is ever refused for lack of money – fundraising for the fees continues throughout the year in a perpetual effort to balance the books. Community service is deeply embedded in the ethic of the school and had been from the outset. The school runs a wheelchair workshop providing wheelchairs and handicapped aids at Third World prices for handicapped people in the local community. As an international and integrated community, Waterford Kamhlaba offers many opportunities for students to experience at first hand the contrasts and potentials of the world in which they live.

Simon Bolivar United World College of Agriculture in Venezuela

Tensions over issues in UWC were strong during the 1970s. They were even stronger than the personalities. Desmond Hoare's was a lone voice in seeking to redirect the aims of the project. His proposal for a vocational school for apprentices in Thailand, which enjoyed some prestigious support locally, was seen as irrelevant in London. He wrote up rather detailed schemes for training schools devoted to Third World agriculture management. They stimulated enthusiastic support from former students, anxious to see the UWC embrace a new ideal, but other topical concerns prevailed. It was not until the mid-1980s that the issue of principles returned. It was the new President, the Prince of Wales, successor to Lord Mountbatten, who found his own ideas on the Third World, traditional agriculture, and the environment to be very closely in harmony with the thinking of many former students.

The result was the Simon Bolivar UWC of Agriculture in Venezuela. Some 150 post-secondary students, all on scholarship, spend mornings in the fields learning practical agriculture skills. In the afternoon, they study languages, accountancy, computing, sciences relevant to agriculture, and international affairs. The College grows most of its own food and has a variety of projects in renewable energy. It also has a most ambitious programme of agriculture, social, and educational assistance to the surrounding village communities. Its aim is to produce farm managers who will have a strong sense of community commitment, will be aware of the international nature of the task of rural development, and will span the classic gap in the developing countries between the laboratory scientist and the peasant. The UWC administration and committees are enthusiastic about this new direction in their affairs and under the energetic pressure of their President, are currently looking for a second site for a similar college in West Africa. How widely, one wonders, may the UWC river flow without losing the force of its current or the clear marking of its banks?

Problems to consider

For some, UWC means selection on merit and entry by scholarship only; focus on the final two years only of secondary education in order to ensure that the social–disciplinary framework can place the maximum degree of responsibility on the students themselves; and a programme of academic studies for the IB combined with activities and community service which is extremely demanding of the able young people who are chosen to embark on it. For others, UWC is enriched and made more relevant by the addition of the colleges in Singapore and Swaziland because those schools are less elitist; they are more representative of the real needs of international community service; children below the age of 16 are equally able and deserving of being inspired by international ideals. Other international schools around the world who would like to hoist the UWC flag should be welcome to do so. As to the Third World needs, all the existing colleges, in different measure, have substantial numbers of students from developing countries, but is the education they provide really suitable and relevant? For the UWC to develop a new type of institution in the Third World itself, explicitly responsive to world issues such as hunger and sustainable development, brings not only a new dimension but a sense of completeness to the enterprise overall. But is UWC wandering with good intentions but lack of expertise into an arena in which experts abound already?

The UWC Board of Directors has more than once commissioned a general development plan. However, though hypotheses are easy to formulate, the most wishful and idealistic thinking does not resolve the question of money, and here the issue is crystal clear. Capital funding can generally be found. The deterrent is the need, year after year, for scholarships. Before a new college can be approved, it has to be shown that it will discover and release new sources of scholarship support. The National Committees as they exist are presently at full stretch. Not all are deterred, and detailed proposals for IB scholarship colleges are at this moment under consideration from Norway, Hong Kong, and Bulgaria. Italy is even contemplating a second college in the south. One or two other countries, already well informed about the scholarship burden, are nevertheless feeling their way forward.

In spite of their 28-year existence, the United World Colleges have escaped serious educational scrutiny from writers or researchers. Literature on the colleges is overwhelmingly press literature, or has been prepared by the colleges themselves for their own purposes. Is there a coherent explanation for their achievements?

Evaluation

It can perhaps be said that UWC planners knew how to catch the tide. In the 1960s, it was clear that the western world wanted to find a way out of the Cold War, a way however which reflected western values. Men of influence in that decade (and they were men not women) had generally fought in the war themselves. A project in education which combined internationalism and peace with the martial virtues of disciplined service to others, together with exposure to the formative benefits of residential life, attracted a supportive response. It cannot have been chance that Hahn found his most enthusiastic allies among military men – Darvall, Hoare, Mountbatten, and their counterparts in other countries.

By the 1970s, the problems of the mobile and expatriate families were sand not oil in the wheels of international trade. An international academic passport was required; it was both a practical and an idealistic target. Throughout this decade, the Atlantic College, joined in 1974 by the Pearson College, was the workhorse of the evolving International Baccalaureate, both as a vehicle for its examinations and equivalence agreements, and as a source of curriculum research and testing. The 1980s have seen expansion (new colleges in the US and Italy), consolidation of the international organization and of working methods, and, more significantly, the entry of the Third World agricultural dimension into UWC affairs. A forecast for the 1990s suggests that the Third World dimension will become more firmly established and expanded; and that the original concept may find itself sought after for new political and cultural environments such as Central and Eastern Europe and the Chinese world.

UWC has been skilful in its search for support, but fortunate too in its success. The Kurt Hahn technique was well learned. The Ford Foundation and the British and West German governments were impressive catches at a time when nothing was proven. The Dulverton Trust and the Bernard Sunley Trust were only two among innumerable other British sponsors who have helped to keep the Atlantic College afloat. Lord Mountbatten, the Prince of Wales, Lester Pearson, and Armand Hammer are world names, among others, who have drawn many into the orbit of UWC. Prince Sadruddin Aga Khan, the former UN High Commissioner for Refugees, and Thor Heyerdahl are two others who as members of the organization have established its prestige. The Canadian government and Canadian industry have backed the name and official memorial of Lester Pearson with remarkable force. The Italian government views the College in Duino as an important expression of what it is proud of in post-war Italian foreign policy. Does UWC deserve all this?

First, it is necessary to believe that internationalism in today's world requires more than lip service and holiday camps in the summer. It requires the commitment of the best. Fundamentally, the colleges work because their students are voluntarily committing two years of their lives to studying away from home, with new classmates, new teachers, in a new curriculum, and, for most of them, in a new language, because they believe that the aims of the college are important. If they fail their examinations, they lose the time they have spent there. Their motivation is high, and explains why they succeed.

Second, the selection is rigorous, and the availability of scholarships makes it open and fair. But the selection has more to do with personal qualities – motivation, idealism, interest in world affairs, proven talent in music, the arts, or other pursuits – than with school grades.

Third, the principles of selection are in harmony with the actual programme of the colleges, because it is above all the activities and community services which create attitudes for life. Alec Dickson, the founder of both Voluntary Service Overseas and Community Service Volunteers, and an influential figure too within UWC circles, used to lament that community service was all too often restricted to the non-academic child or for those children who themselves were in need of some reform. How can talented and intelligent young people remain untouched and unaffected when their education challenges them with the reality of a call-out siren which may, at any time, summon them as experts to deal with emergencies involving serious injuries or even fatalities; with cleaning and redecorating the homes of slum dwellers in Cardiff and Belfast; with responsibility for the welfare and financial security of senile survivors of a small Yugoslavian refugee community in the derelict part of Trieste; with the gentle, very gradual persuading of an anguished Italian couple to lay aside their sense of shame and allow their deformed 16-year-old son for the first time to leave their home twice a week for excursions; with assistance in activities for children doomed to early death by cystic fibrosis; with weekly visits to permanently bedridden and paralyzed young people of their own age?

Fourth, the academic programme is the International Baccalaureate. Just as the community service has shown itself for almost 30 years to be equally challenging and meaningful to the students irrespective of their country and culture of origin, so too the IB has proved itself to be a remarkable instrument for engaging the intellectual commitment of able young people from over 100 countries. It is, we would judge, not a difficult examination in which to achieve passing grades – the safety net is low. But high grades require steady work over two years from even the most able. What are its key features? UWC experience suggests the following: the choice of courses within the given framework which insists on a general, liberal education; the possibility of working at two different levels (three courses at higher and three courses at subsidiary level); IB insistence that all students follow courses and take examinations in their mother tongue language and literature, a valuable statement in a system which could easily have ignored the significance of cultural roots; the amount of personal reading required in most subjects, and the lack of dependence on standard textbooks; the important role of classroom discussion which favours oral presentation and contributes to the continuous internal assessment; the mini-research work necessitated by the guided coursework presentations in subjects such a history and economics; the challenge of the extended essay; the unique and thought-provoking course in the Theory of Knowledge; the constant and evolving contact between teachers and examiners; the fascination exercised by the fact that the majority of the students and a proportion of the teachers are working in a second or third language. For most students from outside the Anglo-Saxon tradition, the seriousness and practical nature of the science courses is a revelation. For those from within the Anglo-Saxon camp, the requirements in the languages are no less a shock and stimulus. For all, there is the excitement of seeing history, economics, philosophy, and other subjects in an entirely new light.

Finally, selection means elitism, and the United World Colleges are saved by their scholarship programmes. If ever the scholarship funds dry up, the colleges must close. But the selection procedures have perhaps been undeservedly free of other criticisms. Selection at the age of 16 or 17 implies a high dependency on school grades, on an assessment of an unformed personality, on the evaluation of performance at interview which gives very great advantage to the precociously mature and articulate. Where does this leave the late developer, the shy candidate, the candidate from the home which lacks a sophisticated cultural background and social confidence, the candidate in many countries, notably in Latin America, whose knowledge of English is poor or non-existent, the candidate for whom loyalty to family and to current friends are the highest values, the introvert? We should, I think, be clearer than we are in recognizing that the United World Colleges have had a natural attraction for ambitious 'action men' and 'action women', a less obvious attraction for the artistic, the dreamers, and the late developers. Kurt Hahn would not be pleased.

Interaction with national education

International education is almost compelled to be independent education. Few teachers in international schools, particularly if they are making a lifelong career in international education, are from countries in which teachers are civil servants. The only regular exceptions are teachers in national schools abroad (the French Overseas Lycées, the German Auslandsschulen), whose international aspects are secondary to the national emphasis, and the schools of the European Community. The difficulties are the lack of freedom to move and respond to openings as they occur, the national career and pension structures, and the general bureaucracy. Most teachers on the international circuit are therefore either British or American. In a small but growing way, this trend is being strengthened by the wish of the IB schools in, for example, Holland and the Scandinavian countries, to recruit British teachers to teach their IB courses in the mother tongue English; and by schools too in Central and Eastern Europe which, among other things, are wishing hurriedly to make up for years of neglect of the English language. Nor do the United World Colleges find it easy to act otherwise as an examination of their teaching staffs, and above all the distribution of the responsibilities within their staff rooms, will show. The residential nature of the Colleges also requires residential school experience, again something more readily available from teachers from Britain and North America. For the UWC, the new Simon Bolivar College is a striking and refreshing exception since it is to provide locally based practical training for managing modern agricultural enterprises and also to promote the principles and objectives of UWC.

Conclusion

The intensity of the UWC experience is not easy for all. Idealism at the age of 16 is an uncompromising sense of expectation. The knowledge that shared humanity means shared weaknesses as well as shared strengths is sobering, in some cases disillusioning. Frequently, UWC students struggle to regain their early sense of perhaps naive idealism in the second year. Two years in a close international and residential community is an extremely testing experience. Those who are strong become stronger. The redeeming feature is, year after year, the quality of the personal concern which the students demonstrate for one another, the calibre, warmth, and durability of the friendships which are created. Then the challenge of entering the College is followed by the challenge of returning to the real world. Almost all require several months to a year to readjust. Certain questions have not yet found their answers. Does the heady, idealistic experience give the strength to challenge the world's conformities and prejudices constantly thereafter? Or does nostalgia for the briefly experienced paradise suffocate the capacity for action? The 10,000-strong worldwide network of ex-students developing their own careers but becoming increasingly active in community service projects in their home country would say not.

In the early days of the Atlantic College, the teachers came from the state schools and the College was proud of the number of colleagues who went on to become heads of schools in the British and in other national systems. The growth in the number of UWC, IB, and international schools generally has diminished this contact. This can only be regretted. For above all, the United World Colleges offer a model of active, committed, unprejudiced political education whose lifetime influence deserves a wide echo in other classrooms. How can it be otherwise when UWC history classes on the 19th and 20th centuries are attended by teachers and pupils from all the world's political creeds; when Lybian pupils struggle with the problem of how to justify to their parents that they have been studying physics under a teacher from Israel whom they love and respect; when a student from the Republic of China leaves a class in economics in protest that what is being taught is not economics but indoctrination and then must justify himself to his classmates and his teacher over the lunchtable; when the Argentinian who has spent two years in Wales anguishes over his duty to his country and his debt to Britain when faced with call-up at the time of the Falklands conflict; when the closest friend of the Eritrean student whose father is a guerilla fighter is the only Ethiopian in the school; when another Ethiopian of a different generation whose 12 relatives at home were all illiterate and with whom he had not been able to communicate for two years, sends his Japanese roommate back to Ethiopia to explain to them that he has won a scholarship to Canada and cannot return because the government would send him to fight against the rebels; when while one brother, a refugee student from South Africa, spent two years at the College the other brother spent two years in the prisons on Robben Island; when a white girl from Johannesburg arrived in Italy she spoke to her first black person, her roommate from Swaziland.

Shakespeare's King Lear cried out to the blinded Gloucester on the heath, 'You see how the world goes,' and Gloucester answers, 'I see it feelingly.' Can we inside and outside UWC teach the young, with Gloucester, to 'see the world feelingly'?

4. International endeavour

John Paterson

Prologue

After the Second World War, the growth in the numbers of diplomats, members of the armed forces (particularly those of Britain and America), and businessmen serving in foreign countries was marked; this growth continued for the next quarter of a century. Increasingly, the personnel concerned were of an age group which included many parents of young children. The armed forces overseas provided schools for such children, British diplomats and businessmen sent their children to boarding school in the UK, and the Americans started overseas schools – often loosely attached to embassies or directly sponsored by large industrial concerns. In Switzerland, boarding schools were set up for the teenage children of expatriates in countries where there were no English-speaking high schools.

Foundation

It was under the aegis of the International Schools Foundation (later to become International Schools Services – ISS) that meetings of heads of American schools overseas, together with some other international schools, were held annually either in Europe or the Near East. In one such gathering in Beirut in 1962, the seed was sown for a new organization: there the representatives of 14 schools in Europe met in the bar (there being no other available room!) to discuss the formation of a local linking organization. In May 1963, at a meeting in Switzerland, the tentative name of Council of European Schools Serving American Students was suggested, and a questionnaire was circulated on fees, salaries paid to teachers, taxes, and host governments requirements. Later, discussions mooted the idea of trying to become a regional office of ISS and also proposed organizing subject conferences for in-service training. In the spring of 1964, it was announced that the US State Department had set up a committee to coordinate the allocation of funds to American overseas schools: this was the root from which sprang the Office of Overseas Schools which, although primarily concerned with schools assisted by the US State Department, has been immensely cooperative with regional organizations of international schools ever since its foundation.

At the 1964 ISS Autumn Conference, Arthur Denyer, the first headmaster of the International School of Brussels, proposed that a worldwide association of overseas schools be set up within the framework of, but independent from, ISS. 'The ISS', he said 'is not a membership organization and cannot, in any case, do many of the things for us which we should properly be doing for ourselves. Nor can we join the US State Department.' Denyer thought that the proposed organization should have local offices and perhaps a central office in Europe to collate and coordinate among other things the services available to schools from ISS and the Office of Overseas Schools. He suggested that the new organization could supply other agencies with advice and with accurate and coordinated information. Membership should be open to schools and to individuals. Dr Denyer proposed the title of 'Council of International Schools'. The proposal was approved and a draft constitution was prepared.

The period of gestation finally reached its climax at a meeting in Geneva in March 1965, attended by representatives of 18 schools and some supporting agencies. Here the name European Council of International Schools was adopted for the first time, together with a draft constitution, and the new organization was born. Its objectives were to be involved with personnel placement, in-service training, evaluation and accreditation, the dissemination of information on curriculum development, methodology, and materials.

Development

In October 1966, when ECIS was registered as a non-profit association in Switzerland, there were 25 dues-paying member schools. The first full-time Executive Secretary was appointed in 1970 and had his home (and office) in Switzerland, where the organization was based until 1974 when the first independent secretariat was established in Surbiton, Surrey with Dr Gray Mattern, a retired headmaster from Massachusetts as the Executive Secretary – a post he occupied for 15 years.

By the tenth anniversary of its foundation in 1975, ECIS had 81 regular school members, 108 associate members (schools outside Europe, and universities and tertiary colleges), 25 supporting members (firms supplying books, equipment, and services to schools), 8 individual members, and 14 honorary members – nominated in recognition of their services to the organization. The most important change in the conference that year was its turn towards offering a diversity of workshops and demonstrations for teachers. Heads of schools and college counsellors continued to attend, as well as exhibitors who wished to supply teaching materials and other supplies to the individual schools. As the ECIS Administrative Office developed, they became involved in more liaison and support activities. They organized, with the Harvard University Graduate School of Education, a successful Summer Institute for Principals, worked with the International Baccalaureate Office, and, more recently, collaborated with the University of Cambridge Local Examinations Syndicate in the development of the International General Certificate of Secondary Education and the training of teachers for this programme.

In the second decade, it became apparent that new categories of membership were needed to accommodate the interest in affiliation to ECIS. The category of provisional membership was created to accommodate newly established schools until such time as the condition of full membership might be met; and in recent years a number of education-related organizations – tutorial schools, summer/winter camps, short-term enrichment programmes catering for special interests – have become affiliated members. But the largest growth of all has been among individual members – professional people worldwide with a specific interest in international education, to most of whom ECIS has at one time or another provided assistance in securing an appointment at an international school. To give some idea of the growth the following figures on membership are of interest:

	March '81	*March '86*	*March '89*
Regular	110	135	154
Provisional	11 (NSS)*	6	7
Associate (sch)	27	83	108
Associate (univ/col)	128	200	236
Affiliate	–	13	11
Supporting	41	43	38
Individual	200	334	440

(NSS)* New Schools are commonly admitted into provisional membership if the ECIS board so votes after their first year of operation: prior to 1985 these schools were affiliated with the Council under the title 'New School Services'.

Additionally, its autumn conferences became more and more multi-programmed three-day mammoths during which, after the opening session, the delegates split up into as many as a dozen different groups at any one time for workshops, demonstrations, and lectures covering most secondary school subjects, primary school activities and techniques, administrative problems and procedures, workshops for board members, computer training, general sessions on health education and the advent of new examinations such as the International Baccalaureate and International General Certificate of Secondary Education. The 1988 conference in Hamburg drew almost 2,000 delegates and 150 exhibitors. The growth of the organization also meant the growth of the support services.

Accreditation

As early as 1965, the subject of accreditation had been discussed as a possible role for ECIS. It was felt that the International Schools had features that were different from US-type schools: for example, frequently they would be using buildings which were not purpose-built but were all that were available; sometimes finances would be precarious with little or no long-term capital investment being possible; and there were difficulties about work permits, customs regulations concerning books and materials, laws concerning admission of host-country nationals, tax laws, and in many areas the need for boarding accommodation. It was felt that such factors, together with differences in curriculum offerings and the huge expense (especially to small schools) of getting visiting teams from America to Europe, made the consideration of US accreditation formidable – in many cases clearly impossible even if the school was worthy. The Middle States Association of Colleges and Schools was the only accrediting agency working in Europe until 1972, and they gave a number of ECIS schools a very necessary service. However, there were schools in Europe – such as the truly international schools (as distinct from the American schools overseas) and, in due course, the British-type international schools – which desired to go through a process of evaluation but did not want it to be American based. In 1968, serious work started on the drafting of documents for ECIS evaluation and accreditation. Great credit is due to the first four schools who participated in the project at a time when it was uncertain whether ECIS accreditation would be recognized by anyone else. When schools expressed an interest in evaluation by both ECIS and the Middle States Association, joint evaluations were based on a single document and with a single visiting team, composed of representatives of both organizations working together. In the ensuing years, ECIS accreditation has become an increasingly valuable credential among international schools; it is now recognized, whether on its own or jointly, and being sought by schools worldwide.

Personnel service

In 1974 the decision to make staffing for schools an active and more important part of ECIS services was taken. It was then that the category of individual membership took on new significance as such members were given the right to maintain full professional dossiers at the Secretariat, from which files could be passed to prospective employers. The ECIS Staffing Service work goes on all the year round to help schools find placements for unexpected vacancies and to provide resources for headteachers who are looking for future staffing needs. In addition to routine work on the files of candidates, the department also carries out specially designed searches for teaching and administrative staff at the request of individual schools. Searches for heads of schools (at the request of school boards) are directed by the Executive Secretary with the support of the Staffing Services Section.

One feature of the section's work has become particularly conspicuous in its attractiveness for schools right around the globe: the Annual London Teacher Recruitment Centre. Its growth is shown in the following numbers: in 1982, 100 candidates and 35 schools participated, but in 1989, 455 candidates and 80 schools participated. The most important statistical measure of the section's success is the number of candidates taking up new appointments as a result of the ECIS placement service at the beginning of or during the school year: 1981/82 saw 62 placements and 1988/89 saw 160 candidates. In 1981/82, the ECIS office had dossiers for 211 individual members: as at April 1989 this had increased to 440. Of these, approximately 55 per cent are of American or Canadian nationality and 30 per cent are British. In recent years, ECIS has worked with about 150 schools each year in connection with staffing, and these schools have been located in some 65 countries.

The College Committee

The College Committee is really two committees: one consisting only of school counsellors and representing their broad concerns across a wide range of students; another concentrating only on activities of US-based institutions of higher education. Each year in the autumn and in the spring, a college tour is held sponsoring a College Day with admissions officers from many universities for two or three schools within the reach of a host city. In the spring, a College Tour representing British universities, polytechnics, and colleges in the UK is also held. In addition, workshops on college–university guidance-related matters are planned at each yearly conference. A new development has been the promotion of tours for college-guidance counsellors in schools to visit universities and colleges in the US and also to see some in Britain.

School services

The mandate of the School Services Officer is to discover and implement programmes of action by ECIS which would enhance the performance of professional staff in member schools. Initially, there were organized meetings of teachers in certain fields to develop ideas for further conferences and newsletters to maintain contact. Later, the committee began, with grants from ECIS, to meet between conferences and cover more subject areas. In 1982, the 13 original committees were enlarged by a system of funded projects to promote in-service training of teachers. The 1988/89 budget of more than £30,000 supported 30 separate events each year, ranging from maths and music competitions to workshops in social studies, special education, science teaching, ESL, and computer studies. Inservice Bulletins are issued twice a year, in October and February, giving full details of the above activities. In 1982, ECIS organized training workshops for teachers dealing with the International Baccalaureate programme. These were so successful that the IB office decided to continue them under their own auspices.

Finally, the International GCSE as a separate examination for students in international schools might never have come about but for cooperation between ECIS and the University of Cambridge Local Examinations Syndicate. The two bodies organized a whole series of training workshops for teachers at ECIS conferences and now run courses in Cambridge to keep up this work.

Publications

Quite early in the development of ECIS, it was recognized that there was a need for a listing of international schools in Europe, mainly for the information of companies sending their employees to this region – employees who needed to know how their children might continue their education in the medium of the English language. From a simple early beginning and with the addition of advertising to support the costs, the directory developed to the point where it became universally regarded as the most accurate and comprehensive source of information about international schools around the world. In 1989 because of increased membership, a separate directory, *The ECIS Higher Education Directory*, of institutions of higher education was also produced.

This list of principal publications gives an idea of the scope of the activities of the organization in pursuing its aim of assisting member schools.

☐ *Guide to School Evaluation and Accreditation*
☐ *International Schools Journal*
☐ *The ECIS Policy Planner*
☐ *The Most Important Decision*
☐ *A Sample Contract for Heads of International Schools*
☐ *Languages and Cultures in English Language-based International Schools*
☐ *Effective Libraries in International Schools.*

Awards and fellowships

Since 1984, ECIS has offered each year the Award for International Understanding to students in member schools around the world who have been nominated by the teaching staff of the school concerned, recognizing meritorious contributions to international understanding. In 1989, 119 awards were made.

In 1986–87, annual fellowships in International Education began to offer financial support to teachers in member schools wishing to conduct original research into some aspect of education having specific relevance to the needs of those working and/or learning in international schools. Three awards are made each year.

Research

The Council conducts an annual survey to gather statistics among its members from which data is collated on enrolment, tuition and other fees, teachers' salaries and benefits; this information is tabulated and provided only to participating schools. A separate document detailing the salary and benefit packages of administrators is also published and issued to participating administrators. From time to time, other research is conducted at the request of the membership at large or of particular members.

Conclusion

At the time of its 25th anniversary, ECIS had member schools (regular or associate) in 82 countries representing every continent on earth. At its autumn conferences, there are regularly over 2,000 participants mainly from Europe but also from America, the Near and Middle East, Africa, and the Far East. Headmasters from all over the world attend the annual London Recruitment Centre, and ECIS publications – especially the *Directory of International Schools* – are read and used far beyond the confines of Europe.

Among the 60 or so schools which have been accredited by the European

Council of International Schools are two in America, four in Africa, and two in Asia for whom the 'European' connotation makes little sense – except that it is the only international accreditation available. Thus the organization has clearly developed to become more and more like the 'Council of International Schools' foreseen by Arthur Denyer in 1964.

At the same time, there is much to be done in the organization's home territory. Recent historic political developments in Eastern Europe, the removal of barriers, and the opening up of frontiers, coupled with the almost equally important if less dramatic changes due in the European Economic Community in 1992, will mean that there are new challenges to ECIS and its regular member schools.

The importance of expanding education in international understanding and the provision of more schools where children of different nationalities and cultures can grow up together will provide a wonderful new opportunity – and a severe test – for a new international endeavour.

5. The International General Certificate of Secondary Education

John Sadler

Introduction

The International General Certificate of Secondary Education (IGCSE) is a curriculum aimed at students aged 14–16 and over. It is rapidly attracting the attention and interest of educators, employers, and publishers from many countries around the world. The IGCSE was developed by the University of Cambridge Local Examinations Syndicate (UCLES) at the request of teachers from a number of international schools, who expressed the need for a curriculum which:

- ☐ Reflected the changes being made in the United Kingdom where the General Certificate of Education Ordinary level and the Certificate of Secondary Education were being replaced by a single system, the General Certificate of Secondary Education.
- ☐ Was genuinely international.
- ☐ Would allow students to follow either A' levels or the International Baccalaureate.
- ☐ Led to a universally accepted qualification.
- ☐ Allowed students and teachers to transfer with relative ease between schools in different countries.

The IGCSE is recognized for matriculation purposes as a preliminary requirement by all the universities and polytechnics in the UK and by a large number of universities and colleges worldwide.

The IGCSE model

The model adopted by UCLES for many of the IGCSE syllabuses in the curriculum is the Core and Extended model. The Core syllabus has a limited content and, when assessed, the grades available are C (highest), D, E, F, and G (lowest). The Extended syllabus has either increased content or greater depth. When the Extended syllabus is assessed, the grades available are A (highest), B, C, D, and E (lowest).

Having a Core and Extended model puts the onus on teachers to enter candidates at the right level of assessment. However, it appears to have caused teachers very few problems. Teachers are given grade descriptions for each subject, and these, together with their own knowledge of their students, allows them to make the 'right' decisions for level of entry. In some subjects, such as history, all students study the same content and are assessed in the same way. Grading is based entirely on 'outcome' – how well the students answer the questions. The assessment takes place in either June or November.

Novel features of IGCSE

There are many novel features in the IGCSE. There are two sets of language syllabuses, 'first' and 'foreign'; first language syllabuses are for native speakers. The language examination papers are written entirely in the language being tested (including all the instructions). There are no translation papers; the skills tested are reading, writing, speaking, and listening. There is also a syllabus in English as a Second Language, designed for students for whom English is a second or working language. Since all the examinations (apart from language examinations) are in English, it is important to have an assessment in the working language. Again, the skills assessed are those relating to communication.

The syllabuses are divided into six groups as follows:

GROUP I: LANGUAGES

First language:

Dutch
English
French
German
Japanese
Portuguese
Lesotho
Spanish

Second language:

English

Foreign languages:

Dutch
French
German
Italian
Portuguese
Spanish

GROUP II: HUMANITIES AND SOCIAL SCIENCE

Business Studies
Child Development
Classical Civilization
Economics
Geography
History
Latin
Literature
Religious Studies
Sociology

GROUP III: SCIENCES

Agriculture
Biology
Chemistry
Combined Science
Combined Science
Additional Combined Science (double subject)
Food Science
Physics
Science (Biology, Chemistry)
Science (Biology, Physics)
Science (Chemistry, Physics)
Textiles

GROUP IV: MATHEMATICS

Mathematics

GROUP V: CREATIVE ARTS AND TECHNOLOGY

Art and Design
Music
Craft, Design and Technology (CDT)
- Computer Studies
- Design and Communication
- Design and Realization
- Design and Technology

GROUP VI: NATURAL ECONOMY

Natural Economy

Students may enter for any number of IGCSE subjects, and they receive a certificate listing the subjects and grades obtained. Alternatively, they may choose to enter for the International Certificate of Education (ICE) certificate. In order to obtain the ICE, candidates must pass in at least seven subjects. These must include two subjects from Group I, one subject from each of Groups II, III, IV and V, and one other subject from any of the six groups. As the reader will appreciate, this group certificate is very similar to the diploma certificate for the International Baccalaureate taken by students at the age of about 18.

The ICE is divided into three categories:

1. *Distinction:* Grade A in five subjects and Grade C or better in two subjects;
2. *Merit:* Grade C or better in five subjects and Grade F or better in two subjects;
3. *Pass:* Grade G or better in seven subjects.

It is believed that a *Merit* award in ICE is an excellent benchmark for deciding whether or not students should undertake further academic studies. If students entered for ICE fail to meet the requirements, they receive an IGCSE certificate detailing the passes obtained.

Another development under consideration is a new certificate which mirrors the IB diploma even more closely. The new certificate might contain seven subjects (two from Group I, and one from each of Groups II, III, IV, and Natural Economy), together with an International Youth Award (such as the Duke of Edinburgh Award or the Crown Prince Award).

Innovative syllabuses

Natural Economy is one of the newer syllabuses, and UCLES believes it should be accessible to all students. It is an interdisciplinary subject, relating human demands on renewable and non-renewable resources to the finite supply of these resources through the natural system. It deals with the patterns of human behaviour necessary to preserve and manage the environment as a self-sustaining resource base. It is a truly international syllabus and will appeal to everyone throughout the world concerned about our planet. It has been enthusiastically welcomed by everyone concerned about the environment. Other syllabuses that are breaking new ground include: Development Studies and the innovative Music syllabus.

Assessment of IGCSE

A variety of forms of assessment are available in the IGCSE examination, ranging from multiple choice questions, short answer questions, essays, orals, aurals, and practical tests to course work. Course work is work carried out by the students in schools and, depending on the syllabus, can consist of a project, folio of essays, field work, art and craft work, design studies, practical work, or any other form of internally set test. The course work is marked initially by teachers. In order for schools to undertake internal assessment of course work in a particular subject, at least one teacher of that subject must have been trained by UCLES and hold the appropriate letter or certificate of authorization. This authorization can be obtained either by attending an IGCSE training course in Cambridge or elsewhere, or by the successful completion of distance training.

Recognition and thanks must be given to the European Council of International Schools and in particular their Emeritus Executive Secretary, Dr Gray Mattern. Without the cooperation and solid support of this superb organization, the IGCSE might not have come about. With the help of ECIS, UCLES has organized INSET training sessions in Brussels, Madrid, Rome, Montreux, Paris, and Vienna. Training courses have also been run in Marbella, Lausanne, Hilversum (The Netherlands), Nairobi, Lusaka, Buenos Aires, Athens, Bermuda, and Dubai. Further training courses and workshops are planned.

Conclusion

Interest in the IGCSE is growing rapidly worldwide. The entries for both the 1989 June and November examinations were double the 1988 entries, while the number of IGCSE centres trebled. The forecast is that this trend will continue until at least 1995. At the time of writing there are IGCSE centres in the following countries:

Argentina	Hong Kong
Papua New Guinea	Belgium
India	Peru
Bermuda	Israel

Portugal
Italy
Canada
Spain
Lesotho
Costa Rica
Sudan
Malta
Egypt
Syria
Mozambique
El Salvador
UK
Nigeria
France
Vanuatu
Gibraltar
Zambia
Pakistan
Brazil
Saudi Arabia
Jordan
Colombia
Sri Lanka
Malaysia
Dubai
Switzerland
Mexico
Eire
Tanzania
The Netherlands
Fiji
USA
Norway
Germany
Yemen
Oman
Greece

It can be safely said that UCLES has achieved its aim of producing a curriculum which is widely accepted by schools, colleges and universities, and which prepares students for both academic and vocational careers. If you would like further details please write to the IGCSE Coordinator, University of Cambridge Local Examinations Syndicate, 1 Hills Road, Cambridge CB1 2EU, UK.

Part 2: The international school experience

Introduction

Patricia L Jonietz

Knight and Leach (1964) describe seven types of international schools:

1. Common Market schools.
2. French and German government schools.
3. ISA member schools with government support (including New York, Geneva, and Ghana).
4. ISA schools without government support (including Jakarta, Kabul, Belgrade, Colombo, Rome, The Hague, Brussels, Zurich, and Tehran).
5. Non-ISA schools (including Vienna, Hamburg, Frankfurt, Hellerup, Saloniki, New Delhi, and Bangkok).
6. Overseas schools (parent owned, English speaking, American or British orientation, and includes the Atlantic College).
7. Private schools operated for profit.

Some of these same categories still exist (some of the schools named are represented among the contributors to this volume), but the biggest growth area is seen in the number of independent, community-based, English language of instruction schools offering education to 'third culture' students (neither a product of the country of residence nor of their original nationality). Since 1964, these schools designed for a population of mobile students and parents have also developed a population of mobile teachers and administrators. Surrounding them are national schools offering special programmes for international students, professional service organizations for international staff, colleges and universities who recruit international students and offer training for international teachers, organizations offering international students summer and holiday programmes, and companies who supply materials purchased by the growing market of international schools.

The question is – what is it like to be part of an international school? Therefore, the aim of this section is to try to explain a 'typical' international school experience from a variety of perspectives. 'Typical' is a difficult word because these schools are in a variety of continents as well as locations (urban and rural), they have different funding bases, their populations represent different national groups, they may be affiliated with different examination boards or national organizations, they may be supported by different national or community groups, and they may be independent or receive some or all state funding. However, they are alike in their international goals and their multicultural, multilingual, and multinational populations.

Keson introduces us to the 'typical' international school and describes the problems and advantages of joining the international school education system.

Davis and Ellwood are on the staff of Vienna International School established in 1978. The school has a long history of cooperation in curriculum matters with the UN School in New York and the International School of Geneva. Associated with the IBO and ISA for many years, Vienna recently served as a pilot study for the development of both ISA and IBO curricula. Davis and Ellwood discuss the following issues: the present IB diploma, the need to establish an international curriculum before the IB years, and the curriculum model constructed by ISA. They also introduce the problem of bringing about major curriculum change in the international schools.

Three students who earned the International Baccalaureate diploma at the United World College of the Adriatic describe their experience with and understanding of an international education in an international school.

Waldron is the parent of a mentally handicapped child who attends an international school. He reviews the progress she has made, and the advantages of international education, and compares her progress to what he thinks would have been the differences in his national educational system.

Koopman, a teacher-administrator, describes the development of a nationally supported international school system. Within the Dutch state schools there are international sections offering both the IGCSE and the International Baccalaureate. These schools are designed to teach international students an international curriculum while at the same time requiring them to learn the language, history, and culture of the country in which they are living.

6. Meet Samantha and Sueng-Won, Ilse-Marie and Haaza

James Keson

Introduction

Samantha, Sueng-Won, Ilse-Marie, and Haaza are all students who can be found at Copenhagen International School, one of half a dozen international schools in Denmark. CIS, founded in 1963, is an independent English-language secondary school. Like many international schools, it is a non-profit organization, governed by a nine-member board, accredited by ECIS, offers the International Baccalaureate, and encourages all students to retain their national roots while developing an international understanding and perspective. A recent survey of nationalities found students from 35 countries, with Danish being the largest national group. How do all these diverse students find themselves in an international school in Copenhagen and not in their home lands? What if you were one of these students or one of their parents?

When you go abroad

A rising executive in Anglo-American Products, you have been given the challenge of creating a new subsidiary. The only drawback is that it will be in a part of the world you have never seen and only dimly remember from geography. You have three years to complete your assignment – too long to be away from your family. Should you take them with you?

Three days to months after hearing the news (six months if Anglo-American is an unusually enlightened company), you land in the capital city with your family. The climate is rather different from what you are used to, the street signs look strange, and the children are worried about missing their favourite TV series.

Fortunately, the Anglo-American staff has put you up in a fantastic hotel, and as soon as you have slept off the jet lag you drive out to the international school to which you have been writing. The school's stationery looked rather impressive, but the actual facilities look a bit, shall we say, makeshift? You can see that the building was not built to be a school, and the playing fields seem to be entirely lacking, but the moment you enter the characteristic smells of books, paste, and children waft to your nostrils. Crayoned drawings and notices of meetings of the drama club decorate the walls, and the children passing by seem to show an alert curiosity. Both pupils and teachers seem to be speaking with a variety of accents, not only British and American but Australian, Irish, and others less easily identified.

The headmaster seems friendly enough, although you wonder how much he knows about the special educational programme of the school from which your children came. But what else can you do – this school is the only school in the English language within miles. You take a deep breath and sign the cheque for the first term's fees.

International schools and the students who attend them

International schools really began to sprout like mushrooms in the late fifties and early sixties. Following the influx of foreigners who were setting up businesses, developing projects, and liaising between newly interdependent governments, groups of parents got together to provide temporary schools for their children. Cooperative or volunteer arrangements formed the beginnings, but it was not long before the schools moved into permanent quarters, hired proper teachers, and developed an integrated curriculum. Presently, most of the capitals of the world have at least one international school, in addition to a British or American or other national style school. In a bewildering variety of exotic locations where there are substantial groups of expatriates – for example, near oil fields, foreign aid centres, or military bases – international schools operate in much the same way as their domestic counterparts.

Often, they were instituted to duplicate the educational experience back home. But as the American and British presence ceased to dominate and as English increasingly became the lingua franca of international trade and relations, schools started to become international in programme as well as in name. Typically, international schools now may have anywhere from seven to seventy different nationalities and follow two or three different curricula.

This rich variety of backgrounds may be pretty intimidating to a youngster out of his or her home town for the first time in his or her life – but most classmates he or she will be meeting can still remember going through this experience themselves and are eager to help him or her feel at home. And since there doesn't seem to be an insistence on one particular accent or style of clothing, it is easier for each of them to maintain his or her own sense of identity. In a short while, the novelty of knowing that one's friends are from Poland, Korea, Denmark, or Saudi Arabia recedes, and students become just Samantha and Sueng-Won, Ilse-Marie and Haaza.

The international classroom

Put a dozen young people from different countries, with different cultures, languages, and customs together – and one might think that they would form a rather stiff and awkward social group. In reality, anyone who has walked into an international classroom probably found it a friendly, noisy, and fascinating place. Visitors (and parents new to the experience) often comment on how well the students get along, how they learn from their classmates, and how considerate they seem to be towards others. As one fifth-grader from 'back home' visiting his transplanted cousin once remarked, 'How come there's no fighting?' Part of the reason why the groups work well together is that the classes are generally quite small and each individual can get quite a bit of attention. The job of teaching is not very bureaucratic, so teachers can actually devote most of their time to the learning process and often spend many extra hours making sure that the needs of each student are met.

A long-time international teacher says, 'International students are fun, they don't feel the enormous pressures of a single-culture school pressing down on them, they relate well to adults, and they can also contribute a unique point of view to discussions. Like the snacks that are shared at lunchtime, each child has a different and often surprising point of view.'

An American parent was surprised when his six-year-old, who was slowly working her way through her ABCs, appeared one evening with her name written in the Greek alphabet. Wondering just what was included in the first-grade curriculum, he asked his daughter where the letters came from. 'From Demitri', she said. 'He sits next to me in class and these are the way letters look in his country.' A six-year-old learning the relationship between Greek symbols and the English alphabet is typical of the unplanned learning that often occurs.

Cultural differences

Parents bringing their children to an international school for the first time generally assume that the academic standards are in order, but they often worry about the possibility of violent political or religious confrontations. At a school which enrols Americans, Libyans, Iraqis, and Iranians, students seem to find politics and religion subjects which should be avoided by mutual consent. Not only do they agree not to discuss things if anyone in the room is sensitive, they gradually learn that their own viewpoint is not the only one possible. Maybe because their own group is most likely a minority when seen in a world perspective, international students tend to stick to the objective facts in discussions rather than blurting out their prejudices.

Students from 50 different countries see themselves differently and also see that what they hope to do when they leave school is extremely diverse. This has the interesting effect that ambitious students (and most of them have high aspirations) do not have to compete against each other. If Eric is trying to get into Harvard and Erika into the University of Tokyo, they find for themselves that cooperation is beneficial to both.

Coming from different countries, international students can bring their own customs to the school, whether it means wearing a sari or sneakers. Actually, a cursory glance around international schools indicates that the preferred uniform of teenagers around the world is probably blue jeans. If there is any common denominator, it must be pop music, which certainly bridges all gaps of nationality or culture.

Young people like these have been called third-culture students by sociologist Ruth Useem since they are neither wholly of the culture of their own country nor of that of the country they are living in. Her work shows that they are a remarkable mixture of innocence and sophistication – they know how to order a meal in five languages but not who was the winner of last year's World Series or FA Cup.

With their mobility many of them have moved half a dozen times before they have completed school, but they work hard at creating a worldwide network of contacts and friendships. When their families move on, they do keep in contact and manage, between new schools, new countries, and new friends to visit the old friends who shared important years with them.

The downside of the international experience

For the overwhelming majority of international students, moving to different countries and changing languages and schools is a challenging and stimulating experience, but there are those who suffer from it, who are numbed by yet another culture, yet another set of classmates..(Here I have to note that parents are more likely to suffer the cultural overload syndrome, and those who are most likely to be affected are mothers who have been torn out of stimulating and familiar environments to be dropped down as housewives and mothers in a strange country where they may be suddenly unemployed.) Among the culturally shellshocked are a very few young people who do suffer from not being rooted firmly in a language or culture of their own. The most extreme case I have met was a former student who, years after graduation, complained about not being totally comfortable in any of his languages (he had attended an English-language school, but talked Cantonese with his parents, and Danish with his friends). The fact that he was driving a BMW at the time makes me think that not even this turned out to be an insurmountable handicap!

A common question from parents new to international schools is, 'What content should be taught to a class of Americans, Belgians, Chinese, Danes, Ecuadoreans, French, and so on?' The answer is not as difficult as it might seem. Pupils need to be able to speak, read, and write the language of the school. As for maths, science, social studies, and physical education – parents from all over the world agree that their children need these skills when they start schooling. The difficulties tend to come at the other end, where each national system and university matriculation scheme insists on a narrow and specific set of knowledge and abilities. In response to a growing number of families returning from abroad in the sixties and seventies, programmes like the International Baccalaureate and the International General Certificate of Secondary Education have developed to provide a flexible yet acceptable curriculum for secondary students.

A serious problem for young people who return to their own country after a prolonged absence is a certain social awkwardness. After a teenager has been out of his or her native culture for a while, he or she loses touch with the language of social discourse – the current jokes, the sports teams, and the top musical groups. An international student who mentions the Swahili word for 'hamburger' or the last time he or she was in Paris may meet with disbelief or hostility. They learn that it is better to keep a low profile for a while, listening to what everyone else is talking about before beginning to unfold.

Sometimes the problems of re-entry are almost amusing – like the boy who was accepted to medical school back home in Mexico City and worked his way to the top of his class – until the authorities discovered that he had been promoted from the seventh grade to the ninth grade at his school in New Delhi and insisted that he go back to complete the eighth grade. (He managed to avoid that fate!)

The students produced by international schools

The students at international schools, because of limited contact with a large and pervasive youth culture, spend more time with their families. They are forced, often because they learn the local language before their parents, to interact with adults more than they probably did back home. People often feel that they seem more mature or sophisticated. Another difference, which is noticed by parents who are abroad even for a short period of time, is that their children's horizons expand noticeably. Not only do they begin to understand complex subjects which might have been difficult if they had not actually seen the Acropolis or a tropical rain forest, their own aspirations undergo a subtle change. 'If the person sitting next to me can study in Athens (or Anchorage or Aberdeen) then why can't I?' Or 'Since the medical profession doesn't seem to have such a bright future in my country at the moment, why not practise it in this country, or on the other side of the world?'

The effects of international schools

International schools, once a temporary solution to a fairly esoteric educational problem, now have a distinct philosophy and character, so much so that often local national families wish that their children could attend the local international school. Part of this is the prestige which seems to be inevitably associated with anything labelled 'international', as well as the results that are possible from dedicated teachers and small classes. But more significant is the ability, partly trained and partly circumstantial, of international children to distinguish between what is superficial and what is essential. Having seen that students from any part of the world have similar pleasures and likes and fears, they come to appreciate the difference, for instance, between the people of a country and its government, between the way a person looks and the way he or she is, and between a person's ability to speak a language and what he or she has to say. Skills like these are of critical value in tomorrow's world, and they quite often come as a natural result of the experience of studying in an international school.

7. International curricula in international schools – a background

Malcolm Davis and Caroline Ellwood

Introduction

The need for and nature of international education at the secondary level are areas that interest parents, teachers, and administrators in international schools. At Vienna International School, we have been closely involved with IBO in developing the International Baccalaureate and with the International Schools Association in developing the International Curriculum for the Middle Years of Schooling (ICMYS). The format of each curriculum will be a significant part of international education in the 1990s.

International Baccalaureate (IB)

The IB is a pre-university curriculum with international recognition. Students sit a group of six IB exams after two years of study. There is a definite distribution of requirements, and all students must study a combination of social sciences, mathematics, sciences, and languages. The balance of higher and subsidiary level exams provides a broad and balanced education. In addition to the full diploma, students may sit one or more IB exams and earn certificates. Assessment for examinations is both internal and external. Full diploma candidates also complete an extended essay which is assessed externally, a course called Theory of Knowledge, and a CASS (Creative/Aesthetic Social Service) project. Although the IB is administered by the Geneva office and a Board of Chief Examiners, local schools play a part in the process of curriculum review and assessment. IBO describes their administrative and management structure as a partnership of schools, administrators, and examiners.

The first students who took the International Baccalaureate examination in 1970 were pioneers in an experiment in international education which has become the rationale for the final years of schooling for thousands of students across the world. It is a complex package that meets the needs of breadth, specialization, coherence, and balance in education. Its aim is to reflect the needs of a mobile international community of students. After 20 years, it has a proven track record, with its graduates entering the very best universities and moving on successfully to all walks of life.

The founders of the IB wanted to improve the quality of international education and reflect the idealism and the philosophy of Kurt Hahn: the hope to develop a new generation of world-minded citizens and a community of people who respected the diversity of cultures and worked together for greater peace and understanding. For the IB pioneers, international education was a necessity in a multicultural and interdependent world.

Today, the International Baccalaureate goes some way towards creating world-minded citizens conscious of the multitudes of interactions within a complex, shrinking world and aware that they will be responsible for the future of that world. However, the IB only covers international education for the final two years of secondary school. This could suggest that international education only exists for the 16+ group. Of course, this is not true and was clearly recognized by the founders of the examination who predicted an eventual need to create a curriculum for the 11–16 age group encompassing the same educational philosophy and ideals of internationalism.

A vacuum in the pre-IB years

A truly international programme is possibly even more important when students are at a much more impressionable age, and many internationally minded schools across the world have attempted to fill the gap. Usually this involves a marriage between national systems and the needs of the more international examinations. The French in their overseas Lycées, the US Department of Defense schools, and the overseas national schools (British or American) which offer national examinations like the O level now GCSE exams have all provided possible 'marriages of convenience'. Nor have such adaptations taken place in a static situation: across the world curricula reform is being discussed and carried out. Educators, parents, administrators, politicians, and students all realize that new roles and responsibilities are in the making as dynamic economic, environmental, and culture forces demand new responses.

So the need for a new curriculum comes not just from the downward push to prepare students more appropriately for the International Baccalaureate, but also from an upward force in an area where curriculum reform is already providing discontent with the present programmes. Thus, international schools have an ideal opportunity to harness the present desire and need for change to their special circumstances. Furthermore, if the curriculum as a whole presented a response to social and technical change, had a philosophy which was applicable in terms of global education, and had sufficient flexibility to be adaptable to different local situations, then it could appeal not just to international schools but also to a growing number of internationally minded national systems.

Philosophies of international education

Philosophies of multicultural and by extension global education are very much in the process of discussion, experimentation, and change (Lynch 1989). Any distillation of values aiming at a universal human with a universal moral code would negate the appreciation of cultural variety that is the richest part of an international education. What has to be arrived at is some philosophical framework in which many educational philosophies can operate, reconciling areas of similarity and difference. International humanism with the aim of amelioration of the human condition could be the core of this philosophy, offering a stable centre. The difference of response, interaction of cultures, and their impact on the environment can then be used to show the richness of diversity, and, it is hoped, to produce respect and understanding.

All schools can aim for such a programme; where the international schools have an immediate advantage over many (though not all) national schools is in the vital resource presented by the diversity of individual backgrounds, languages, cultural biographies, and cognitive styles of their students. There in the schools is the basis for an awareness of the problems of the real world and the need for communication in one's own language and the languages of others. Modes of learning and thinking styles are complicated by the multicultural nature of international education. Any innovative curriculum model will have to consider the following aspects of language: the problem of students with no real mother tongue to help create identity, the methods of reinforcement of the mother tongue, the frequency of instruction, and the variety of foreign languages on offer; not to mention the complex issue of bilingual instruction of content areas. Learning how to learn rather than what to learn will also be a major concern.

None of these philosophical aims are peculiar to international schools, the aims of international education are all possible for any school so long as the perspective of the students at the end of the process includes: understanding and tolerance of other cultures, a sense of being part of the global family as opposed to just a national family, a belief and understanding that the action of individuals in one part of the globe have impact on all other persons, and finally a belief in cooperation and not competitiveness at the expense of others.

This 'internationalism' should create a spirit of self-worth and acknowledge that all persons warrant respect and care. Idealistically, we believe - with many other educators from the earliest pioneers of the International Baccalaureate to today's developers of the ISA curriculum - that if such values are implicit within the educational process then we will ameliorate the human condition.

International Schools Association Curriculum (ICMYS)

This philosophy and other issues were part of a ten-year discussion among international teachers and administrators across the world, and led to the development of ISA's innovative model for the middle years of schooling. What is important about the model is the recognition that the knowledge base is ever growing and changing, and it involves value judgments as to what should be conveyed. Indeed, the barriers of knowledge are being pushed back at such a speed that any school science lesson which dwells on facts is in effect a lesson in the history of science. The same is true of literature and history which have, since the sixties, undergone crises of purpose and methodology. Marxist interpretations, regardless of their merit or veracity, have created new emphases and approaches to the study of both subjects. The influence of anthropology on the humanities has changed rigid attitudes within subject areas, and teaching has moved from Aristotle's misleading grouping together of poetry, philosophy, and history to cross-referencing through music, art, and languages, or any area that is relevant to the enquiry. Selling a particular point of view, political philosophy, or series of facts has given way to hermeneutics as the heart of the critical debate, and to problem solving as the most useful skill. This is especially appropriate in the international school where 'cultures' and 'ideologies' must not be manipulated for particular ends. As international teachers, our business is to develop the mental capacities of all our students. We must create a sense of the world as a place where no one people have or had a monopoly on greatness; where no one environment is better than another.

Such a move away from knowledge to skills is part of the basic aim of the subject experts who created the syllabuses for the ISAC. What has been attempted with the whole series of subjects is a balance so that the academic is not stressed at the expense of the creative. Students will have a broader education than is presently the case in many schools, but the emphasis will not be on learning more but on employing different skills in practical studies. Models of assessment are left to the individual disciplines, and continuous assessment, the production of interdisciplinary projects and interview, will be used extensively so that strengths and potential can be established. The child is at the centre and is for everyone the purpose of the curriculum.

Introduction of international curricula in schools

Change is by its nature difficult to introduce in schools. Although often perceived as agents of change, schools are usually conservative institutions that are happy to stay within the traditions in which they have grown, and to continue time-proven methods. The new is seen as dangerous and frightening, and its introduction is often expected to produce a fall in standards. Teachers often feel that they themselves will not cope with new methods and ideas, and therefore they will fail. They are busy people and see curriculum changes as involving time and talk, both of which take energy and initiative out of the classroom where it should be and into committees, which is not productive. Correspondingly, the initiator of change is faced with resistance and/or apathy, the latter on the basis that no participation might result in the change not being implemented.

When introducing curriculum change on the scale of the IB or ICMYS, all the above factors are writ large. Therefore, it follows that when introducing a new curriculum there needs to be a hard core of staff who believe in the idea sufficiently to encourage and convert the rest. The motive for change must be clearly identified. The centrally produced syllabus outlines, which have been agreed by teams of teachers from different continents, should be open to modification where necessary. This process of adaptation to the local needs will produce a degree of ownership and, it is hoped, convert the hearts and minds of the majority of the staff to what will now be the school's own programme. The general approach could be to form committees that reflect key areas. All department areas should be made aware of what others are doing.

Conclusion

The International Baccalaureate began with high ideals of creating a pre-university programme for the mobile international student community. ICMYS takes the ideal one step further and offers to the younger age group an educational programme that is suited to the needs not just of mobile students but to all students who are preparing to enter the world of tomorrow: a world of fluctuating international relations, a world of rapid change, and a world of hope. IBO and ISA have the fundamental belief that international humanism will produce a person whose aim is to use knowledge to ameliorate the conditions of other humans. As we look to the 21st century, there is now available a whole international curriculum for students aged 11–18. Future planners in international education will now look to the elementary levels so that the child of the future will have an education programme K–12 that has as its aim world citizenship.

Bibliography

ISA Handbook and Curriculum Guides 1986 to 1990, ISA: Geneva
Lynch, J (1989) *Multicultural Education in a Global Society* Falmer: Lewes
Skillbeck, M (1990) *Curriculum Reform* OECD: Paris

8. The multicultural, multilingual, and multinational school: the student perspective

Cesare, Yonas and Anna from the UWC of the Adriatic

Cesare, Italian – my multicultural experience

It was a community where everyone seemed so hopelessly different from me: different culture, religion, colours, and languages. How could I fit in coming from a small Italian village of less than 180 people where the 'foreigners' were those coming from the other side of the banks of the river Po? Well, it did not take longer than a day to be drawn into the college life, facing my German and Chinese roommates, having to choose my own subjects, being confronted by new names, faces, smiles, nationalities, a challenge to anyone's memory. Consider that I did not know more than ten sentences of English at the time. The pace of college life never did slow down. My favourite activities were photography (taking pictures around the Carso region), speleology (visiting the fantastic caves around Trieste), and my social service (visiting a blind boy every week in an institute who became one of my best friends).

No, it was not always easy and fun, but you could learn how to manage your new life by trial and error – many, many errors – supported by friends who would be as close as a new family, teachers who were always present for any need, and an open new environment based on no strict rules but mutual understanding and respect. At the end of two years, it all seemed to have been far too quick. Close friends parted to different corners of the earth and being thrown back home was a real challenge. I knew I wanted to study more about people and places, and it was difficult until I came across Human Sciences (a mixture of genetics, anthropology, human ecology, and demography) at Oxford University.

Before UWC, going to university in a country different from Italy was something I would never have dreamed possible, and it is a great experience. I do not know what I will do after my degree, but plans are the one thing I never lack. It will have to be something to do with people and culture. Maybe working with handicapped children like the social service I am now organizing in Oxford or in the field of international education. Whatever it will be, I know that the experience of those two years in a small sea village near Trieste will never fade in my memory. It will always influence me and all the people I meet on my way.

Yonas, Eritrean – my multilingual experience

I would like to describe the life of a student in the Adriatic College with particular reference to my own background. I am an Eritrean refugee student from the Sudan. Having successfully done my O levels, I became interested in the UWC and being a refugee I had to apply to the United Nations High Commission for Refugees (UNHCR) education office. The UNHCR selection committee, like the other national committees, is in two groups. In the regional selection, I and another friend were selected from 50 candidates. The next selection was at Khartoum UNHCR branch office; three out of twenty refugees were qualified. As one of the three, I went to Adriatic College.

I joined 200 students from different parts of the world, over 50 nationalities. The college life and the academic programme are integral. The academic programme leads to the International Baccalaureate diploma. The IB is particularly suited to the ideals of the college, with an academic programme composed of six subjects. One of these, Language A, gives each student an opportunity to study in the student's best language. In my case it is particularly interesting. My best language is Tigrinya; as a result of the political problems between Eritrea and Ethiopia, I had never had the opportunity formally to study my own language. In the college, I studied Tigrinya, and I had an official examination at the end.

Second, in addition to the academic programme there are important extra-academic activities which are obligatory to all students. Students are required to do a social service activity – helping the mentally and physically handicapped in the local community, visiting and entertaining old people at home and in institutions, teaching English or other languages, and involvement in environmental services (cleaning and collecting glasses and plastics). A physical activity of some kind of sport such as soccer and baseball offers closer contact with the local community through a series of matches organized throughout the year. The third extra-curricular activity is an aesthetic activity.

The students in the Duino college live in residences spread out in the village. They share rooms in groups ranging from two to five. In my first year, I shared a room with an Italian, a Swiss, and a Turk and in my second year, with two Italians, a Bolivian, and a Chinese from Hong Kong. Not only in rooming, but also in specially arranged national evenings, is there contact among the diverse nationalities.

After college, the students are kept with their ideals and memories through a network organization centred in London. There are also ex-students' associations which meet to discuss current problems and help with other students. In this way, the UWC's offer a life of international understanding and coexistence and also promote individual tolerance towards others.

Anna, Bulgarian – my multinational experience

> '. . . the only people for me are the crazy ones, those who are crazy for life, crazy for salvation, those who want everything at the same time, who neither yawn nor babble banalities, but burn, burn, and burn . . .'
>
> Jack Kerouac

The UWC students and the crazy people have in common the fact that both are absolved from any kind of barriers placed upon their thinking and behaviour. We come young to the college, without having entrenched cultural, political, or racial prejudices, without being familiar with the necessary social decorum, and without having the detrimental experience which leads to redundant precaution, and we are left on our own. All these qualities which initially may be called 'inexperience' become an inherent part of our personalities.

A UWC college is a big challenge to our imagination and creativity. We are given an unlimited number of opportunities, and the only step we have to make is to take them. We have to be willing to risk and experiment.

We come together, 200 individuals, and we can enjoy the bliss of being together, of being able to talk to each other whenever and wherever, and of being able to live together. The UWC experience triggers our desire to get to know the world. Without losing our national identity, we switch from the notion of 'my country' to the notion of 'my world', and we subconsciously assume the responsibility of taking care of it.

Unfortunately, by the time one realizes the essence of the college, one has to leave it, but it may be that this is the necessary thing to get the initial spark, and our vocation is set on fire.

9. International schools: perspective of a parent with a handicapped child

Mike Waldron

In today's highly mobile society, the opportunities to live and work abroad are probably greater than they ever have been. What was once the domain of a privileged few in diplomatic or military circles is now available to a wide range of the employment sector. In the 'multinational' world a willingness to travel is often a springboard to career advancement.

Obviously, the career aspect is one of a number of factors which have to be taken into account when contemplating such a move. Those with families need also to consider how the various family members will be affected by the move, how they will integrate into the new country, how they will feel about leaving friends and extended family behind, and particularly, how the children's education will be affected.

In the English speaking community, these decisions have been made easier in recent years with the spread of international schools designed to cater for this more mobile community. These schools very often have the kind of curriculum which enables a child to slot back easily into school in the country of his origin. At the same time, naturally enough, the curriculum generally takes a more 'international' view of the subjects taught.

Given the availability of these schools and their excellent facilities, there is still one group who are faced with difficulties when it comes to considering a move abroad: those with handicapped children. I use the term 'handicapped' in its widest possible definition to include mental and physical disabilities and remedial-type learning difficulties. Many of these parents will already have experienced problems in finding suitable schooling for their children in their own country. Legislation now exists in the United States and Britain providing for the integration of handicapped children into normal state schools, but as many parents can attest, there is often a considerable difference between the legal provision and the reality. Resources are not abundant and the shortage of funds and trained personnel often means that integration programmes are not fully implemented, and facilities such as speech therapy are not as widely available as they might be.

So if the parent of a handicapped child is often faced with a hard task in finding suitable education at home – what does he or she do when he or she is asked to go abroad? Obviously, if they speak the same language in the country concerned, the problems are greatly reduced; there should be some sort of equivalent facilities available. However, if we are talking about a foreign language, the choices become very limited indeed. I should stress here that for the purposes of this article I am dealing with the situation for an English-speaker who is asked to travel abroad. The choices essentially are: (a) not to go, (b) to go but leave the child in a suitable school/institution at home, or (c) to go and try to make suitable arrangements upon arrival in the new country.

In the past 20 to 25 years, the evolution in the care for the handicapped has been considerable. There have been greater moves to integrate the handicapped into the community, and the benefits in most cases have been remarkable, particularly in the area of mental handicap. Years ago, mentally handicapped children were cut off from the general public and consigned to institutions, where to all intents and purposes, although they were generally well looked after, they vegetated. It has since been shown that if these children can live in a normal environment, they respond tremendously to the stimulus of daily contact with their family, their peers, and, where possible, teachers and students in 'normal' schools. Every year, the frontiers of their attainable potential are rolled further back. For example, 25 years ago doctors would have said that it would be impossible for a person with Down's Syndrome to write a book or to learn to drive a car. Both of these things have now been achieved.

The one aspect which the experts consider of paramount importance in realizing the potential of these children is that they get a solid foundation in the mother tongue. So yet another factor is introduced into the equation when considering the move abroad, and however good the local facilities might be, they are not necessarily going to be appropriate.

When we made our move to Brussels our daughter who has Down's Syndrome was only nine months old, so we had some time to consider what options were open and to hope that, in the words of Mr Micawber, something would turn up. From the aspect of international schooling, Brussels is probably quite a good place to be sent for there is a choice of English-speaking schools, including several private primary schools, the European Schools catering primarily to the children of the European Community, the British School, the International School, St John's International School, Le Verseau, and the EEC School. In addition, there is a US Department of Defense School, mainly for the children of NATO personnel.

We were very fortunate in that something did 'turn up'. In 1983, the International School of Brussels (ISB) decided to open up a special unit to cater for handicapped children. Recognizing that there were certain types of problems the school would not be able to deal with, they first decided to cater for less severely mentally handicapped children, such as those with Down's Syndrome. In fact, they soon expanded their horizons, and since then have also admitted children into the programme with cerebral palsy, autism, non-specific brain damage, and visual handicap.

The initiative for setting up the unit came from the then Superintendent, Robert Ater, who felt that a school such as ISB should try to reflect not just the high intellectual echelons but as broad a spectrum of society as possible. He argued that the setting up of the unit would have a two-way benefit: the handicapped children would have greater possibilities to fulfil their potential in this environment, and having the handicapped in their midst, the other children would realize that those less advantaged than themselves still have a role to play in society. The philosophy was based on the reasonable expectation that the international children who attend ISB will probably in their home countries be among the leaders of tomorrow in whatever field they choose to enter. Having had the experience of dealing with and even helping the handicapped during their school lives, they will be in a better position to encourage and to influence the fuller integration of the handicapped into future adult society.

In practice, the special education unit accepts children across the whole age range. It has a separate classroom in the Elementary School, and the optimum number of students it can handle is six to seven. It is staffed by one qualified special education teacher and one to two assistants. In addition, it can call on the services of a speech therapist and a music therapist, as well as specialists in such fields as art and physical education. The timetable is structured to give the students such one-to-one tuition as they can comfortably handle; it must be remembered that one-to-one tuition is very demanding, both for the teacher and the pupil. The children are sent out into the mainstream of all sections of the school for whatever is considered to be the appropriate level for their abilities. The mainstreaming is reviewed regularly. Other students in the school are also encouraged to come and visit the unit and to help out with lessons like reading and structured play. In addition, where it is appropriate, those children in the school who use the school bus are given a 'minder' who has the responsibility to make sure they travel without difficulty across the large campus, get to and from class safely, and behave reasonably on the school bus. It is interesting to note that occasionally children who have had problems themselves in adapting to school life are given particular responsibilities in helping with the handicapped children – often with beneficial effects on both sides.

Personally, I must say that we are delighted with the work of the unit and the progress that our daughter has made there. In many ways, she is better off than if we had remained in England. For example, she receives daily speech therapy which would have been difficult to achieve in even the best resourced areas in Britain. There have of course been some problems along the way. In the initial stages because of the normal mobility of the community, there was quite a lot of staff change. Both the parents and the school have come to appreciate the importance of staffing continuity.

I have talked from personal experience of the special unit which ISB set up, but it should be noted that at different times all the international schools in Brussels have tried in their own way to help all educationally handicapped children. Obviously, there are some types of disabilities which by their nature simply cannot be catered for in the normal school environment, and there are cases where schools have felt obliged to abandon their attempts to integrate a particular child. It is nonetheless encouraging to see that efforts are being made to deal with this problem.

Under the auspices of a parent advocacy group called Brussels Support for the Handicapped (BRUSH), a seminar was organized in 1985 to discuss the question of integrating handicapped children into normal schools, with particular emphasis on the problems faced in countries such as Belgium which have large international populations. This seminar succeeded in gathering representatives of all the international schools in Belgium together under one roof, to air their own views on problems and to hear those of experts on the subject. One interesting outcome was that although the schools had differing views on tackling the problem, there was general consensus that they should all look at ways in which information and expertise could be shared, and even how resources might be pooled.

The last aspect of this question which I want to mention is literally the bottom line – the cost. The schools we are discussing here are, for the most part, in the private sector. There is very little state intervention or support. In Brussels about 90 per cent of the school fees are met by the parent's employers as a part of the financial package to get prospective employees to come and work abroad. Because of the individual nature of the tuition, the cost of special education in a unit such as that at ISB is particularly expensive – at least the equivalent of pre-university level schooling. Perhaps not surprisingly, there are employers who baulk at this kind of expenditure, and I know of at least one case where the employer, a well-known multinational, obliged the parents to transfer to another country because they were unwilling to pick up the tab. Cost is a difficult factor for international schools when it comes to making any kind of long-term provision in the field of special education. For the normal school population, although there may be some fluctuation in numbers due, for example, to changes in the economic climate, the schools know there should be a fairly steady stream of new students. As far as the handicapped are concerned, it is much more difficult to predict how many and what type of handicap might arrive. This has an enormous influence on the sort of facilities that could be provided: from regular staff teachers and specially adapted computers, to physical changes in the fabric of the building to accommodate wheelchair access.

I am encouraged that there are schools which, although in the private sector and under no obligation to provide for other than the normal catchment, do make an effort to integrate handicapped children. To me this is an important reflection of the changes in recent years in society's attitudes towards its more disadvantaged citizens. I hope that more international schools will move in this direction and thus, in doing so, offer opportunities to individuals in today's international and mobile community who up to now have felt obliged not to take them.

10. State-subsidized international schools in the Netherlands

Jeff Koopman

Introduction

There is a great variety of international schools in the Netherlands, and most of them have in common the use of English as the language of instruction and a multinational student population. However, this is about as far as the comparison can go. There are schools with a predominantly British or American curriculum and schools with a combination of a foreign and Dutch curriculum. Since 1984, there have also existed mainstream Dutch state schools with international departments that are partially subsidized by the Dutch Department of Education and Science (DES). In a number of cases, these schools are also subsidized by local government during the starting-up phase.

The first such section in a Dutch school was established in 1974 and is the first manifestation of cooperation between the DES and the international business community in the Netherlands. The curriculum was modelled on the British system, and the section was given the name 'English Stream'. Soon, there followed at the initiative of the DES an experiment to offer International Baccalaureate courses at a number of secondary schools. This experiment ran until 1989 when the DES increased the number of state-subsidized IB courses to a maximum of seven. A parallel development in this period was an increasing call for international education in the provinces. In many cases, the driving forces behind this trend were the international business community, the various provincial industrial development banks, and the local governments.

In cooperation with secondary schools, international sections (then still known as 'English Streams') were started in a number of cities. Two types of departments arose in this way: one was the British model English Stream with an IB course, and the other was a four-year pre-IB course leading to entrance in the IB diploma class. Though different in many respects, these schools have in common the fact that they are all subsidized by the DES, a unique situation in the world of international education.

Importance of internationalism

The DES was pursuing a clear policy when it introduced the International

Baccalaureate and international departments into Dutch schools. The role of the Netherlands in international business and commerce made it desirable that Dutch schools should offer facilities for internationally orientated education. The pupils involved were, in the main, those with little or no Dutch who were therefore unable to attend normal Dutch day schools. Internationally orientated schools would promote the acculturation of these children who would otherwise remain entirely excluded from Dutch society during their stay in the country. The five points of the DES policy can be summarized as:

1. The regional distribution of subsidized international education.
2. Optimal cooperation between the schools in specially established consultative bodies.
3. The introduction of preferably one other examination system alongside the IB.
4. A form of financing which does not favour the international pupil.
5. The initiation of the participation of the international business community, for example via the Department of Economic Affairs.

In this way, Internationally Orientated Schools (IOS) were born. The majority of these IOS decided to implement the International General Certificate of Secondary Education (IGCSE) administered by the University of Cambridge Local Examination Syndicate (UCLES) in the UK. Most of these schools now have an IB at the upper end and work in cooperation with a state-subsidized international department of a primary school. These schools are referred to by the DES as 'English–Dutch Departments'. As the size of the subsidy is related to the number of pupils, the smaller departments in particular are financially dependent on the international business community operating in their area. Most schools have a sponsor trust which actively attempts to stimulate local government and business interest in this form of education. The structure of a typical Dutch school with an IOS department could be depicted as shown in Figure 10.1 and Table 10.1.

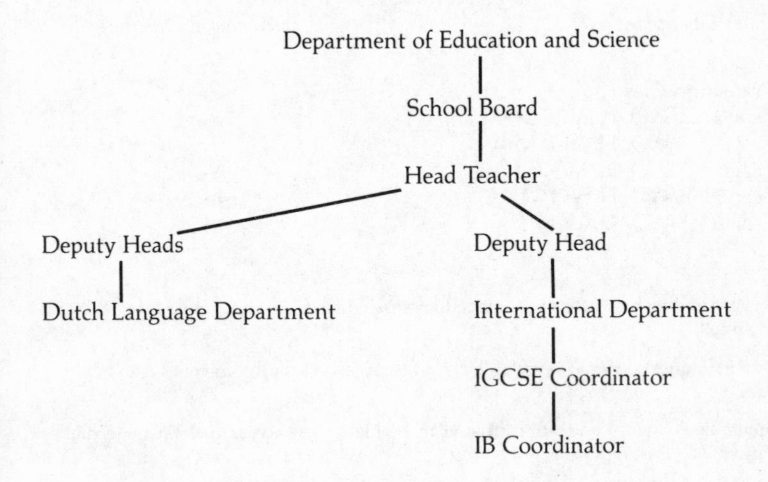

Figure 10.1 *Organizational structure*

Table 10.1 *Educational structure*

YEAR 1 All subjects compulsory
YEAR 2 All subjects compulsory
YEAR 3 All subjects compulsory
YEAR 4 Subject choice for IGCSE
YEAR 5 IGCSE Examinations
IB 1 Subject choice for IB
IB 2 IB exams

Dutch secondary internationally orientated schools

Table 10.2 gives a comparison of international departments and mainstream Dutch schools. The IGCSE gives students access to higher vocational education on condition that certain demands are met with regard to the grading achieved. The IB diploma is recognized for entrance by all colleges and universities as well as higher vocational courses. Obviously, there are consequences to the DES of financing international departments in mainstream secondary schools. In particular, those departments which started from 1984 were affected by a number of conditions of the subsidy. They were not allowed to enrol Dutch nationals, and 50 per cent of the lessons had to be taught in Dutch. The school could not receive more subsidy for an international pupil than for a mainstream Dutch pupil. However, DES had overlooked a number of matters. It is impossible to educate children in Dutch for an English-language exam, and it is difficult to administer a 'school within a school' without extra financing.

Table 10.2 *The Dutch secondary IOS department: secondary non-vocational education in the 11–18 years age range*

AGE	*TYPE OF EDUCATION*		
	Dutch Department		*International Department*
11			Year 1
12	Transition Class		Year 2
13	Year 2	VWO, HAVO, MAVO	Year 3
14	Year 3	VWO, HAVO, MAVO	Year 4
15	Year 4	VWO, HAVO, MAVO	Year 5
16	Year 5	VWO, HAVO	IB 1
17	Year 6	VWO, HAVO	IB 2

KEY:
Transition Class: a year in which an attempt is made to assess which form of secondary education is best suited to the pupil.

VWO: pre-university education (six years) which gives access to both university and higher vocational education.

HAVO: senior general secondary education (five years) which gives access to VWO and higher vocational education.

MAVO: junior secondary education (four years) which gives access to HAVO and senior general education.

The change to Dutch as a subsidiary language

In various consultations with the DES, the Internationally Orientated School departments contested both the subsidy formula and the 50 per cent requirement for teaching in Dutch, but the results were modest. The 50 per cent requirement was reduced to 30 per cent; some schools have attempted to comply by among other things combining international and Dutch department classes in drawing, music, drama, and physical education. When it became obvious that this would not work, the 30 per cent requirement was replaced by the requirement of Dutch as a compulsory language, what IB calls the subsidiary language.

In 1968, the DES set up a working group to prepare a definite programme of Dutch/Dutch Studies for the benefit of international departments in Dutch secondary schools. Compulsory Dutch/Dutch Studies and Practical Dutch would be offered alongside optional Dutch as the mother tongue and Dutch as a foreign language and the course would be initiated in the school year 1992–93. The so-called Cambridge Committee was formed to work in conjunction with UCLES to compose a syllabus and exams in IGCSE Dutch as the mother tongue and Dutch as a foreign language. Both these exams are now offered by UCLES at the core and extended level which is a feature of all ICGSE subjects. The Dutch/Dutch Studies group identified two types of pupils: those joining the department and being confronted with Dutch for the first time and those joining the department with some command of Dutch.

Lesson tables

The working group proposed three lesson tables (see Table 10.3). Table A is intended for the non-Dutch-speaking intake from the second form upward and also includes pupils from the fourth and fifth forms who have not chosen Dutch in their exam package. Table B is intended for pupils with Dutch as their first or mother tongue. Table C is intended for those pupils taking Dutch as a foreign language.

Table 10.3 *The three lesson tables*

Year	*Table A*	*Table B*	*Table C*
	Practical Dutch *Dutch/Dutch Studies*	*Dutch* *1st Lang.*	*Dutch* *Foreign Lang.*
1		3 periods	3 periods
2	3 periods	3 periods	3 periods
3	3 periods	3 periods	3 periods
4	1 period PD 2 periods DS	3 periods C/E	3 periods C/E
5	1 period PD 2 periods DS	3 periods C/E	3 periods C/E

KEY:

1 period = One 50-minute lesson
PD = Practical Dutch
DS = Dutch Studies
C/E = Core/Extended

If the above tables are introduced into all IOS school departments in 1992, Dutch will have achieved the central role that the DES initially envisaged for the language. The curriculum will have a balance between internationalism and local national recognition. It will be clear that the introducton of these subjects will have to be accompanied by a substantial increase in the available state subsidies.

Course descriptions

For Practical Dutch a textbook has been developed illustrated with drawings and covering 25 themes which relate to language situations occurring in daily life: home, school, clothing, sport, and leisure. The structure of the lessons is recurring. After a short story on tape as starting point, the students work on expanding their vocabulary, learn simple rules of grammar, and follow listening, speaking, reading, and writing exercises.

The programme for Dutch Studies is interdisciplinary: containing material from history, geography, economy, art history, and sociology to develop a wider European and global context. It preceded the IGCSE course which students follow in the fourth and fifth forms. A new textbook has been written containing units which are to be supplemented by field trips and visits to exhibitions, companies, and institutions. Whether Dutch is the first or the foreign language, the student selects the appropriate IGCSE syllabus from UCLES.

Conclusion

IOS departments occupy a unique position in the world of international education. Pupils of international departments are part of a Dutch-speaking community. One condition for these pupils to be able to function properly in their environment of school and society is a knowledge of Dutch language and Dutch history and culture. The fact that the Dutch Department of Education and Science subsidizes these departments, and the requirement that Dutch occupy a central place in the curriculum, testifies to insight into the rapid changes and internationalism of the national education. It is also an indicator of the importance the DES attaches to the notion that children from various countries being educated in the Netherlands should (regardless of their nationality, language, or length of stay) leave with a clear awareness of the country they have lived in and the place of that country in international affairs.

Part 3: Curricula issues in international education and international schools

Introduction

Patricia L Jonietz

A recent catalogue of publications from UNESCO identifies some of the topics of importance in international education and international school curricula: adult or continuing education, special needs, science and technology, literacy and language competency, and lifelong learning. UNESCO hopes that their documents will facilitate understanding of common needs and increase communication at an international level. Their organizational goals are akin to the goals of this section.

However, language mastery seems to highlight the core of many problems within the international curriculum and the international school. Mutual understanding rests on the possession of a common vocabulary. How in a school with 16 nationalities on the faculty and 40 nationalities in the student body do you find common vocabulary for mutual understanding? Is that the purpose of the school language of instruction? If the school language of instruction is English, how do we describe the non-native speakers of English in the population? Are they EFL or ESL students and teachers? Actually these acronyms mean different things and reflect the complexity of language in the international curricula. EFL is English as a Foreign Language, and ESL is English as a Second Language. Often, the choice of the term used in a curriculum plan only reflects the educational training of the teacher or area coordinator in a particular school and not the needs of the population.

The *ECIS Guide to School Evaluation and Accreditation* (1987) proposes for ECIS international schools not only Language of Instruction and Second Language but also the combined term English as a Foreign or Second Language. This implies that if the school language of instruction is English, then a second language is *any* language other than the language of instruction, and that a foreign language is *any* language other than the maternal language. Thus for some students English may be a foreign language *and* a second or third or more language. What do we label English for a native speaker of Japanese living in Spain but attending an English language of instruction school where she chooses an IB Language A exam in Japanese, a Language B exam in Spanish, and all the other examinations (history, science, and maths) in English? If you think these students do not exist, ask the shop assistant at the British Museum who was bewildered by five Japanese women needing to purchase Spanish language museum guides before beginning their tour. How do we label the Italian native teaching maths in English in a school located in French-speaking Switzerland?

Confusing? Complex. Controversial! Rather than take sides here in a discussion of the 'appropriate' label for language analysis in an international school, it is suggested that an understanding of why ECIS is careful in chosing terminology is probably related to the goal of developing mutual understanding and sharing information at an international level.

Beyond the question of ESL/EFL, all language teaching holds an important place in the curricula planning of international schools. Perhaps, this importance is related to the relationships among maternal language, language of instruction, foreign language, and environmental language. For our Japanese women visiting the British Museum, Japanese is the maternal language (assuming both parents speak Japanese), English is the language of instruction, both English and Spanish are foreign languages, and Spanish is the environmental language. For our Italian teacher in Switzerland, Italian is the maternal language (assuming he did not live in German-speaking Italy or have a non-Italian parent), English is the language of instruction, English and French are foreign languages, and French is the environmental language. Consider the multiple problems of students who, even if they do not study the environmental language at school, need some level of competency just to live in and understand their environment. Consider the pressing problems of the parents in arranging to maintain the fluency and quality of the maternal language. Consider the myriad problems for the teachers presenting chemistry in English with supplies labelled in Spanish to Japanese-speaking students.

What is literacy for these individuals and for international schools? In international schools, is language a basic life-skill and continuing education for all participants? Is it necessary to be bilingual to have an international perspective? How do language problems affect the international school definition of special needs? At what level does mastery of the language of instruction allow students free participation in classes in the regular academic curriculum? In budget planning, which is more important to an administrator: an EFL/ESL techer or a new music class? Should an international school refuse admission to a student for not possessing 'enough' English, or is the purpose of an international school the education of multinational students in a common language through the teaching of that common language at all academic levels? Is it any wonder that the complex topic of language teaching and learning assumes a position of importance in international education?

Paddy Carpenter is the director of the European Community's Lingua Programme, which is a support plan for the teaching and learning of foreign languages in the EC member states. Mr Carpenter believes that an emphasis on language learning and teaching signals two important messages from the European Community Council of Ministers:

1. that language learning is important in the further development of Europe; and
2. that language teaching and learning will encourage us to leave our national educational ghettos and broaden our horizons.

Again we can see a relationship between an organization's goals and the goals of this section. Language learning is important to the further development of international education and international schools, and a broadening of an understanding of language teaching and learning will broaden our curricula horizons.

Tosi reviews the topic of language learning in the international context: bilingualism, home language, school language, and environmental language. He also compares the language learning plan of the schools sponsored by the European Community and the typical international school offering the International Baccalaureate.

Horsley reviews the operation of the bilingual education programme developed by the Atlanta International School, which though a private American school has support from the French and German governments in developing a curriculum to lead students to mastery of two languages.

Carder deals with the way in which the 'ESL problem' has developed into an integral part of the curricula of international schools. He outlines how the ESL programme should become integrated into the total school curriculum, which models can be adopted, and how five key groups participate. He summarizes the latest research on language learning and its direct implications for all who are involved and for students who are hoping to achieve success in curriculum subjects in a language that is not their mother tongue.

Davis and Ellwood move to content subjects taught in English to a multinational population and discuss the IBO's new curriculum proposal: History and Culture of the Islamic World. This course opens up the possibility for students to study a wider span of history than is often the case. The argument for encouraging students to take this course is put forth and some of the problems of teaching it are explained.

Glover looks outside the academic classroom and says that the value of the extra-curricular element in the educational development of the international individual is rarely fully recognized and, as a consequence, schools have seldom bothered to develop such a programme fully. When dealing with international schools, this is a serious failing, as these institutions should be at the forefront of educational innovation. Having always required some extra-curricular involvement as part of its diploma, the International Baccalaureate Office has recently strengthened this requirement and published new guidelines on its CASS (Creativity, Action, and Service) programme. The United World College of the Atlantic, since it was founded in 1962, has steadily developed a comprehensive programme which involves all its students. Glover describes the functioning of the programme in some detail as he hopes that it could suggest solutions to schools involved with IB and CASS activities, although it is acknowledged that special conditions do prevail at the college which is a boarding school.

11. Language in international education

Arturo Tosi

Introduction

It is not at all obvious what international education is, but it is clear that it is a consequence of national education, and is likely to exist as long as national education does. International schools often are – and many argue that they ought not to be – private, but seldom describe themselves as providing a privileged alternative to state-maintained education. As one of its pioneers put it, international education is a special system for those otherwise at risk of becoming underprivileged by national standards (Peterson 1977). However, together with the members of that mobile community, who should be the major target population for every international school, there are also other students. Some may be sent from developing nations seeking an alternative to colonial traditions, others are sponsored by governmental or parental schemes so that they can experience, outside their national context, the educational excellence of some international curricula (Maillard and Malingre 1980). All these students are usually considered to be privileged compared with those schooled by national systems: the claim is that they receive an education directed to meet individual or small group needs through a curriculum designed to avoid national bias and cultural generalizations.

Today, there is an increasing number of international schools with a multinational staff and a multilingual population of students that offer a multicultural curriculum enabling both staff and students to see the world from a much wider perspective than that generally adopted by national systems. But there are also overseas schools serving parochial groups of expatriates, who do not mind if the curriculum perpetuates old-fashioned colonial or national traditions under the guise of internationalism. In the former schools, international education would include multicultural studies and international understanding (Gellar 1981), while in the latter schools it would mean nothing more than a multinational agreement to recognize qualifications obtained abroad by students conventionally educated according to a national tradition. While it is an obvious interest of all international schools to protect their common curriculum leading to qualifications recognized by colleges and universities in different countries, some difficulties have arisen from the coexistence of diverse national approaches within the same system. These can be summarized by the question 'how can a general philosophy of international-mindedness develop the criteria needed to define the diverse competence of culturally and linguistically different students?'

History and geography seem, of course, the most sensitive areas of knowledge and their curricula have traditionally attracted most concern and discussion. Yet many educationists repeatedly argue that it is not history and geography, but mathematics, physics, and other sciences which are the most controversial academic areas of an international curriculum. The argument is that most people and educators willingly admit the ethnocentricity of their view of history and their knowledge of geography. Very few would be prepared to accept instead that a different emphasis in physics, or different practices of teaching mathematics, may be as legitimate and worthy of consideration as different views on the study of man and mankind (Mayer 1968). One area of international education where controversies stem from transmitting knowledge as well as evaluating competence is languages or rather language. It is interesting, however, that after the initial consultations between schools (the International Schools Association Conference in Milan, 1963) and with international organizations (UNESCO 1964 and Council of Europe 1964 and 1967, as reported in Leach 1969), the general approach to the treatment of different mother tongues, the teaching of modern languages and the evaluation of competence in both has remained virtually unchanged over the past 20 years. This is surprising when one considers that it is during the past two decades that the contributions of applied linguistics have made the teaching and evaluation of language learning more effective, especially in multilingual and multicultural settings.

The purpose of this chapter is to provide a critical review of the most prominent issues in language teaching that are currently found in international schools. It begins with terminological and conceptual clarification of bilingualism. Then it introduces the main issues pertaining to the planning, instruction, and assessment of language in international education, and it goes on to discuss them with reference to the specific programmes of the European Schools and the International Baccalaureate. In the final section, these two international curricula are compared, and some conclusions are drawn in connection with their protagonists: the students and their diverse languages and cultures.

Terminology

In education, any debate about language and language study is complicated by the fact that people, ordinary people too, like to talk about 'language' and this has developed a terminology of language in everyday life which is different from the more precise terminology concerned with the scientific study of it. A fundamental notion which recurs in the debate about international education – and one which must be defined – is that of the 'mother tongue' of students, which an important UNESCO report (1953) identifies as 'the language acquired in early years . . . which normally becomes the natural instrument of thought and communication'. 'First language' and 'second language' can also be misleading if the educational context in which they appear is not carefully qualified. Is the first language of the student the 'first acquired', or her or his 'best' or 'dominant' language? The problem, of course, does not exist when education is provided for a homogeneous population of learners within the same national context; but it is more controversial to refer to the 'first language' of students who have a mixed linguistic background as a result of their heterogeneous language experience and education in two or more countries. For many clients of international education, in fact, 'first language' can mean exactly the opposite whether one refers to it as the 'first acquired' or the 'dominant language'. Likewise, 'second language' is a confusing term, and it incorporates a further element of confusion since certain national contexts (especially the US and countries academically affiliated to it) use it interchangeably with 'foreign language'. Conversely, in British discussions all definitions are consistent in explaining 'second language' as 'a language which is not the mother tongue of its speakers, but which is a language of the country in which they live and which they use regularly in day-to-day business within their country' (Brumfit and Roberts 1983). The same terminological source specifies that 'foreign language', on the other hand, is 'a term usually applied only to languages spoken outside the boundaries of the country in which one lives or, more critically, to languages learnt only for communication with those living outside one's own community and not used for everyday communication within one's own community'.

The range of definitions considered so far clearly indicates that 'mother tongue' and 'foreign language' are unambiguous when referred to in a national context or a monolingual community of speakers. When speakers live in a community with more than one language, or experience education in more than one language or in a medium different from their home and community language, the qualifications 'first' and 'second' are related to so many variables when the criteria are not specified, that they become virtually meaningless.

Definitions and factors of bilingualism

For a long time, bilingualism was believed to be 'the native-like control of two languages' (Bloomfield, 1933). In the late sixties, however, this notion of bilingualism was challenged on practical as well as on educational grounds. On the one hand, the majority of bilingual speakers throughout the world showed an unequal knowledge of the two languages and this made it impractical to continue to apply a theoretical definition which was socially irrelevant. On the other hand, the rapidly growing body of bilingual research demonstrated that among the minority who achieved balanced bilingualism or equilingualism, the native-like command of two languages embraced merely the phonetic control: that is to say, accent and intonation. The conclusion was that as far as other aspects of language competence are concerned, a balanced knowledge of two languages is extremely rare when education is bilingual; it is virtually unattainable when education is monolingual. Today linguists have finally agreed that bilingualism is not an all or nothing property: that the repertoire of bilinguals does not normally comprise the repertoires of two monolinguals and that the bilingual's knowledge of one language hardly if ever equates to her or his competence in the other. This means that in some educational contexts an old and a new notion of bilingualism coexist. The former is a narrow notion that restricts its meaning to equal mastery of two languages, while the latter, which has gained wider acceptance in professional circles, identifies bilingualism as a characteristic that may vary from minimal competence to native-like mastery of more than one language.

In international schools, when the whole or part of the curriculum is offered in a medium different from the home and community language, and often different from that of previous education, students develop bilingualism through a learning experience which professionals refer to as either 'immersion' or 'submersion', according to the educational support or lack of support attributed to the native language by the school curriculum. These are the two most common situations in which bilingualism develops in national as well as international schools, whether they do or do not provide 'bilingual education' ('the use of two languages, one of which is (usually) the native language of the student, as mediums or vehicles of educational instruction', UNESCO 1978).

There are two conclusions which can be drawn from this terminological discussion.

1. Many of these notions have only recently become relevant to education administered by a national system where ethnic minority pupils develop bilingualism, though not necessarily equilingualism, as a result of monolingual education in a language different from their native tongue. In international education, where a multilingual population has always been the norm rather than the exception, the pupils' language diversity *vis-à-vis* the curriculum should never be taken as an accident.
2. Since it is normal rather than exceptional for pupils to experience education in more than one language or in a medium different from their home and community language, it is more meaningful to refer to their 'first academic language' and 'second academic language', spelling out the academic use of the languages, *not* the sequence in which they acquired them. *Bilingualism in international education therefore can best be defined as the competent academic use of two languages.* This study refers to it in this sense, and the following discussion is intended to make explicit the role of the language of school, home, and environment in the development of bilingualism.

School language

Recent research and comparative studies carried out in many multi-ethnic, mainly English-speaking societies, have consistently demonstrated that the home–school language switch does not produce bilingual proficiency automatically. At one extreme, there are those pupils who are non-native speakers of the school language as they are educated via a second language from the primary level, their native language no longer receiving support from the home, the community, or the school after that time. In this case, the prolonged use of the school language, often extended to the peer group, makes competence in the second language surpass the knowledge of the first or native language. Increasingly, however, families are found to exert pressure on the schools and to motivate their children with a view to developing their knowledge of the home and/or national community language. When this is the case, intensive exposure and instruction in a second language leads to bilingual proficiency with no detrimental effect on the first language. The attention paid by parents of mobile families to the factors which develop or hinder bilingualism in their children has already increased the awareness of teachers and administrators in many international schools. This awareness is related to the diverse opportunities for the learning of a non-native language, which vary enormously according to environmental circumstances as well as the personal motivation of students: take for example (a) a Saudi Arabian pupil learning English in an English medium school in England, and (b) an English pupil learning French in an English medium school in Saudi Arabia.

Clearly the reason why the non-native speakers of the school language enjoy better opportunities is that they combine the best motivation with the best resources. Thus, all pupils who succeed in complementing the academic use of the school language – which is their non-native language – with the development of the language of their home and national community, prove that in international education too, the conclusion of many recent studies holds true: ie once the development of the native language has been secured, the most efficient means of promoting bilingualism is instruction in a non-native language (Swain and Cummins 1979).

Home language

The home language is the language acquired in the early years and which normally becomes the natural instrument of thought and communication. 'Normally' in this case refers to continuity between the home and the school language. But some children grow up with two languages resulting in a linguistic mismatch between home and school, as far as (a) basic competence for everyday communication, mainly tied to informal situations, and (b) linguistic proficiency for cognitive operations and academic use. These two properties of language competence are likely to become compartmentalized in two separate languages. Cummins and Swain (1986), who have investigated these conditions among bilingual minority children and monolingual majority children educated bilingually in Canada, have made an important distinction between the different nature of the competence in the home language and in the school language. They say that competence in the home language tends to develop in 'context-embedded communication' where participants can actively negotiate meaning (eg by providing feedback that the message has not been understood) and the language is supported by a wide range of meaningful paralinguistic and situational cues. On the other hand, the activities and demands of the classroom involve 'context-reduced communication which relies primarily on linguistic cues to meaning and thus successful interpretation of the message depends heavily on knowledge of the language itself'.

Naturally, language competence – any language competence – develops within a cross-fertilization of the cognitive with the communicative and vice versa. It is also indisputable that for many bilingual pupils who have achieved considerable fluency in a non-native language, this distinction no longer holds. This achievement, however, is by no means automatic for children whose school language is different from their home language.

There are conditions of language training which must be met by the school and the family to ensure that native fluency in the home language develops the cognitive ability and linguistic accuracy of the school language, and vice versa. If these conditions are not met, the potential bilingual will remain limited to the academic use of only one language though she or he has developed native fluency in the home language. When this is the case, some schools tend to refer to pupils whose home language is different from the school language as 'not truly bilingual'. What this popular definition really means is that the child has developed linguistic accuracy and/or academic proficiency in only the school language, though she or he has native fluency in the home language. What is often overlooked, however, is that unless the school provides the cognitive training for the academic use of the home language, it does not develop automatically from native fluency.

Environmental language

The third variable that facilitates the development of bilingualism is the language of the environment outside the home, when this is different from the home language and/or the school language. When this is the case, and the environment language is also studied as a second or non-native language in the school, pupils enjoy an additional learning opportunity that is not available to genuine foreign language learners who struggle to practise a non-native language solely within the artificial communication of the classroom. Just as the home language and the medium of education have a different impact in the development of bilingualism according to personal circumstances (ie active parental supervision of the native language and duration of the school immersion programme for the non-native language, respectively), the positive role of the language of the environment is also subject to circumstances: namely individual motivation and duration of exposure. The former concerns the inclination of the learner to involve her or himself in social interaction with the community of native speakers of the language of their own country. This is, however, a facility which is mediated by the status of the national language and the social status of its speakers: two factors that notably produce less interest and involvement among Western people resident in the East than Eastern people resident within the Western world. There are, of course, exceptions like that of European and North American families resident in Japan who encourage their children to learn Japanese as a second language. But on the whole, the number of Western families interested in social and linguistic interaction outside the Western world is not anywhere near that of Easterners interested in becoming socially and linguistically involved in Western countries. Similarly, within the Western world there is a stronger inclination to learn the language of the environment in a European country among other Europeans than among North Americans. To them, English medium schools still tend to offer French as a foreign language rather than the language of the host country that is spoken outside the school. When this is the case, pupils who could have been brought up with bilingual abilities in an environment rich in exposure and facilities for a language different from that of their home and school, have remained monolingual in English with only a smattering of French.

A recent survey of bilingual research, which is also specifically concerned with the different degrees of bilingualism developed by diverse curricular approaches (Swain and Cummins 1979), reaches this important conclusion. When the school language is different from the home language and this tends to be denigrated by others and by the speakers themselves, and is taught only a little or not at all, bilingualism is rarely associated with school success, especially when bilingual pupils are tested in their school language, in which they are weaker than monolinguals. However, when the home and the environment can protect and promote the first language, the school can best develop academic success associated with bilingualism by offering education via a second rather than the native language.

Language planning – main issues

Language planning is regarded as essential to language education for two reasons: it highlights the problems and uses of different languages for intranational and international purposes, and it provides the appropriate long-term policy necessary to equip members of a national or international community to solve communication problems (Kennedy 1982). There are of course strong relationships between language planning and other types of planning, for example in the economic and cultural spheres. These relationships are always political by nature, although their purported objective is educational. Indeed a language policy requires planning in order to assess resources, assign preferences and functions to one or more languages, and develop their use according to previously determined objectives. The language policy of bilingual communities or multilingual societies provides an exemplary situation for problem solving within language planning: eg it may involve the continued maintenance of two cultures and their associated languages or it may mean temporary maintenance, where it is assumed that maintenance is a transitional stage towards eventual cultural assimilation and loss of the first language. The crucial initial choice is whether the native or the other language will function as a subject or as a medium of instruction at various educational levels. Policy responses can be very different, ranging from systems involving three or more languages, which obviously put heavy demands on pupils, teachers and resources, to arrangements whereby one second or foreign language is taught as a subject entirely through the context of another content subject (Widdowson 1968).

Since language planning solutions influence all aspects of language instruction and assessment, awareness of planning activities places one in a better position to appreciate the role of language in education and to relate the academic achievements of students to the long-term objectives of different types of curricula.

European Community Schools

The system of European Community Schools (Scholae Europeae 1973) operates an international curriculum which is based on the principle of language equality in order to meet the aspirations of all national groups who work for the same political and economic confederation: the European Community. The pupils who form the multilingual population of European Schools are all nationals of EC member states and their languages, by constitution, enjoy the same status in all European Schools. Within each school students from the same state are taught together in their national section through the medium of the official language of their country of origin, which in most cases is their mother tongue. Everyone, however, is expected to learn certain curricular subjects through the medium of another European language, and to study a third language as a foreign language.

The European School model is designed to develop bilingualism: there is an emphasis on the maintenance of the native/national language and in the development of a second European language which is taught like the first language for academic use, in addition to a compulsory foreign language which is taught as a subject. The concept behind the European Schools is that students should be in a position to be able to reintegrate into their respective national education systems, to move to another European School, or else to a national school in a different member state. Hence everyone is expected to function academically in two languages: ie to be able to learn content matter and take examinations in another European language in addition to their own. This curriculum is the same in every European School, as it was founded on the principle that language equality is needed to fulfil the aspirations of all European national groups. By constitution each European language enjoys the same status, and their equal treatment is intended to safeguard the multilingual partnership of the European Community, to protect the multinational equality of its citizenship and to promote multilingualism among European citizens with three languages, of which at least two can be used for academic purposes.

International Baccalaureate

The language curriculum of the IB schools is very different from that of the European Schools since it adopts monolingual not bilingual education. The IB programme originated from the efforts of some schools to agree a common curriculum that could be made available to mobile students and that could be recognized for university entrance in as many countries as possible. The constitution of this international curriculum (International Baccalaureate 1967) stipulated that for the two-year pre-university upper secondary course only English or French were acceptable vehicles to study other subjects and to be media of examination. Thus the major problem of language planning the IB needed to solve was the treatment of languages other than English and French, and subsequently to provide a suitable structure for their examination. In addressing the first problem, the IB specified that 'the language of instruction in an international school is not necessarily the candidate's native tongue', and the subsequent curriculum was one whereby every student was expected to undertake 'the study of another language, called second language, and defined as one usually but not necessarily a foreign language'. Within this approach the IB readily acknowledged some of the drawbacks and gave some indication as to how to minimize them:

The most complicated problem arises from the different linguistic back-

> ground of the students. By choice or by necessity, many of them use a language of instruction which is not their mother tongue; at the same time their mother tongue may be taught to them as a foreign language or they may use it only at home or in private lessons. Consequently, instead of talking of 'mother tongue' on the one hand and 'foreign languages' on the other, it seems more desirable to call the first means of expression (of which a pupil should have complete command at the end of his secondary school studies) Language A, and the second (of which he should have an adequate knowledge) Language B.
>
> (International Baccalaureate 1967)

The original framework of one Language A and one Language B (where two Language A programmes were accepted but not two Language B programmes) underwent an important political change when a new facility was introduced to allow candidates to offer any language they wished, in either a Language A or a Language B programme, provided that it had a written literature. However, this new opportunity in practice restricted the number of languages which could be offered in the Language A programme when its syllabus introduced a compulsory selection of world literature to be studied in translation. In theory, this innovation was introduced to expand the number of languages within the international curriculum, but in practice the world literature requirement reinforced the trend whereby native speakers of the languages of developing countries could not be examined for their competence in their own mother tongue (ie by a Language A programme), but only for their knowledge of it as a foreign language (ie in a Language B programme). This is a surprising policy decision if we are to believe the Twentieth Century Fund report that the International Baccalaureate received its initial grants from them and the Ford Foundation on the basis that 'an international syllabus and examination would be particularly useful to developing nations seeking to escape formerly colonial ties'. (Mayer 1968)

Language instruction – main issues

The professional definition of bilingual education is education where two languages are used as media of instruction, but bilingual schools are not the only schools which produce bilingualism (Tosi 1990). There are many students educated in monolingual international schools who are committed to using their native language at home and/or within their national community abroad. Many of them achieve bilingual proficiency approximating very closely to an equal command of the two languages in accent, fluency and cognitive operations. On the other hand, there are many students who are brought up and educated in their own country who become immersed in second language education for a few years before university and achieve cognitive operations and linguistic fluency in two languages with a native accent in one and a near native accent in another. Bilingualism, therefore, can also be the outcome of education which is imparted through a second language: it requires curricular planning including teaching and evaluative instruments which are different from those adopted in monolingual schools, which teach mother tongues and foreign languages to students who are native speakers of the school language.

Many monolingual international schools, of course, would wish to offer bilingual education though they are unable to provide the vehicular use of more than one language because of the wide range of native languages spoken by pupils. When this is the case, it is very important for teachers and administrators to appreciate the different outcome of bilingualism with and without the academic mastery of one of the two languages: the classic explanation provided by Swain and Cummins (1979) refers to the diverse types of bilingualism they found when comparing the bilingual competence attained in 'immersion' programmes with that of children in 'submersion' programmes. Immersion students, they say, achieve a privileged 'additive' form of bilingualism; other bilingual children attain only a 'subtractive' form of bilingualism when they are not taught their mother tongue or they are not taught it in the right way and at the right time. The latter, Cummins points out (1984), is not a satisfactory and competitive form of language competence as it incorporates limitations which become difficulties when the language is used for academic purposes rather than for daily communicative operations.

European Schools

The European School model of bilingual education adopts as a first medium of instruction the student's national language and as a second language of instruction one of the so-called vehicular languages which can be French, German, or English. Most education takes place in the student's first or national language, with native-speaking teachers. Each of the national sections of the school follows the same timetable and the same curriculum, and the same compulsory subjects are taught through the medium of the second or vehicular language right up to the final examination. The primary level (five-year programme) includes bilingual education in the national language with a good grounding in the vehicular language. This involves the second language being taught as a subject for the first two years and for the third year onwards the programme contains European Hours, which are conducted in one of the vehicular languages. The vehicular language is a language with a privileged status from the nine available, in that it serves both as a medium of instruction and as a lingua franca for inter-student contact.

At primary level, the vehicular language is taught by concentrating exclusively on the spoken language, written competence being left to the secondary school. At the secondary level, the vehicular language plays a more important role: it is taught as a subject for almost an hour a day in the first three grades of secondary education and for two hours per week for the last four grades. During the first two years Human Sciences (history and geography) are taught in the national language, and in the vehicular language from the third year onwards. Artistic subjects and physical education are also taught in the vehicular language, and it is also used for Complementary Activities (eg Electronics, Informatics, etc). Half-way through education, the instruction not imparted through the first or national language has increased to the advantage of the vehicular language, amounting to almost half of the curriculum. At the same time, a third language is introduced as a compulsory subject for all, while a fourth language becomes optional in the fourth and fifth years of secondary education. In these final years, the only subjects taught through the medium of the national language of the section are the language itself, philosophy, mathematics, natural sciences, and a classical language if this is chosen instead of a fourth European language (Baetens Beardsmore and Swain 1985).

International Baccalaureate

Only one language of instruction is envisaged by the IB curriculum, although it is obligatory for every diploma student to learn another language alongside the school medium of education. The aim of the IB programme is also bilingualism, but whether it involves the academic use of two languages or of one only, with a smattering of a foreign language, depends on the diverse treatment of the native tongues of pupils. Since the IB curriculum treats the native speakers of its official working languages differently from those who are not native speakers of the school medium of instruction, only the latter can develop bilingualism with the academic use of the second language if they have already developed academic proficiency in their own national language outside the international school. This approach originates from an early international philosophy of the 1960s when the IB was founded, and many international educators were more concerned with the support of the so-called world languages than with the development of individual bilingualism. Accordingly, world languages only were introduced in international schools as vehicles of knowledge because of their extraordinary supernational status.

Today, the IB curricular structure still includes two language programmes which are based on assumptions relevant to mother tongue (Language A) or foreign language learning (Language B): a curriculum that is tailor-made for the monolingual native speaker of the school language. What this structure still ignores is the language learning process of those students who are not native speakers of the school language, and who develop bilingualism by adding to their native competence in their home and national community language a near-native competence in the school medium of instruction. The mastery of the school language is regarded merely as a function of exposure to it, hence the attainment of competence is seen as a process necessary to the learning of other curricular subjects or to the study of literature, but it is neither recognized nor evaluated as an experience of learning a non-native language. The assumption is that all pupils have the same mother tongue and all languages other than the school language are foreign languages. When the IB programme was set up, this was in tune with the times. Until the 1970s, there was a general confusion between the processes of learning a second language and a foreign language. International education inherited this confusion from national education, and subsequently the process of second language learning by bilingual pupils, who were not native speakers of the school language, was either interpreted as the phenomenon of adopting English as a mother tongue or confused with genuine foreign language learning.

In the light of the growing international commitment to bilingualism and biculturalism in national as well as international education, it is unlikely that this state of affairs will meet the aspirations of parents, students, and staff in IB schools for much longer. When the IB programme was established a quarter of a century ago, it was considered normal to examine native competence only in the school medium of instruction: all other languages were examined as foreign languages. The early documents of the IB international programme could not be more explicit about this practice: 'The Language A is the mother tongue or the *adoptive* language of the student [my emphasis] which is his basic means of communication and culture.' The Language B, which was designed as a foreign language programme, was considered to provide a suitable examination also to its native speakers since 'to them mother tongue may be taught as a foreign language' (International Baccalaureate 1967 and 1968).

Language assessment: main issues

The previous section discussed why bilingualism with the academic use of two languages is accessible to students who are educated via a second language and are taught their mother tongue with a view to maintaining or developing a similar academic proficiency. This section discusses further why bilingual proficiency of second language immersion students involves a cognitive and academic competence in the second language which is not normally accessible to genuine foreign language learners. These learners acquire basic communicative skills, when the foreign language is taught as a subject within the limited time-frame of the curriculum, that are less competitive than the bilingual proficiency of second language immersion students. It may be argued that when the school offers structurally different language learning programmes to diverse categories of students (eg the native speakers and the non-native speakers of the second language), and the examination system does not treat them as separate populations, the test validity can be compromised.

For the purpose of assessing language competence in international schools, a fundamental distinction needs to be enforced between the notion of second language academic proficiency and that of knowledge of a foreign language. The first notion relates specifically to the academic use of a non-native language which is practised through the study of curriculum subjects. The second notion refers to an ability to function in communication with speakers of another language outside the school. The emphases are different. In the case of a second language proficiency, the emphasis is on the high levels of competence required for academic use. In the case of the knowledge of a foreign language, the linguistic competence is expected to be confined to basic communicative tasks rather than sophisticated cognitive operations.

The subsequent distinction between language tests, which contain emphasis on the cognitive and academic activities of second language users, and tests which are more sensitive to communicative skills of genuine foreign language learners, should be understood on educational grounds. The concept does not suggest an alternative type of language competence. It suggests, instead, a practical framework for a more reliable measurement of the standards achieved in two worthwhile but different learning programmes (Tosi 1986).

European Schools

The examination structure of the European Schools reflects the diversity of language competence developed by its multilingual curriculum. The examination criteria are similar to those of schools in national systems, and their contents are harmonized across the national sections of the European Schools for many subjects. Tests used in mathematics, natural sciences, philosophy, and classical languages, which are taught in the students' national language, are identical irrespective of the language in which the examinations are taken. The rest of the curriculum, which involves history and geography, is examined through the medium of the vehicular language. All national languages which are taught as first academic languages are examined by five written and four oral tests; the examination of the vehicular language, which is the students' second academic language, consists of tests measuring cognitive use and clarity of expression as well as oral and written comprehension of literary style. In theory, the levels of achievement in the first and second academic language are expected to be similar; in practice, simpler syntax and less sophisticated vocabulary are tolerated as long as they are not found to threaten accuracy. The third as well as the fourth language, when the latter is chosen as an option, are examined separating the population of learners who have studied them as curricular subjects from the students who have used them as vehicular languages. On no account are genuine foreign language learners allowed to sit the same examination with students who speak the same language as a mother tongue, or those who have learnt it as a second academic or vehicular language.

International Baccalaureate

In the IB schools as in European Schools, there are three different language learning processes at work with their multilingual population:

1. Mother tongue learning for the native as well as the non-native speakers of the school language;
2. Foreign language learning for the native speakers of the school language;
3. Second language learning for the non-native speakers of the school language.

Unlike the European Schools, IB examination structure requires from every diploma candidate two instead of three languages, and these are examined respectively by one set of tests of mother tongue (Language A) and one set of tests of foreign language (Language B). The option of two Language A tests is also available, but this is taken up by virtually no students because it demands the study of an impossible literary load, and expects from each bilingual candidate standards of language competence comparable to those of two monolingual students.

The lack of a special examination for bilingual students who have developed the academic use of two languages has consequences for the validity of the examination system as a whole. In one option, when those who are not native speakers of the school language choose to enter the examination of the language of instruction with its native speakers (Language A), they end up being examined in their mother tongue together with genuine foreign language learners. Naturally in a system operating with norm-referenced language tests, the top marks are awarded to native competence. In the other possible option, when those who are not native speakers of the school language choose that their native competence should be examined by a mother tongue programme (Language A), their second language achievement is examined by the foreign language tests (Language B). In this case, the performance of students who have learnt another language within the most favourable curricular opportunity – that of using it as a medium of education – is allowed to set unrealistic standards against which is measured the achievement of those candidates who have studied it only as a foreign language, within the limited time-frame of a curriculum subject.

Either option introduces inconsistencies of standards, and the situation is further complicated as the majority of IB students who are not native speakers of the school language is almost evenly divided between the two options. Their decision to take one combination or another depends on a number of personal and contextual factors. For example, some schools have a policy whereby all students are free to choose the language they wish in the Language A and in the Language B programme. Others do not allow native speakers to enter a Language B programme. Some practically oblige native speakers to do so, since they offer only the Language A programme in the school medium of instruction. Moreover, there are language programmes which can be 'untaught', others which must be taught, and this is further complicated by the fact that all diploma candidates need a certain number of High and Subsidiary options: in the IB credit system a Language B High rates higher than a Language A Subsidiary, which is more challenging but less rewarding. This explains why the programmes of Language A and Language B, which have such different definitions in practice, include the same wide range of performances: from the ablest native speakers to those who struggle with a second or foreign language having no exposure to that language outside the school (Tosi 1989).

The models compared

A recent study summarizes the differences between the European Schools and the vast majority of what the writers describe as the 'so-called international schools' in this way:

> [These] quite often are only international in pupil composition, occasionally provide bilingual education, but usually function as monolingual establishments. Moreover most international schools are fee-paying and élitist, and most are independent and not controlled by government organizations.
>
> (Baetens Beardsmore and Kols 1988)

By contrast, the writers emphasized the diverse language planning priorities of European Schools which are (a) the maintenance of the national language, culture and identity and (b) the European supernational experience that is promoted, among other things, with the vehicular use of a second language that is different from the national language. Accordingly, all European Schools adopt two languages of instruction, with students developing bilingualism enriched by academic use of two languages. In addition, all students are expected to acquire a functional knowledge of a third European language which is taught as a foreign language for several years. Moreover, the multilingual population of

European Schools is examined homogeneously according to diverse types of language learning experiences in the curriculum: native speakers are isolated from second language immersion students and the latter are not mixed with the genuine learners of a foreign language, which is studied as a third language by all candidates and as a fourth language by some.

Instead, when the International Baccalaureate planned its language curriculum in 1967, it decided that only two languages of instruction and examination could provide education with the necessary international status: French and English. These were the principal languages used in international diplomacy; also they were the languages most in demand for commerce as well as cultural exchange; finally, they exercised great appeal to non-native speakers in Europe as well as to students in former colonial territories and developing nations. The situation was modified in 1982 when it was decided to add Spanish to the two official working languages in response to the growing interest in the Hispanic world, especially in Latin America. Since this time, all the IB administrative work has been carried out in these three working languages; also the IB curriculum can be studied through one of these three media of instruction; and the examinations in all subjects are carried out and can be taken using the medium of one of the three languages. All schools in the IB with the exception of one, however, are monolingual and students cannot opt to be taught in another of the IB working languages. Although the knowledge of two languages is a requirement for all IB diploma students, the minimum level to be achieved in a second or foreign language to pass the final examination is indeed very low. This level of linguistic ability in a second language in many cases corresponds to the competence attainable in only two years of an *ab initio* course. This provision has been introduced *de facto* for many native speakers of the school medium of instruction, who in the IB are overwhelmingly English speakers, with a view to compensating the poor interest and facilities for the study of language and cultures other than their own which prevails in many English-speaking societies and schools. This decision, of course, raises the political issue of the status of the English language in international education, and the subsequent professional dilemma – do some customers of international schools receive a privileged treatment, or vice versa, are they underprivileged by virtue of being native speakers of the world international language?

Language status

Today, most planners and practitioners of international education are reasonably convinced that no language is inherently inferior to another, that they all have academic value, and that any native tongue should be used in the education of its speakers. Therefore, should the two languages – the national and the international language – be given equal status throughout the curriculum, or should they be given different status? The former strategy is adopted by European Schools which make available to all students two languages of instruction – one to develop native competence and education in the national language and culture, the other to promote cognitive functioning and European identity through the academic use of a second language. The curricular cost for students is not as high as the resource cost for schools: the time spent on the second academic language does not cause the first academic language to deteriorate, and the reward is a population of educated bilinguals, equally at ease with two languages, their own national culture and the supernational European identity. Though European Schools are not private, because of its high cost their curriculum is offered only to communities of technologists and administrators working for the European Community institutions, and is not made available to communities of ordinary European families working outside their own countries. It is true that unlike in private international schools, education is free. This does not mean, however, that it is less exclusive: it simply means that children from non-civil servant families are admitted to schools in order to avoid social ghettos. Indeed the high cost of these schools has not prevented this privileged European education from being made accessible to a few powerful families; but so far, the high cost has been an obstacle in the spread of the same model to other areas of Europe where urban concentrations of non-nationals are made up of less fortunate and less powerful families.

The second strategy is adopted by the International Baccalaureate schools, most of which are private and need to be concerned primarily with resources and cost-effectiveness. Accordingly, they do not adopt expensive measures of bilingual education with two or more media of instruction, but they attribute to one international languge, overwhelmingly English, the exclusive role of vehicular language and culture-carrying medium. Within the limited time-frame of another curriculum subject, some IB schools teach a foreign language to the native speakers of English and to its non-native speakers teach their mother tongue. The risk of falling into monolingualism or imbalanced bilingualism with cultural assimilation and cognitive operation predominantly in the English language is greater in IB than in European Schools, and this is proven by the functioning of the system if not by its pronouncements. Certainly, native speakers of English have no facilities to develop bilingualism with an academic use of another language in any English medium school. On the other hand, all those who are non-native speakers of English can study English as their native or adopted language and their mother tongue as a foreign language. If they feel inclined to maintain and develop the academic use of their mother tongue, they cannot find the appropriate facilities within the IB schools. Thus the IB curriculum works well as an immersion programme for those who have firm grounding in any language other than English, and wish to add the academic mastery of this language to their competence in the national language. But for those who have many years of education outside their own country, the IB curriculum speeds up the alienation from one's own cultural and linguistic origin, unless the family takes the appropriate precautions privately outside the school.

Student achievement

It is quite clear that if the European Schools believed in bilingual education to promote bilingualism right from their origin in 1958, the IB programme which was set up ten years later emphasized more the privilege of being educated in a world language rather than the educational value of learning to function successfully in two languages and cultures. The IB emphasis is still on assimilation rather than on diversity, and this is a pity since the latter is precisely the emphasis that is rapidly taking over in most international circles, if not in the Third World and Developing Countries then certainly in Europe. To put it crudely, many Europeans see bilingualism, and not Esperanto or English, as the passport to international relations. Significantly, 'English is not Enough' is the title of a manifesto/article published by the leading British linguist Randolph Quirk in *The Times Higher Educational Supplement* of 11 December 1987.

It is not surprising that in this changing climate of international education, the native speakers of English in the English medium schools that adopt the IB curriculum are no longer advantaged. On the contrary, they are at a disadvantage as their schools cannot provide second language immersion and they cannot help them develop the academic use of another language. Since the condition of the native speaker of the world language is rapidly becoming recognized as a disadvantage in education, international schools would do well to think further about the expectations and aspirations of those schools who care for the international awareness of many of the families they serve. Is the advantage of international education today the mere qualification which is recognized by many countries around the world, or do families and students expect a different cultural and linguistic experience from that available perhaps in some of the best national schools? Moreover, if that international qualification is available at the expense of the strong grounding of a national cultural and bilingual education, how far and for long how will it satisfy the European population?

Certainly both systems of European Schools and the International Baccalaureate today experience new problems and this is the way they seek new solutions. The former, due to government control, might not be able to enjoy expansion if it is felt to be insufficiently cost-effective for a wider sector of the European population. But the latter, because of its private status and the pressure for cost-effectiveness, must rid itself of its Anglocentric cultural and linguistic biases if schools wish to avoid the criticism of those governments which are seriously committed to bilingualism and language equality within the European Community.

Bibliography

Baetens Beardsmore, H and Kols, J (1988) Immediate Pertinence in the acquisition of multilingual proficiency: the European Schools *The Canadian Modern Language Review* **44** (2), 240–60

Baetens Beardsmore, H and Swain, M (1985) Designing bilingual education: aspects of immersion and 'European School' models *Journal of Multilingual and Multicultural Developments* **6**(1), 1–15

Bloomfield, L (1933) *Language* Holt, Rinehart & Winston: New York

Brumfit, C J and Roberts, J T (1983) *An Introduction to Language and Language Teaching* Batsford Academic and Educational Ltd: London

Cummins, J (1984) *Bilingualism and Special Education: Issues in Assessment and Pedagogy* Multilingual Matters: Clevedon, Avon

Cummins, J and Swain, M (1986) *Bilingualism in Education: Aspects of Theory, Research and Practice* Longman: Harlow

Gellar, C A (1981) International education: some thoughts on what it is and what it might be *International Schools Journal* 21–6

International Baccalaureate (1967) *The International Baccalaureate* International Schools Examination Syndicate (ISES): Geneva

Kennedy, C (1982) Language planning *Language Teaching* **15** (4), 264–84

Leach, R J (1969) *International Schools and their Role in the Field of International Education* Pergamon Press: Oxford

Maillard, J P and Malingre, D (1980) *Guide Français de l'enseignement International* Librarie Editions des Echanges Internationaux: Paris

Mayer, M (1968) *Diploma: International Schools and University Entrance* The Twentieth Century Fund: New York

Peterson, A D C (1977) The program of the International Baccalaureate *The Journal of General Education* **28** (4), 276–82

Quirk, R (1987) English is not enough *Times Higher Educational Supplement* 11 December

Scholae Europeae (1973) *Schola Europeae ex foedere novem nationum* Office for Official Publications of the European Communities: Luxembourg

Swain, M and Cummins, J (1979) Bilingualism, cognitive functioning and education *Language Teaching and Linguistics: Abstracts* **12** (1), 4–18

Tosi, A (1986) Home and community language teaching for bilingual learners: issues in planning and instruction *Language Teaching* **19** (1), 2–23

Tosi, A (1989) *Feasibility Study No 1: Bilingualism in the IB* International Baccalaureate and Institute of Education, University of London. Unpublished report

Tosi, A (1990) Bilingual education. In R Kaplan (ed) *Annual Review of Applied Linguistics* Volume X Cambridge University Press: New York

UNESCO (1953) *The Use of Vernacular Languages in Education* Monographs on fundamental education, Paris

UNESCO (1978) *Meeting of the Experts on Language Teaching in a Bi- or Pluri-lingual and Multicultural Environment* Final Report, Paris

Widdowson, H G (1968) The teaching of English through science. In J Dakin, B Tiffen and H G Widdowson (eds) *Language in Education* Oxford University Press, 115–75

12. Bilingual education in the international school – dream or reality?

Alex Horsley

Introduction

It is sad that in this modern and interdependent age we still find ourselves deploring the lack of genuinely bilingual educational opportunities throughout the world. The supreme irony is that less than one quarter of the 700 schools listed in the index of the international schools worldwide in the *ECIS Directory of International Schools* make any claim to teach students using the medium of more than one language. This is ironic because virtually all of these institutions claim to represent a fully international community and strive to present an image of international education prowess.

The sad fact is that English-as-the-sole-language-of-instruction schools dominate the international school scene. Most of these schools offer either a British or American curriculum, sometimes a combination of both. At the secondary level, many of these schools prepare students for the International Baccalaureate examinations, which require reasonable levels of achievement in a second language, but foreign language is treated as an academic subject, rather than the language of instruction and general communication.

In addition to English language international schools, there are networks of national schools throughout the world. The most extensive of these is the French, with 500 schools worldwide. There are also significant numbers of German and Japanese schools in various parts of the world. Basically, these schools offer a purely national curriculum, using the national language as the medium of instruction. In most cases, the language of the host country is taught as a foreign language. In this category, however, there are a few schools which have developed a fully bilingual curriculum. For example, 10 of the 26 member schools of the Association des Ecoles Françaises d'Amerique du Nord are listed as being fully bilingual.

The purpose of this paper is to demonstrate that it is not only desirable but possible to undertake a completely bilingual educational programme, even for students who enter as monolinguals. Schools which offer immersion programmes (full or partial) in a second language can point to significant levels of educational achievement in both the student's native language and his or her acquired one. Specific examples from Atlanta International School will be given to prove this point.

Bilingual models

First, however, we should describe how such programmes work in practice. There are several basic models for bilingual elementary schools, of which three can be readily identified:

1. Full immersion in the second language. This is the favoured approach in many schools in English-speaking parts of Canada. Here students are fully immersed in the French from kindergarten level, and undertake complete reading/writing/mathematics programmes in French right from the beginning. English is introduced progressively into the classroom from Grade 2 or 3, with a complete 50/50 split by the end of fifth grade.
2. Partial immersion in the second language. This is the approach at Atlanta International School and many other bilingual schools in the United States. Here, students spend exactly half of their time in each language from kindergarten through at least Grade 5. In effect, students have two home-room teachers, one in each language.
3. Individual subjects in the second language. In this model, students remain in one home-room, but have specified subjects in the second language. Subjects often taught in this way include social studies in addition to the obvious reading and writing, but often exclude mathematics and science.

Each of the three models has its own advantages and attractions, but this paper will deal most specifically with the second model. This is because of the ready availability to the author of specific data from a school operating such a system.

Atlanta International School

Atlanta International School has a total enrolment of 350 students, of whom 250 are in the fully bilingual elementary section; 45 per cent of the students are American, with the balance representing 48 different countries. There are three distinct language tracks: English–French, English–Spanish, and English–German. The school was founded in 1984 to offer American and foreign children resident in the Atlanta area the possibility of a fully bilingual education. The English part of the programme generally follows a US curriculum, although the approach includes something of the British. For example, European-style exercise books are used, rather than the American looseleaf and tear-out workbook approach.

The French programme, fully recognized by the French Ministry of Education, uses teachers and materials imported from France, Quebec, and the Ivory Coast. The following is from the French Chief Inspector's report on the school to the Ministry in Paris in February 1989:

> La reconnaissance de l'ensemble des classes elementaires peut être des a present accordée .... Un élève qui aura commence ses études a l'Ecole International d'Atlanta pourra s'inserer dans une autre scolarité française sans difficulté s'il est francophone avec un effort minimal d'adaption s'il ne l'est pas.

The German section follows closely the programme of the German province of

Baden-Wurttemberg. The teachers are all trained German Grundschule teachers, using materials supplied in part by the section of the West German government which deals with German overseas schools. Students have transferred easily from Atlanta International School into schools of all kinds in Germany.

The Spanish section has teachers from Colombia and Puerto Rico. Students have transferred to Spanish-medium schools in Mexico and Spain without difficulty.

From kindergarten through to Grade 5, students spend exactly half of their time in English and half in their second language. The school operates a unique 'Short Day/Long Day' schedule, specifically designed to maximize the exposure to both languages. 'Short Day' runs from 8.30 until 10 am. After a 20-minute break, 'Long Day' commences at 10.20 and runs until 3 pm.

Bilingual schedule

To illustrate how the schedule works, let us take as an example a student in Grade 3 English–French. On a given day (say Monday) this student may spend 'Short Day' in her or his French home-room and 'Long Day' in her or his English home-room. During 'Short Day' French, she or he would cover the basic academic parts of the curriculum in the French language – reading, writing, and mathematics. During 'Long Day' English, she or he would again have a period of basic academics, but she or he would also have exposure to other aspects of the curriculum, such as science, social studies, art, physical education, or music. The next day, Tuesday, she or he would have the same timetable, but this time with 'Short Day' English followed by 'Long Day' French. This alternating daily cycle would continue through the school year.

There are several reasons for the 'Short Day/Long Day' system. It maintains an exactly 50/50 split between the two languages, while preserving daily exposure to both. It allows an extended period in one language to develop project work in science or social studies, without taking away from the basic reading/writing/mathematics time. It allows for exposure to subjects such as art, music, and physical education in both languages.

Assessment

Results from students who have been in this system for four or five years are impressive. Educational Records Bureau, American-style standardized tests, are administered to students in Grade 3 and above with consistently good results. ERB is part of the Educational Testing Service of Princeton, New Jersey, which is the major US testing agency. Other branches of ETS produce the SAT and many other college-level tests. The ERB tests are given in virtually every major independent school in the United States and in a few public schools. Given the fact that students have only spent half of their time in a classroom where English is the language of instruction, these scores are most impressive. Table 12.1 gives the scores for the first class of students to pass through Atlanta International School's bilingual elementary programme.

Table 12.1 *ERB test scores, 4th grade, May 1989 (22 students)*

ATLANTA INTERNATIONAL SCHOOL: PERCENTILE RANKINGS BY CATEGORY

	National Norm			*Independent School Norm*		
	High	Median	Low	High	Median	Low
Verbal Aptitude	99	79	41	99	40	6
Quantitative Aptitude	99	84	46	98	50	10
Vocabulary	99	83	28	99	52	2
Reading Comprehension	99	81	52	96	53	14
Mechanics of Writing	99	77	43	94	39	9
English Expression	99	95	36	98	74	7
Math Concepts	99	91	61	98	55	23
Math Computation	99	88	42	95	54	13

The students represented in this table entered AIS in 1985 as First Graders and in February 1990 were in the fifth year of the programme. The 22 students include 12 who arrived as monolingual English speakers, 6 who arrived as monolingual speakers of other languages, and 4 who were already bilingual when they arrived. The National Norms refer to United States national norms (ie public schools). The Independent School Norm figures refer to percentile rankings of students in academic private schools, where all of the graduates are destined for four-year college and university programmes. The scores indicate clearly that students in this class are well above national average norms, and of average levels when compared with students in other academic private schools. The scores in areas of *achievement* (reading, writing, and mathematics) are slightly higher than those for *aptitude*, indicating that students may be over-achieving in relation to their level of aptitude.

In the German and French sections, tests have been administered which indicate that Atlanta International School students are on a par with their counterparts in Germany and France. In French, our Grade 3 students take the 'Evaluation a l'Entree au CE2' tests given by the Ministry of Education and scored well in the average plus range of students in France. Following accreditation by the Ministry of Education, students from AIS are readily accepted into French government schools without the need for further testing. In German, the AIS Grade 4 students take the 'Aufnahmeverfahren in Weiterfuhrende Schulen, Hauptschule (Vocational School), Realschule (Intermediate Schools), and Gymnasium (Academic/University Preparation)' examinations given to students in the province of Baden-Wurttemberg. Around 50 per cent of our students would qualify 'without need for further test' into the Gymnasium. Of the remainder, most come into the second category of 'further test needed to enter the Gymnasium'. Very few students tested at the level where they would have no chance of entry into the Gymnasium. As yet, students in the Spanish section have not been given similar tests, but the fact that within the past two years students have transferred into government schools in Spain and Mexico without any difficulty indicates appropriate levels of proficiency.

It is important to re-emphasize that AIS students attain these levels without regard to their linguistic background. In French 'Entree au CE2' tests taken in

1989, the two highest scoring students were English-speaking Americans with absolutely no family background in French. Likewise, the top scoring student on the 4th Grade ERB tests was a German student who arrived at AIS with no knowledge of English. This student also had the highest score in mathematics and essay-writing in the German examinations. The students transferring to schools in Spain and Mexico include native English speakers as well as native Spanish speakers.

Bilingual effects

Of course, test scores alone do not represent the success or failure of a particular programme. Far more important is the students' knowledge and conceptual level, and the ability to express and use that knowledge. In a bilingual setting, the student is exposed to different approaches to study and knowledge. Intrinsically, this adds to the student's experience by challenging him or her to see the world from two different angles.

In *social studies*, the student obtains information from two completely different sources. A student in the English–Spanish track uses fairly standard American texts in the English classroom, giving a broadly based US approach to history and geography. In his or her Spanish classroom, where his or her teacher and text is from Latin America, he or she will study the history and geography of the Americas from that perspective. Similarly, the French and German sections bring their approach to these subjects. The teachers work closely together to ensure a common thread to this process, but nevertheless the students do readily understand the different perspective on the world.

In *mathematics*, there are significantly different approaches in various countries throughout the world. In a bilingual setting, it is quite possible for a student to grasp quickly mathematical concepts using two different approaches provided that the teachers work closely together in planning their timing and introduction of new concepts. Figure 12.1 shows examples of work in mathematics from a 5th Grade English–German student in both languages. In both cases, the same concept is involved (double-digit division), but the differences in approach are clearly apparent. Nevertheless, the student has mastered the concept and demonstrates ease in approaching a similar problem in the two different ways.

In the bilingual programme, *language skills* development, being immersed in the second language, means that much language skill development is achieved by osmosis. When a child begins an immersion programme at kindergarten or First Grade level, there is no real need for specialist attention to the learning of the second language. By being immersed in the language from such an early age and by taking part in the early reading, writing, and mathematics programmes, language skills will develop naturally. For a child who enters at Second or Third Grade level, there is a clear need for specialist attention to enable the child to function in the classroom with other students.

Statistics from the Ministry of Education on the English-speaking Canadian province of Ontario, where there are many full and partial immersion French programmes, shows the following time periods that are necessary for the

Figure 12.1 *English–German mathematics*

English section

The fifth grade sold boxes of cards to earn money for a class trip. 23 students sold 851 boxes.

a) Approximately how many boxes were sold by each student?

n = 851 ÷ 23

n = Each child sold 37 boxes

```
     37
23 ) 851
    -69
     161
    -161
       0
```

b) If each student turned in $109.15, how much did each box sell for?

n = $109.15 ÷ 37

n = Each box sold for $2.95.

```
      $2.95
37 ) $109.15
      -74
       351
      -333
        185
       -185
```

German Section

Eine Kabinenbahn hat eine Tragkraft von 1200kg oder 16 Personen.

a) Von welchem mittleren Gewicht einer Person wird ausgegangen?

Rechnung: 1200 kg : 16 = 75 kg

```
1200 kg : 16 = 75 kg
-112
   80
  -80
   00
```

Antwort:
Eine Person kann 75 kg wiegen.

b) Für die Versorgung der Bergstation werden 8 Kartons mit je 25kg eingeladen. Wieviel Personen dürfen noch mitfahren?

Rechnung: 8 · 25 kg = 200 kg

```
 1200 kg
- 200 kg
 1000 kg
```

```
1000 kg : 75 kg = 13
- 75
  250
- 225
   25
```

Antwort:
13 Personen dürfen noch mitfahren.

development of second language skills:

> *Basic level of proficiency*
> Defined as a vocabulary of up to 3,000 words and about 100 basic sentence patterns. This level can be achieved in 1,200 hours of instruction, 1,200 hours is equivalent to 45 minutes per day for nearly ten school years. In a 50 per cent partial immersion system, 1,200 hours are covered in two-and-a-half school years.
>
> *Intermediate level of proficiency*
> Defined as being able to carry on a basic conversation in a familiar subject area; being able to read and write (with the help of a dictionary) at a reasonable level; being able to undertake study of other academic disciplines in the language. This level can be achieved in 2,100 hours, which is reached after four-and-a-half school years in a 50 per cent immersion programme.
>
> *Advanced level of proficiency*
> Defined as being able to carry out serious conversations in most subject areas; being able to follow freely radio and television broadcasts and to operate freely in a country where the language is spoken. This level can be achieved after a minimum of 5,000 hours.

These time-frames demonstrate that it is impossible to develop real fluency in a second language by the traditional approach of one class period per day. Such an approach, which is the norm in virtually every secondary school in the world, can only provide a grammatical base, which in turn can serve as a foundation for developing fluency more quickly when immersed in the language.

Conclusion

To develop true bilingualism through a school system, it is imperative that the bilingual approach be adopted from the elementary level. Once the student has reached a fair degree of proficiency, it is important that the language be used as a medium of instruction for at least a part of the day. This reinforces basic linguistic skills and provides a vehicle for the student to develop complete use of the language.

Schools which strive to develop true bilingualism are relatively rare. There are such schools in major cities in Latin America, in parts of Canada and in parts of the United States. In Europe, outside the EC schools, there is a sprinkling of bilingual schools, especially in Spain and France, but sadly many opportunities for bilingual education are missed. In Great Britain, there are virtually no such schools. Likewise in Asia and Africa, English-only schools are the norm in the international school scene.

There is no doubt that persons with complete fluency in more than one language have a real advantage in our modern world. Unfortunately, even in international schools, foreign language teaching is still seen as just another academic discipline. Those persons who have developed bilingualism have done so either through their natural background or by going to live in another country following their regular schooling. Yet, there are sufficient examples throughout the world that show that it is indeed possible to create bilingual citizens through school systems. It is hoped that such programmes will become available to far more people in the future. To achieve this, it is important that educators concerned with international education should give very serious consideration to integrating some kind of bilingual programme into their institutions.

13. The role and development of ESL programmes in international schools

Maurice W Carder

Introduction

'We have two teachers who help out with extra English, but the students pick up the language quickly anyway. We don't stop them speaking their own languages on campus anymore, but there's really rather a fuss made about this language thing.' Far-fetched? Fortunately in most international schools today, this is not the line that would be taken by any serious administration interested in education. It does, however, represent the views that many teachers have and feel that they ought to suppress for the sake of professional respectability, and therefore needs to be addressed. We are fortunate in one respect, great advances based on widespread research have been made in the field of language acquisition in the last ten years; this area includes that of bilingual education. However, in international schools we are less fortunate in that little research has been carried out in international schools in this or any area, as has been shown by a recent study (Matthews 1989). Can the findings of the more nationally based investigations be related to the special circumstances of schools that consist of pockets of international clientele, each with its own idiosyncratic composition of students and host-country culture and language, scattered around the world? Perhaps not directly, but there are many useful pointers which, combined with the experience of those who have worked for a period of time in ESL (English as a second language) teaching in international schools, will indicate the best solutions.

Background

International schools developed for various reasons: international business, United Nations, Armed Forces abroad, diplomatic missions, and other sectors. Because of the development of English as the lingua franca, especially since the war (1945), it is almost universally the language of instruction in these schools (in 93 per cent of schools offering the International Baccalaureate in 1989). Inevitably, it was taken for granted that those requiring information in these schools wanted the cultural model of the country of the school language of instruction, ie British or American, especially where the Armed Forces and businesses were involved. Those who did not speak English were probably seen as 'foreigners' and expected to fit into the English or American 'way of life' as quickly as possible. The student's mother tongue was possibly seen as something of a nuisance and not to be encouraged. At this stage, there were probably few non-speakers of English involved. Schools began to focus more on this 'problem' with the development of modern world communications and the greater movement of those working for international companies and agencies. In some schools (especially the United Nations schools), it is not unusual to find a minority of students who have English as their mother tongue. Clearly attitudes had to change, and curricula and teaching methods had to be adopted to cater for this situation.

Not the least of the reasons why most schools did not tackle the 'ESL problem' were the financial implications. Each international school has its own peculiar financial base – some firmer, some shakier; to employ extra staff specifically to 'teach extra English' seemed to be an unnecessary burden on an already stretched budget. Surely if the parents were lucky enough to get their children into the school, they would not mind if their progress in English was not as rapid as that of their English-speaking peers! Even large schools with minorities of mother-tongue English speakers are still apt to point to their ESL teachers with pride; these teachers are not entirely accepted as a necessary, regular, and integrated part of the school curriculum. There are no easy solutions here; every headteacher has to balance the budget. It is to be hoped that by the end of this article, school directors will be better persuaded to support the linguistic needs of their students.

Some facts about language learning

Thirty years ago it was thought that growing up with two languages would limit personal ability in all areas, ie individuals would not speak either language well and would feel disadvantaged. They would not be able to learn school subjects properly and would therefore get poor marks. The solution to this 'problem' was to force the child to speak only one language. If the parents were of different nationalities, they would agree on which language to speak to the child; this often meant that a mother would talk to her own child in a language she did not speak well, having unthinkable effects on her ability to interact naturally with her child. If this sounds exaggerated, could you imagine talking to your child every day in a language in which you were hesitant? Many people still believe that a child will be disadvantaged by being brought up bilingually (I know of at least two families where either the mother or father never speak their own language to their own child for fear of the effect it will have), and it is time this superstition, for it is no more than that, was laid to rest. One surprising 'fact' is that a minority of the world's inhabitants are monolingual; ie most people regularly speak two or more languages. This is perhaps not so surprising on reflection. Frontiers are usually established after wars, and they are not often drawn up by the people living in those areas on the basis of what language they speak; thus groups of speakers of one language are splintered and forced to speak the language of the 'host' country, which carries all the undertones of power relationships and lurking nationalism and racism.

Another 'fact' about bilinguals is that research has shown they are not disadvantaged in academic success by learning in more than one language. In fact, it is almost certain that by having the greater flexibility of working in two (or more) languages they probably do better than their monolingual counterparts.

English is sometimes thought to be an 'easy' language because the 'grammar is easy'! True, it does not have the word endings or different cases that distinguish many languages, but the area of English that usually causes a stumbling block for so many learners is its strict and complex rules of word order. Precisely because many languages have a system that shows internally whether a word or phrase is subject or object, or whether it is connected to another part of the sentence, it is not so important as where in the sentence it is placed. Take the sentence 'all of the information you have in front of you is relevant to the matter under discussion', and see if you can move even one word to another place and retain 'correct' English (without making any other changes). It does not work, implying that there is a rule which insists on 17 items appearing in one and only one order – surely a very complex rule.

There are also still those that believe English to be a 'superior' language; 'no other nation has a literature like ours'. There are two misconceptions here; first, that some languages are intrinsically better than others, and second that language and literature are the same. First, no language is more advanced than another: some languages are spoken by primitive peoples, but they are just as complex, subtle, grammatically developed, and contain as large vocabularies as any other language. Second, a particular language group may have produced a body of literature that is highly valued, but this is due to historical circumstances that may involve the wealth of the nation involved, its development, its expansion, and its contact with other countries and their perceived power; that does not mean there is anything intrinsically 'better' about the language.

There is also at present much clamour about the relative quality of British or American English (with the implication being that the former is somehow 'purer'). This does not stand up to any sort of serious discussion; it has already been pointed out above that languages are all complex and different in their own ways. The English language is rapidly becoming accepted as 'the' international language, which will mean that it increasingly 'belongs' to all those who speak it. There may be those who protest that it is 'losing' its 'purity', that it is no longer 'the language that Shakespeare spoke', but to no avail. Latin is now dead – that 'lingua franca' developed into modern Portuguese, Spanish, French, Romanisch, Italian, and Rumanian, and had a profound influence on other languages (not least of which is English). English is developing in the same way; it is common now to speak of the different 'Englishes' spoken in the world, each developing its own separate grammar, intonation, and pronunciation. Indeed, one particular 'English' which I have become familiar with (and which my own children speak) is international school English, with a vaguely mid-Atlantic accent and particular quirks of expression and grammar, most of which come from the host country language.

Finally, another misconception that needs to be demythologized is that of the 'perfect bilingual'. No one ever talks of the 'perfect monolingual'; there are speakers of a language who have larger or smaller vocabularies or control over particular areas of language. A well-educated person might be quite lost in a conversation between two lawyers, two engineers, or two mechanics. Every individual has a daily repertoire, a fund of words that suffice for most situations, but is perhaps better acquainted with some subjects than with others. The same applies to a bilingual; in fact, from the time that a monolingual acquires one word of another language, he or she has become a bilingual, a process that will gradually develop. Definitions of bilingualism need to be established for different purposes; in international schools, a useful definition of bilingualism is where a student can successfully perform academic tasks in the languages in question.

BICS and CALP

The understanding of these two concepts (Cummins 1985) is essential to those involved with educating students whose mother tongue is not the same as the language of instruction in a school. BICS is Basic Interpersonal Communication Skills. CALP is Cognitive and Academic Language Proficiency. Before explaining them further, a few anecdotal references may help. In the past, it was frequently the case that when a new student came to an international school and was interviewed for placement in the appropriate course and year group, the student was judged on English ability entirely by performance in the spoken language. 'Oh, she chatters away in English, she'll be fine; she certainly doesn't need any special courses or tuition.' This has been shown to be patently untrue. In school, it is largely a student's performance in written work that gains merit, and for which grades are given. Cummins' work opened up the whole field of identifying which areas of school work were more or less cognitively demanding, which were taught in a more interactive way (thus containing more interplay of language and facilitating learning for the non-English speaker), and which in a transmission mode (eg teacher lecturing to class, implying no cognitive peg to hang the language on).

Thus, BICS are the types of language a student acquires for ready communication – for social purposes, for use around the school, and for communication with the peer group. This level of native-like proficiency generally takes students two years to master, and cognitive tasks during the period of time between BICS and CALP are not very cognitively demanding.

CALP skills, on the other hand, involve language which is context-reduced and highly demanding cognitively. A brief explanation of terms may help at this stage. A context-embedded pedagogical model will be one where the student will be able to understand new language as it is introduced as this immediately makes clear what the language refers to; for example, a PE teacher says 'run when I blow the whistle', and then demonstrates what is meant by blowing the whistle and running. The student will also see other students performing the actions. In this way, words and actions are connected and learned. A context-reduced model will be where the student has no means of connecting the words with their meanings; a typical example of this will be a teacher standing in front of a class talking about 'the Reformation' without the use of blackboard, overhead projector, or text books. Figure 13.1 illustrates clearly where the different school subjects come, and helps the teacher to develop strategies for more helpful isntruction for non-speakers of English (or the school language of instruction)

(Rojas 1990). The numbers are placed approximately, refer to the student's language proficiency, and are taken from Rojas' explanation of the 'ESL Academic Language Proficiency Scale'. You can spend a few minutes placing school subjects on this chart – PE will probably go on number 1, Science on 4 or 5, and History and Literature on number 9. In this way, you can develop a clearer idea of when, where, and why the ESL student will have more difficulties in learning a particular area and plan strategies accordingly.

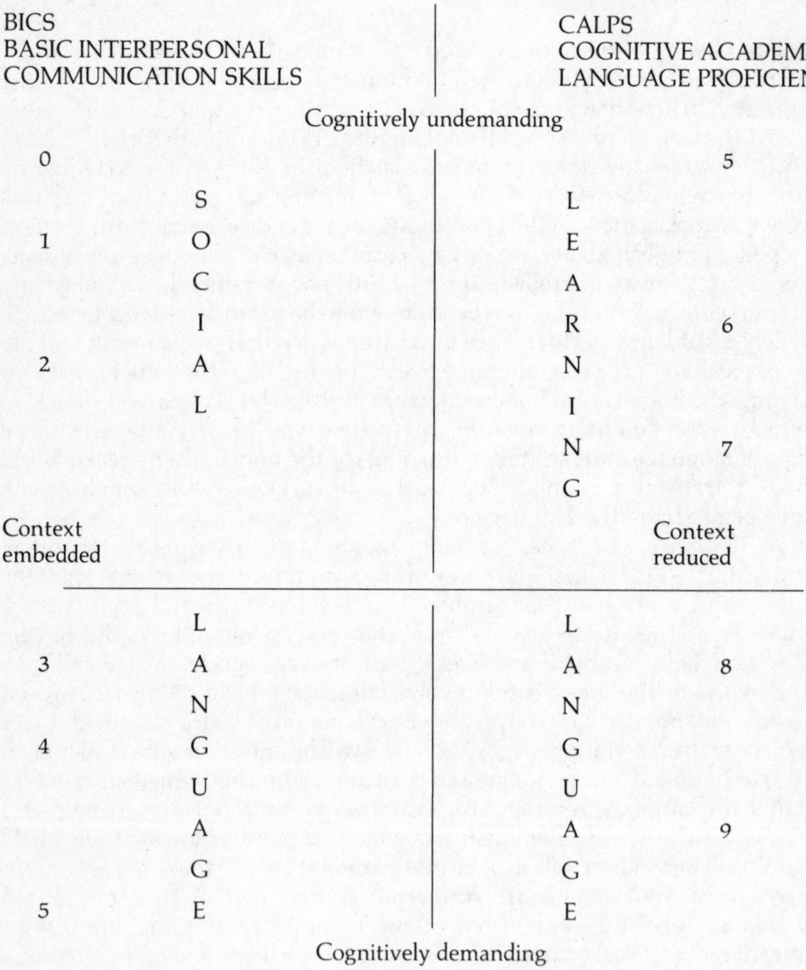

BICS
BASIC INTERPERSONAL
COMMUNICATION SKILLS

CALPS
COGNITIVE ACADEMIC
LANGUAGE PROFICIENCY

Cognitively undemanding

0	SOCIAL	LEARNING	5
1			6
2			7
Context embedded			Context reduced
3	LANGUAGE	LANGUAGE	8
4			9
5			

Cognitively demanding

Figure 13.1 *Typology of language skills*

ESL ACADEMIC LANGUAGE PROFICIENCY SCALE – (ROJAS 1990)

Student's name ______________________________

Native language ______________________________

Date ______________________________

9. *Bilingual and literate*
   Comprehends academic discourse with little difficulty. Speaks fluently with few errors. Reads and writes both concrete and abstract materials. Manipulated language with relative ease and evidences metaphorical expression. Able to work up to potential in all academic subjects.
8. *Fluent and literate*
   Comprehends much conversational and academic discourse. Idioms can still present a little difficulty. Makes occasional spoken errors (eg prepositions and articles). Reads and writes materials commensurate with cognitive development. Works up to grade level.
7. *Near English fluency and literacy*
   Comprehends substantial parts of academic conversations. Sometimes requires repetitions in context-reduced discourse. Has confidence in speaking but some errors are common. Reads and writes texts containing complex vocabulary. Some difficulty expressing abstract language. Nearly up to grade level.
6. *Threshold level of proficiency that separates BICS from CALPS*
   Experiencing dramatic increase in vocabulary recognition, both oral and written. Idioms are difficult. Knows what he or she wants to say but gropes for utterances. Frequent errors in grammar, word usage, and pronunciation.
5. *Uses language to exchange social information and to extract meaning from simple texts*
   Some difficulty with comprehension. Speaks hesitantly making frequent errors in grammar, word usage, and pronunciation. Lapses into silence. Reads very simple texts. Writes with fairly restricted structures and vocabulary. About two years below native speakers in language skills.
4. *Adequate conversational skills in highly contextualized settings*
   Decodes written symbols. Writes dictated items.
3. *Routine conversational exchanges*
   Comprehends when speaker repeats, gestures, and uses concrete referents. Speaks haltingly, if at all. Shows some recognition of written segments. Not literate in English.
2. *Basic survival English*
   Receptive and somewhat expressive. Occasionally comprehends chunks of discourse.
1. *The silent period*
   Receptive vocabulary but depends almost entirely upon gestures, facial expressions, objects, pictures, a phrase dictionary, and often a translator.
0. *No English*

One startling fact that has emerged from research studies on language-minority students is that when they work academically only in their second language, ie English, it takes them from five to seven years to master commonly accepted age-grade norms in context-reduced aspects of English proficiency (Cummins 1985). This figure is immediately questioned at gatherings of international school teachers and administrators as their gut feeling tells them that their students seem to be getting there much more quickly. However, a recent study (Collier 1989) confirms the initial findings. To control the important variables of mother-tongue schooling and socioeconomic status, only those students who were at grade level in the first language when they entered the United States and who were from a middle- or upper middle-class background were included. This last point is important, as it is generally accepted that international school students come from such a background. No research data is yet available on international school students, though a project has recently got under way under the auspices of the ESL and Mother-Tongue Committee of the European Council of International Schools (ECIS), the umbrella organization for most international schools in Europe and elsewhere.

Another point which must be made here is that the most effective instructional programmes for ESL students are those that take place in their mother tongue. This is because the cognitive skills developed in the students mother tongue transfer automatically to the second language (English). All current linguistic research supports the theory that there is a common underlying proficiency (CUP) for both languages. Cummins summarizes these findings as follows:

> The results of research on bilingual programs show that minority children's native language can be promoted in school at no cost to the development of proficiency in the majority language. The data shows that well-implemented bilingual programs have had remarkable success in developing English academic skills and have proved superior to ESL-only programs in situations where direct comparisons have been carried out.

The main difficulty with bilingual programmes in international schools is the number of languages involved – it is quite possible to offer a French/English bilingual programme in Canada, but in an international school where 50 or 60 languages are spoken it is clearly impractical. This means that ways must be developed for ensuring not only that an ESL programme is successful, but that all areas in the school – teachers, parents, students, and administrators – are made aware of the situation and what they can do to help.

ESL: programme for students

It might seem ironic that this heading appears as one out of four. Isn't the whole purpose of a school to teach the students? Isn't the trend for them to become lost under a flurry of paperwork, teachers' careers, and shifting trends in educational policy? It should by now be clear that an international school with large numbers of ESL students must be necessarily committed to involving everyone in the process of educating them; it is no longer acceptable to adopt the conservative, traditional attitude of 'they don't speak English – well, they'll soon pick it up.' The whole community must become involved and must become more 'language-aware'.

The area of different types of ESL programme models has been amply dealt with in the recent book: *ESL: A Handbook for Teachers and Administrators in International Schools* (Murphy 1990). This book was written by teachers and administrators currently practising in international schools and gives the most useful, up-to-date information available about setting up an ESL programme, employing ESL staff, testing, and choosing materials – the whole area of ESL teaching. It would be superfluous, therefore, to repeat or summarize what has been said at length elsewhere. What would be useful is to consider the way forward, to see how to realize more fully the, at present, largely untapped language resource of the non-English mother-tongue students, and involve everyone in an awareness of what it means to study in a second language.

ESL students need to be involved as much as possible in the regular life of the school; they should not be made to feel like refugees, like learning-disabled students, or in any way different or left out. Cummins (1985) shows clearly that students who are coping with the whole curriculum in a language they have only just learned deserve to be treated as especially gifted rather than disabled. Thus at a primary/elementary level, it is advisable not to withdraw children from classes, but rather for all staff teaching this age-group to have an ESL qualification. ESL teachers can assist by taking part in an 'ESL push-in' component, ie they visit the regular class and team-teach as necessary. Even for complete beginners, the idea of a 'Reception Centre' is questionable; this is where children are placed in a half-day or all-day ESL classroom where they only study English. This leads to isolation from the main body of students and can create an 'ESL ghetto' mentality. If practised at all, the children should be filtered back into the mainstream class at certain times of the week (activities), and by the second half of the year be more fully assimilated with their peers. The following table from Rojas outlines the most common ESL models:

ENGLISH AS A SECOND LANGUAGE PROGRAM OPTIONS

1. *ESL reception centers* – students can be placed in a half-day or all-day ESL classroom where they only study English until sufficient mastery has been attained. This type of program is commonly used with refugee adults in resettlement programs. It is inappropriate for us in international schools.

2. *ESL pull-out classes* – students are 'pulled-out' from classrooms for a specified time period each day. They receive English instruction from the ESL teacher while trying to keep up with classroom instruction. This is the most commonly used ESL program in settings where the number of limited-English proficiency students is much less than the number of English-proficient students.

3. *ESL submersion classes* – students are 'submerged' into classrooms and expected to perform in the English language without any assistance. The stated goal is for students to replace their native language with English. Submersion occurs when the number of native English-background students is greater than the number of ESL students. As such, ESL students are in the minority. This type of program frequently occurs in stateside American schools.

4. *ESL immersion classes* – students are 'immersed' into classrooms where the language of instruction differs from their own. Immersion implies that all of the students are second language students, and the stated purpose of the program is to teach them in another language. The goal is to add a language to students' native languages so that they are bilingual. Examples of this are English-speaking children attending French-language schools in Canada and the American School of Valencia.
5. *ESL sheltered classes* – students are 'immersed' into classrooms where the language of instruction differs from their own. Sheltered classes are unlike other immersion classes in that students come from several different linguistic and cultural backgrounds and include students that are English-proficient. They are similar in that the goal is to add another language. Classroom teachers are trained in second language methodology and are familiar with the cultural background of their students. The curriculum is based upon a cognitive academic language learning approach. Materials and instructional activities are intended to teach subject matter while simultaneously enacting the acquisition of English as an academic and cognitive tool. A corollary option is to have an 'ESL push-in' (ESL teacher goes into classroom) program component. Many of the American-sponsored and international schools could appropriately house this type of program.

In the Middle School (age 11–14), the most useful approach for beginners is to have a largely 'pull-out' system for the first half of the year, concentrating on BICS at first, with students going to PE, art, music, and other activities with their peer group. ESL teachers can teach the basic language of maths, science, and geography at this stage. In the second half of the year, students should be filtered into mainstream classes where possible: science, maths, and geography.

For intermediate and advanced students, a combination of 'pull-out' and 'sheltered' classes is appropriate. How this programme is devised will depend upon the staffing of a school and its policies. Many students are 'pulled-out' while others are learning foreign languages; in fact it would be more logical for them to be pulled out during language arts (mainstream English) and history, as these are the most cognitively demanding and context-reduced subjects (ranking as number 8 or 9 on the 'Typology of Language Skills'), whereas the early stages of a foreign language rank as number 1 or 2. Furthermore, it is important for students newly arrived in the host country to learn the host country language at an early stage to enable them to 'survive' in the environment.

The ESL teachers' aims in pull-out classes should be to incorporate into the general ESL programme materials that are specially devised to provide both background knowledge of the main subjects and the specific types of language that may be useful for understanding them in order to assist the ESL student in making up ground quickly in the transition to mainstream subjects. (It should always be remembered that as long as the ESL student is spending time 'learning English' he or she is missing whatever is being learned in the mainstream subjects.) ESL students are forever aiming at a moving target. The aims of ESL teachers are not to teach material actually being covered in mainstream subjects; this would be an impossible task as materials would need to be constantly revised to keep pace with mainstream curricular changes.

In the 15–18 age-range, some schools do not take ESL students, but where they do they have to take account of what the students' aims will be after leaving school; will they be able to acquire enough English to follow courses successfully? If not, special courses will have to be devised.

One reason why sheltered classes do not provide a complete solution is that, from my experience, ESL students benefit greatly from working in a small group of similar students in a pull-out class with an ESL teacher who takes a special interest in their progress. The initial culture shock, settling-in problems, and then a carefully monitored process of language and personal development, give the ESL teacher a special role which is invaluable to the children of international parents who are often rootless and move with their families every few years.

ESL teachers

It goes without saying that these will be qualified in their chosen speciality (ie ESL). The days of 'those who can speak English and can therefore teach it' are hopefully over; international schools do not, I think, employ as maths teachers those who can add two and two together, but expect a little more competence and some further training. Native speaker status need not be a prerequisite; some of the best ESL teachers can be those who have learned English as a second language themselves; they have been through the process and understand the problems. Ovando and Collier (1985) give a good definition of the ESL teacher:

> An ESL teacher is expected to teach English at breakneck speed, provide meaningful content-area instruction in all subject areas, solve all problems of limited-English-proficient students, and serve as a mediating link between home and school. In other words, ESL staff are to be superpeople! But let's get back to reality. Somewhere, in between the ideal vision and the complicated school world of proposals and administrative superplans, we as teachers have to deal with day-to-day working relationships with the group of live human beings who have been assigned to us.

ESL teachers are usually those who have first graduated in foreign languages, ie they have been through the language learning process themselves. This, added to an experience of at least one other culture than their own, usually adds to their qualities of 'teacher as understanding, helpful person' in relation to the ESL class. It is often the case that ESL students feel more trust in and companionship with the ESL teacher and will turn to that person in moments of emotional upset or stress.

Content area teachers

The day may come when all teachers at international schools are themselves bilinguals, products of the very schools they are now teaching in! But until that day comes, there needs to be a regular programme of in-service training. Administrators could help here by employing only staff who have some sort of ESL qualification or at least experience of teaching in multi-cultural schools. In addition, new staff could be given a short introduction to what is involved at the beginning of the school year, and the ESL staff should embark on a regular process of in-service training on a department basis. This is described in detail in Murphy (1990) and includes information culled from ESL students themselves about what their needs were in class, plus a summary of points gained from video viewing of teachers working with ESL students.

The annotated bibliography of this article has a reference to the model developed by Chamot and O'Malley (1986). The Cognitive Academic Language Learning Approach (CALLA) is a programme to provide a model for all the content area subjects for ESL students, and deserves serious consideration in international schools, especially those with majorities of non-mother-tongue English speakers. If the curriculum, at least, is on the right rails, then there is more chance of the ingrained habits of 'the whole world should speak English' attitude being dissipated.

However, this area deserves a few words of comment. Some teaching staffs are perhaps becoming carried away by their enthusiasm and are over-reacting to what they perceive as an Anglo-Saxon domination of international schools. Partly, this is due to the transitional period such schools find themselves in; having been established as English language schools, they became, by extension, English language culture schools – the ethics of the Anglo-Saxon world being transmitted to the student body. Some schools are beginning to re-examine their philosophies, and this is an exciting time where there is much potential for a more truly international school philosophy where language and languages could play a greater part. However, it would be useful for international schools who are claiming to be truly 'international' to have an argument ready to refute the claims that they are involved in 'linguicism':

> The ideologies and structures which are used to legitimate, effectuate and reproduce an unequal division of power and resources (both material and non-material) between groups which are defined on the basis of language (ie of their mother-tongue). (Skutnabb-Kangas and Cummings 1988)

'Linguistic imperialism' is seen by Skutnabb-Kangas and Cummings as:

> An essential constituent of imperialism as a global phenomenon involving structural relations between rich and poor countries in a world characterized by inequality and injustice. 'Linguistic ideology' has affinities with the way racism is affirmed: it essentially involves the dominant group/language presenting an idealized image of itself, stigmatizing the dominated group/language, and rationalizing the relationship between the two always to the advantage of the dominant group/language.

Strong stuff, and not the type of discourse associated with the more genteel clientele of international schools, perhaps. A brief survey among students (at the Vienna International School) revealed that they wanted to learn English, did not in any way feel threatened by it, and accepted that English was the passport to success.

The counter-argument to this could be

> 'just as colonialism has been superseded by more sophisticated forms of exploitation, the crudely biological racist ideology has been superseded by

ethnicism . . . and linguicism. The 'higher and better view' of the West is now less represented by the gun and the Bible than by technology and the textbook. Western products still come wrapped in a Western language and in Western thought.

It is not enough simply to discuss these statements with a 'but parents and students want to have an English language education – it's clearly the best thing for them.' English has 'cornered the market' in most parts of the world, but there is hardly an international school nowadays that does devote a large amount of time and space in the curriculum to environmental issues and the broader political issues of five billion people sharing one planet. Languages are also threatened, are dying out, and need support; there is more than one set of values in the world, and truly international schools should focus in depth on the balance of cultural and, by implication, language awareness, which they inculcate in order to create leaders of tomorrow's world who have an objective, unbiased view of the situation.

ESL programmes and parents

This area is also dealt with in detail in Murphy's *ESL Handbook* (1990) already mentioned. The important thing is to make parents aware of what is involved in their children studying in a language other than their mother tongue and to encourage them to support their children as much as possible. They need to be encouraged always to speak their own language with their children; misguided but well-intentioned attempts to speak English with them should be discouraged. The advantage of learning school subjects through the mother tongue should be pointed out (especially for beginners in English) so that there is not a gap in knowledge for the months or years when their English is not good enough to understand the content of the mainstream subjects. An excellent book to recommend to parents is *The Bilingual Family* (Harding and Riley 1986), which does much to remove fears and encourage parents that if they are doing what is 'natural' then it is probably right.

ESL programme and administration

Having the right framework in which to work is three-quarters of the battle. In the past, ESL teachers have often felt undervalued and peripheral. In ECIS schools this situation is now much improved, and ECIS has done a great deal to assist in this respect by sending out memos on the necessity of ESL support to member schools, including a comprehensive section on ESL in the Accreditation Guidelines, and giving support to the ECIS-ESL Committee, which publishes a regular newsletter and organizes a conference every two years.

Another external body, which is well on the way to providing more recognition and by implication more suitable instructional programmes for ESL students, is the International Baccalaureate Organization. It is in the process of a language reform which will replace the present Language A and Language B with a Language A1, Language A2, and Language B programme. This is not the place to go into detail about the contents of the syllabus for each exam, but given that the new scheme will no longer treat second language immersion students either as genuine foreign language learners or as native speakers, but recognize them for what they are, the effect of an appropriate exam will inevitably have positive spin off for the instructional programmes in schools by the 'backwash' effect. This is the name given to the influence exerted by tests and examinations on the teaching.

Individual schools can do much to support ESL students by setting up clear frameworks; ESL departments will not be 'submerged' in English departments, they will be separate, and treated as a full academic subject department like other foreign language departments. They might be named 'ESL and mother-tongue departments' to encourage an awareness of the other facet of ESL teaching and to give mother-tongue staff, who are often part time and rather excluded from the main body of the school, a base and a feeling that they are as much a part of the faculty as others.

Larger schools, with large numbers of non-mother-tongue English speakers, can consider wide-ranging reorganization of all language departments. The traditional 'English' department can become a Language A1 department (in IB terminology), where students will be taught either English or their mother tongue, including the literature, and the 'humanizing' aspect traditionally associated with this area. There would then be 'Language B' departments which would teach foreign languages (the ESL department taking care of the English B area). Such decisions will depend on staffing and other considerations, but need to be given serious thought in today's multifaceted world of political change and global awareness.

Conclusion

It has not been my intention to talk in depth about ESL programmes in international schools today; this information can be found in other sources (Murphy 1990). Rather it is important to question some assumptions about ESL students, ESL teachers' roles, and the ESL structure within the framework of an international school. More families are on the move around the world than ever before, and there will be an ever-increasing need for expertise in the area of language planning. It is important that the right decisions are made, and that the right people are consulted about how to make them if we are really to provide a meaningful education for the clientele of the schools which may produce those who come to be tomorrow's decision makers on the world stage.

Annotated bibliography

Baker, C (1988) *Key issues in Bilingualism and Bilingual Education* Multilingual Matters: Clevedon, Avon

This book is valuable for classroom language teachers for several reasons. First, it is the most recent survey of the present state of our understanding of bilingualism and bilingual education. Second, the book handles theoretical problems from the perspective of classroom teachers rather than that of field theoreticians. Finally, the book offers simple comparative descriptions of policies and practices of bilingual education in English speaking countries (ie Britain, Ireland

and North America) which have witnessed a remarkable growth of interest in bilingualism. As such, it is a very useful starting point for anyone wishing to become acquainted with the current academic debate.

Chamot, A U and O'Malley, J M (1986) *A Cognitive Academic Language Learning Approach: An ESL Content-Based Curriculum* National Clearing House for Bilingual Education

The Cognitive Academic Language Learning Approach (CALLA) is an instructional programme for limited-English-proficient (LEP) students who are being prepared to participate in mainstream content instruction. The programme is designed to assist LEP students' success in school by providing transitional instruction between English as a second language (ESL) or bilingual education and mainstream instruction. The transitional instruction is designed to further academic language development in English through content area instruction in science, mathematics, and social studies. In CALLA, students are taught to use learning strategies derived from a cognitive model of learning as aids to comprehension and retention of concepts in the content areas. In brief, CALLA is designed to: meet the academic language needs in English of upper elementary and secondary level LEP students; provide a programme of content-based instruction that can serve as a bridge between the English as a second language or bilingual programme and mainstream education; provide instruction based on a cognitive model of learning.

Cummins, J (1984) *Bilingualism and Special Education: Issues in Assessment and Pedagogy* Multilingual Matters: Clevedon, Avon

This book is central to many of the theories and practices on which today's ESL classrooms are based. It examines the effectiveness of alternatives to traditional assessment and pedagogical practices for bilingual children. A central theme of the book is that progress can be made in improving practice only by means of a thorough re-examination of the assumptions underlying the entire special education enterprise. It is argued that despite its laudable intentions, much special education practice with respect to bilingual students is fundamentally misdirected. Concrete suggestions are made both for changing the structure of special education services for bilingual students and for instituting more appropriate assessment and pedagogical practices.

Harding, E and Riley, P (1986) *The Bilingual Family – A Handbook for Parents* Cambridge University Press

This book provides parents with the information and advice they need to make informed decisions about what language 'policy' to adopt with their children. The authors, who are professional applied linguists, draw on their own experience as parents of successfully bilingual children and on interviews with other bilingual families.

The book is divided into three main parts. In the first part, the authors help parents identify the factors that will influence their decision to bring up their children as bilinguals. The second part consists of case studies of bilingual families which illustrate a wide range of different 'solutions'. The third part is an alphabetical reference guide providing answers to the most frequently asked questions about bililngualism.

Murphy, E (ed) (1990) *ESL: A Handbook for Teachers and Administrators in International Schools* Multilingual Matters: Clevedon, Avon

Produced in conjunction with ECIS specifically for international schools, this major reference work will be of concern to all involved with children who are being educated in a language other than their mother tongue. In particular, the book addresses the issues which arise where English-medium international schools accept non-English-speaking students and therefore enter into an obligation to provide a special programme to enable these students to pursue their education and fulfill their potential in English.

The contents are as follows:

1. The international school ESL challenge
2. Some theoretical considerations
3. Setting up the ESL department: primary and secondary
4. Organizing the ESL programme: which model to choose?
5. Features of the programme: primary and secondary

6. Assessing the ESL student
7. The teacher's task: the work of the classroom
8. Some common difficulties and how they can be avoided
9. The ESL student with special needs.
10. Appendices:
    - I Professional journals and other periodicals
    - II Professional societies and organizations
    - III Obtaining ESL materials – bookshops and publishers
    - IV Books for the ESL departmental library
    - V Computer software: primary and secondary
    - VI Teaching materials: primary and secondary
    - VII Materials for testing and assessment
    - VIII Appendix glossary
    - IX Glossary

Ovando, C J and Collier, V P (1985) *Bilingual and ESL Classrooms* McGraw-Hill: Maidenhead

Although aimed more specifically at the US situation, this is a comprehensive guide to the methods of teaching in bilingual and ESL classrooms, and addresses the challenges that face teachers and administrators. Each chapter combines theory with practice, and teachers in all subject areas will find valuable information on methods of teaching ESL students. Methods of teaching first and second languages, social studies, science, maths, music, and art are described and reinforced with specific examples. A wealth of references and recommended readings are provided for those who wish to explore the topics in greater depth.

Pinter, H (1988) *Mountain Language* Faber and Faber: London

Not a reference book, but a play which deals with the use of language as a repressive instrument. Lasting only 25 minutes on stage, it deals with a fictional state where a group of women are waiting to see their imprisoned male relatives. They are told they must not speak their mountain language. An elderly woman is permitted to visit her son and is initially instructed to speak the language of the capital. By the time the rules have changed and the mountain language is officially accepted, she is unable to communicate with her tortured, trembling, and beaten son.

Siguan, M and Mackey, W F (1987) *Education and Bilingualism* Kogan Page in association with UNESCO: London

This book presents brief descriptions of the main issues related to bilingual education including individual and community bilingualism, psychological and educational problems, and planning and evaluation of programmes. The approach adopted by the two authors is that of summarizing research, placing much emphasis on the constraints and success of bilingual education in different contexts. In addition, this book has two qualities. First, it rejects the simplistic view that bilingualism as such has good or bad effects with the argument that it functions as an educational asset or disadvantage according to individual cases and contextual circumstances. Second, it provides a short but authoritative introduction particularly useful to novices in the field of bilingual education which is also available in French and Spanish in the Educational Science Series of UNESCO.

Tosi, A (1988) *Project Reports Nos 1–10* Prepared for the Bilingualism and Language Testing Project of the International Baccalaureate Organization in conjunction with the University of London Institute of Education.

The question 'why should international education be concerned with bilingualism?' produces various answers. The findings of several surveys show it to be a twofold problem. Some such students only attain basic communicative skills in a non-native language, while others achieve high levels of bilingual proficiency, international schools have lately become concerned with the diverse nature and standards of language competence available to the two groups. The International Baccalaureate, which provides all international schools with a common curriculum, is concerned with the promotion and certification of bilingualism. The IBO believe that this requires the introduction of syllabuses and examinations for bilinguals (mainly second language immersion students) that are different from those currently available for genuine foreign language learners. This series of reports outlines the background to the ways in which international education is concerned with bilingualism, and the steps that should be taken to ensure its certification and encourage a higher awareness of all that is involved in students, teachers, and administrators.

Tosi, A (1989) *Feasibility Study No. 1: Bilingualism in the IB* Prepared for the Bilingualism and Language Testing Project of the International Baccalaureate Organization, in conjunction with the University of London Institute of Education.

The most up-to-date findings on the situation of bilingualism in the IB in international schools. This study, based on a survey of students' bilingualism in IB schools, discusses 'the fallacies and reality of bilingualism', reviews the present language testing structure in the IB, and goes on to outline the findings of the survey. Finally, the implications for Language A and Language B, IB terminology, the Bilingual Diploma, the IB language curriculum, and IB internationalism are discussed.

Tosi, A and Kaplan, R (ed) (1990) *Bilingual Education in 1990* Annual Review of Applied Linguistics

A comprehensive review of developments in the field of bilingual education over the past two decades. It reveals how complex the dynamics of language spread and language change are in diverse sociopolitical contexts, and concludes with the view that the most important legacy of past researches is the realization that bilingualism in itself is neither a deficit nor an asset, as so much of its functioning in education depends on its definitions, status, and treatment.

Wallace, C A (1988) *Issues in Teaching English as a Second Language, in Bilingualism and the Bilingual* Nelson: Windsor

This article explores the development of ESL in Great Britain. The first part reviews the history and development of the provision of ESL in the UK. The second part discusses recent developments in language teaching and second language learning in general, to help the reader judge the merits of various approaches and assess the syllabuses and materials currently available.

Unannotated bibliography

Abbot, G and Wingard, P (eds) (1985) *The Teaching of English as an International Language: A Practical Guide* Collins: London

Baetens-Beardsmore, H (1988) The European Schools *Canadian Modern Languages Review* **44** (2), 240–260

Baetens-Beardsmore, H and Swain, M (1985) Designing bilingual education: aspects of immersion and 'European school' models *Journal of Multilingual and Multicultural Development* **6** (1), 1–15

Chamot, Ana *CASA: Context Academic Skills Assessment*

Collier, V P (1989) How long? A synthesis of research on academic achievement in a second language *TESOL Quarterly* **23** (3), 509–531

Cummins, J (1981) The role of primary language development in promoting educational success for language minority students. In California State Department of Education *Schooling and Language Minority Students: A Theoretical Framework* National Evaluation, Dissemination, and Assessment Charter, California State University, Los Angeles

Cummins, J (1985) Education and cultural and linguistic pluralism; theory and policy in bilingual education. Paper written for the National Seminar on Education in Multicultural Societies, Ljubljana, Yugoslavia

Curtain, H and Pesola, C (1988) *Languages and Children – Making the Match* Addison-Wesley: Reading, MA

Gibbons, J (1982) The issue of the language of instruction in the lower forms of Hong Kong secondary schools *Journal of Multilingual and Multicultural Development* **3** (2), 117–28

Los Angeles County Office of Education *Sheltered English Training Guide* Los Angeles County Office of Education, Los Angeles, California

Matthews, M (1989) The uniqueness of international education *International Schools Journal* **17** 7–17

Northcutt, L (1989) *Sheltered English Teaching Handbook* Available from: P O Box 1429, Carlsbad, California 92008, USA

Rojas, V P (1990) Sore spots and hard parts: ESL and learning disability. Handout given at the Eastern European Schools Association ESL/LD Conference, Prague

Skutnabb-Kangas, T and Cummings, J (eds) (1988) *Minority Education: From Shame to Struggle* Multilingual Matters: Clevedon, Avon

Swain, M (1978) Home-school language switching. In J Richard (ed) *Understanding Second and Foreign Language Learning: Issues and Approaches* Newbury House: Rowley, Mass, 238–51

Tosi, A (1986) The evaluation of language competence in international education. Study prepared for the International Baccalaureate Organization, Geneva

Tosi, A (1987) First, second, or foreign language learning? Political and professional support for bilingualism in national and international education. University of London (Institute of Education): London. PhD thesis

Widdowson, H (1990) *Language and Languages in the National Curriculum* Institute of Education, University of London: London

14. An alternative history within the International Baccalaureate – a history and culture of the Islamic world

Malcolm Davis and Caroline Ellwood

Introduction

The first experimental examination of the fledgling International Baccalaureate (IB) was in history, and that subject was chosen because of its sensitivity to the cultural heritage of each student, the opportunities for political and aesthetic judgment, and an understanding of the process of an awareness of bias. It is all the more strange then that for 20 years, with the exception of a number of school-based syllabuses, the IBO has paid only lip service to internationalism in terms of the content and approach of its World History papers. It can be argued that a World History course reflecting trends in the 20th century is implicitly international, but it must also be noted that within this the stress is on the development of the western tradition, and certainly the emphasis is on a western perspective of events. Critics, who are looking for a more international approach and also the opportunity to break out of the time trap of the 20th century, may therefore be interested in a new course of study that breaks the western mould – an IB course centring on the History and Culture of the Islamic World, now in its pilot form. Four schools, two from the Middle East, one in the Indian subcontinent, and one in Europe have offered their students an opportunity to view the world differently.

Objectives

History courses in the last two years of secondary education traditionally focus upon the events of the 19th and 20th centuries and do not give students an opportunity to look at either broad sweeps and/or very distant happenings in the past. This new course allows the student to do both. The objectives are to introduce students to the history and culture of the Islamic world and to expose them to the contributions of this culture to world civilization. Implicit within the courses are the overall aims of a Group Three Subject (Study of Man in Society) for the International Baccalaureate, and also the opportunity to practise the skills of the historian and to debate controversial issues of the past. This last point will be explored later as it raises in itself something of a controversial and debatable issue.

Course content

In the mid 1970s, the North East London Polytechnic launched a total history course for their undergraduate students, and within the IB History and Culture of the Islamic World course the same principle of *total history* is applied: the course content includes components on pre-Islamic Arabia, the life of the prophet, the Qur'ān, the five pillars of Islam, the expansion of the Islamic world, its interactions with other cultures in the form of the Crusades, the Mongol contacts, and the study of a modern Islamic state. In addition, there are modules on art and architecture, the growth of the Muslim city, and the changing role of women. Clearly, with such diversity of topics spread over a time period of more than 1,500 years, selection must take place. The criteria used to guide such selections must be left to the individual teachers, reflecting their own strengths, interests, and available resources. However, the structure of the examination does make both teacher and student look at both the early time periods and more recent events.

It would be impossible to teach this course without some reference to religion. Perhaps, one can teach aspects of a course in Western Civilization without recourse to the influence of the Catholic church or the impact of Luther, but the effect of religion on Islam is integral. The words of the Prophet and the Qur'ān penetrate and mould the culture so much that any students must at least have an understanding of the rights and duties of a Muslim and the social importance of the five pillars. Karl Marx suggested that religion was the opium of the people, with Islam it is not so much an addictive drug, as a life-force flowing through the blood of the culture as a whole. As the International Baccalaureate course itself is deliberately designed to appeal to both Muslim and non-Muslim students alike (if only Muslim students pursue the course then one of its hidden aims is lost) teachers of a non-Muslim background may be hesitant in tackling the religious aspects. The solution lies in team teaching. Often our international schools are as diverse in teacher background as student background, and this course creates an opportunity for teaching staff to share knowledge and methodological expertise. A team teaching approach also avoids the possibility of inadvertently causing offence or constantly making references to Christianity. By tackling the religious bull by its horns, it also enables the student to realize some of the myths that have grown up about the beliefs of Islam and similarly to expose many misrepresentations that appear in the modern media coverage of Islam in the 20th century.

Additional benefits

A careful choice of components within the course can also result in interaction with other departments within the school. Not all of us feel happy to deal in depth with the arts and architecture, but many schools will find interest and support within their fine arts and literature departments. It is possible that when conceiving this course the IBO did not appreciate fully the opportunities for both staff and students that they were creating.

Similarly, the IBO did not perhaps realize how the course could transform the teaching of other historical areas. A change of perception and a realization of built-in expectations comes about. To illustrate this consider the idea of the Middle East or the Near East - middle and near in relationship to what and whom? Clearly, the observer is sitting in Paris or London and not in Jerusalem or Baghdad. Likewise, the notion of democracy or constitution are western concepts that have no place in the Muslim mental world until the 19th century (Ayalon 1987). In the context of teaching beyond the confines of this course, increased awareness of the importance of Islam as an intellectual force results in a more balanced presentation of different perspectives of knowledge in Theory of Knowledge, discussion of Arab philosophies in a philosophy course, and an appreciation of the contribution of Islam to art and architecture. Lower down in the school, there is more recognition of the contribution of Arabic mathematicians and an integrated course between computers, arts, and history on the Vedic square is possible. A complete reteaching of the Crusades to younger children is a necessity.

It would seem that a small step to increase internationalism at the IB level could make big steps for internationalism at other levels. However, two problems remain to be resolved. The first is the practical question of resources; an appeal to compilers of primary material and publishers must be made for materials to be made available from more easily accessible sources. Many that are available are labelled as 'Orientalism' (Said 1985), presenting all materials with traditional western values. There is certainly an opportunity for Arab publishing houses to widen their marketing and also for publishers of those weighty tomes printed by western universities to realize that there could be a market at a lower academic level. Yet, the whole question of who publishes what and from what perspective and with what value judgement opens up the second problem - the one mentioned earlier which in itself is a controversial and debatable issue: the difference between Arabic/Muslim intellectual tradition and that of the West.

Conflict

Many teachers have experienced the problem of students who persist in memorization with little critical thought and complete mastery of facts but apparently no personal insight. Of course, in some cultures such an ability is rewarded and considered a high achievement, but the International Baccalaureate reflects in the assessment procedure and performance criteria a Western intellectual tradition, which the international schools to a very large extent support. Therefore, how can this dilemma of two seemingly conflicting traditions be resolved? If the IB offers a course studying another culture can it entertain the practice of that culture's values and incorporate them, or will it be merely a cosmetic change and judge one culture by another's values. This issue must be faced and resolved. Not, it is to be hoped, with the conclusion that one tradition is superior to another. A review of Arab philosophical tradition does reveal a way out of this dilemma for the philosophers themselves were aware of the problem and discussed it. So far as history is concerned at the end of the 14th century, Ibn Khaldun (1967) wrote:

The inner meaning of history involves speculations and an attempt to get at the truth, subtle explanations of the causes and origins of existing things, and deep knowledge of the how and why of events. It takes critical insight to sort out the hidden truth; it takes knowledge to lay truth bare and polish it so that critical insight may be applied to it.

Conclusion

The IBO has innovated and is creating an opportunity to widen its international base. It is for internationally minded teachers and students to take up the possibility of studying The History and Culture of the Islamic World. If Muslim and non-Muslim alike do not take up this offered chance then another attempt to give the future generation a wider understanding of a rich, diverse, and influential culture will have been lost.

Bibliography

Ayalon, A (1987) *Language and Change in the Arab Middle East* Open University Publication: Milton Keynes

Khaldun, Ibn (1967) *The Mugaddimah* Translated by F Rosenthal, Routledge and Kegan Paul: London

Said, E (1985) *Orientalism* Penguin: Harmondsworth

15. The extra-curricular programme – from margin to mainstream

Deon Glover

Introduction

Near an age when thoughts of the future would naturally start turning towards retirement in less than a decade, I applied for a senior post in an educational establishment. It struck me as more than somewhat strange when I was asked about my academic qualifications or, more precisely, what degree I had achieved at university. It was the sheer irrelevance of the question that staggered me. Was I still to be judged on how well I had performed in an academic context at a stage when I was barely beyond being a pimply teenager? Had everything that had passed since then remained of such little consequence? Was there no place for some recognition that experience was of more practical value than the quality of my degree? I wish I had known that this would be the case while I was enjoying the freedoms of university life. Perhaps then some of the pints of beer could have been converted into obtaining a slightly better degree that would have assured job fulfillment for a grey-haired teacher years later!

Was mine a unique experience, or did it represent an attitude that still remains prevalent in society as a whole? There can be little doubt that far too much emphasis is placed on purely academic performance with little more than lip service paid to achievements that cannot be supported by some formal academic documentation, preferably in script embossed on vellum. This attitude is all the more worrying when it is being implicitly encouraged at the school level where youngsters are often being spurred on to better grades by promises of entry to exclusive universities. The schools themselves are encouraging competitive assessment only on the basis of the number of their students who gain entry each year to the handful of these prestigious centres of higher learning.

Education must have more than simply an academic function and success can no longer afford to be measured in terms of the length of time that noses remain buried in textbooks. We should be moving forward from the point where evaluation of worth is based solely on performance in the academic field to where the development of the individual as a whole is of greater concern. It is the role of the educator to ensure that this happens. There can be some debate about whether education should merely follow society or lead it. Believing firmly in the latter, it is reassuring to note that there is a shift in emphasis. This is evident even in those bastions of conservatism – the universities – where there is a growing recognition that the potential of applicants should also be measured in terms of the contributions they have made in areas outside the classroom. It is of particular importance that international education is in the forefront of encouraging this development.

International education

By definition, international education finds itself needing to satisfy requirements that span several national systems. The demand that it should be acceptable worldwide, means that international education has to include in its curriculum a range of elements designed to prepare its candidates for entry to further education in more than one country. The choice of these elements cannot be determined by choosing the lowest common denominator in a set of local systems. On the contrary, international education finds itself under an obligation to develop curricula that are widely relevant. Curricula that are a synthesis of the best of national systems. Curricula that extend the philosophies of national systems. Where opportunities are grasped, international education could and should be in the vanguard of educational thought and development, willing to accept the challenge of educating the 'complete person'. This implies that what happens outside the classroom is of equal importance to the educator as what happens inside it.

Since its inception, the International Baccalaureate Office (IBO) has fostered the concept that the complete educational experience should include 'experiential and unassessed parts of the curriculum (which) are of comparable importance to the traditional academic and assessed subjects' (IBO 1989). Although, in all honesty, IBO has paid little more than lip service to it, and only recently introduced tighter regulations to ensure compliance with the requirement that all candidates pursue a CASS programme comprising activities in three categories: Creativity, Action, and Service. Involvement in these activities should continue for the duration of the two-year course, occupying a recommended two to three hours per week. The commitment, therefore, is now quite substantial and indicative of the value the IBO attaches to this element in the curriculum.

Current attitudes towards extra-curricular work

There must be a variety of reasons why many schools, even some of those involved in international education, thus far have paid little attention to what happens beyond the classroom walls. Usually, they offer elective opportunities for sport and team games (a relic of the British public schools' emphasis on these activities as character building?) or a small number of clubs and societies. There is rarely a structured extra-curricular programme aimed at developing the individual in which all students participate. Some schools may simply lack the physical facilities, while others (better endowed and often with residential students) who do offer a greater range of activities seem to be motivated only by the need to keep idle hands occupied. Parental pressure on the importance of gaining good grades may mitigate against any additional time spent in non-academic pursuits. There are also the schools located in cultures where extra-curricular involvement is unknown (although this should not provide an excuse for any international institution).

A major obstacle facing many schools is the logistical one of attempting to integrate a time-consuming programme into an already overfull timetable – gallons into pint pots (or, in the international context, the metric equivalent). Still, the problem may be less real than imagined, as analysis of the aims of an extra-curricular programme such as the IB shows:

- To complement the academic disciplines of the curriculum.
- To challenge and extend the individual student by developing a spirit of discovery and self-reliance.

This suggests that it is a weakness to consider any such programme as separate from the mainstream academic work, either in concept or in operation. The possibility exists that much of what the student does beyond the formal teaching period potentially could be redirected and presented in a more challenging manner and thus qualify as a valid component of the CASS programme.

United World Colleges

The United World Colleges, independently of the IBO, have always recognized the necessity for and benefits of a strong extra-curricular programme – particularly in the area of community service. This aspect, together with a commitment to the promotion of international understanding, is fundamental to the movement's philosophy. Atlantic College, as the first UWC to be developed and also the largest, has had more time and opportunity to develop a comprehensive programme, which may be worth examining in detail. It cannot provide a model, as too many conditions at the college are special, but its experience could help to illustrate examples and suggest possible solutions.

United World College of the Atlantic

Atlantic College was started in 1962 by, among others, Kurt Hahn the German educator who had fled to England from Nazi Germany. He held very strong views on the dangers facing young people, in particular from the 'declines' caused by the cynical and exhausted culture of the post-war world. These dangers could be combated by what he referred to as the 'moral equivalent of war', namely challenging young people to become involved in lifesaving and physically demanding, even dangerous, activities such as rescue work. From its inception, students at the college were responsible for providing safety cover for a stretch of the Bristol Channel by operating a beach patrol and manning (as it was in those non-coeducational times) the lifeboat and cliff rescue team. A social service group also visited the handicapped, the elderly, and the disadvantaged in the local community. When the college became the first institution to offer the IB as the only external examination, the extra-curricular requirement posed no problem and has not done so since. As the programme itself has expanded considerably over the years and the IBO has made recent changes, the impetus for further development in the area appeared.

The UWC Atlantic extra-curricular plan

The college soon saw that the obligation that all students should make a commitment to community services soon led to the realization that this could only be effective where a larger choice was available. Not all students were attracted to the physical challenges of the rescue services. This realization had nothing to do with the entry of girls to the college. They still opt in large numbers for the rescue services. The college has had the distinction of presenting the first female crewmembers and boat captain for registration with the Royal National Lifeboat Institution. (Something that hasn't helped the image of the grizzled lifeboatman.)

Expansion of the college's range of services occurred whenever a new need was identified. At present, in addition to the traditional rescue and social services, students are helping with a community arts centre on campus, in the local environment, on the college farm, and in the extra-mural centre also on campus which caters for disadvantaged groups on day visits or short residential courses. The latter is an excellent example of how student involvement can contribute to the success of an undertaking, providing skilled manpower to the benefit of both the students concerned and the enterprise. The centre developed from what was primarily a summer vacation course that offered English classes to foreign students, with ex-students employed to cover sailing instruction as a recreational activity.

Although some disadvantaged groups were also invited along during this period, the demand from the latter was such that the whole summer programme is now based on these groups and run by a number of ex-students from all the United World Colleges, under the direction of qualified staff who are responsible for continuing the courses throughout the year, but helped by the current term's students. In all the services, including rescue, new students who have just joined the centre are taught all the necessary skills to cope with their responsibilities by their peers in the second-year group.

It is part of the college policy that all students learn to swim and complete at least a basic course in First Aid, although the skill levels demanded will be considerably greater if students opt for particular community services. The lifeguard unit, for instance, will train its members to achieve award standards set by outside organizations such as St John's Ambulance, the Surf-Lifesaving Association, and the Royal Lifesaving Association.

In addition to these service commitments, students are also expected to participate in two to three further activities each term. The choice is often difficult to make as more than 50 different interests are on offer, ranging from the artistic through the cultural to the physical; from madrigals to oriental cookery to bandy (an oriental ball game), for example. Most of these activities are organized and run by students themselves and all that is required to have one accepted officially as part of the programme is some interest and enthusiasm on the part of the instigators, with any knowledge or skill being an additional bonus! Team games fall into this category. It is not unusual to witness the absence of some major sport from the programme in some years as the interests of each intake change. Students are encouraged to select activities over the two-year period which ensure that they always have a physical activity and additionally an involvement in something of both an artistic and an international nature.

At present, all students at the college are required to give a commitment of the equivalent of eight to ten hours per week to the CASS programme. While they will complain readily about the pressures on their time, the commitment is extraordinarily wholehearted and effective. Given the opportunity to reduce their load, many invariably add further 'unofficial' activities to their programmes, explaining that they felt that 'this would probably be the only chance we have of learning origami/ballroom dancing/knitting/etc'.

However, it is not only the participation in these regular activities which is considered to be of value. Involvements in one-off events can be equally rewarding, and these can be just as varied: making a major contribution to the annual international show which is open to the public and consists of a variety of different acts reflecting the multicultural composition of the college; organizing the two-day world development conference which addresses a major issue; practising an item at the weekly music concerts; and probably amongst the most rewarding of all, some of the activities undertaken during the two ten-day project periods each year, during which many will spend the time living and working in inner-city schools, hospices, special institutions, and with charitable organizations.

Special considerations

The involvement with outside organizations is obviously the key to the success of the project periods. They provide quite extraordinary opportunities for the students, but their role is of equal importance in other areas. Much of what is achieved, particularly with the 'outside community' would have been impossible if the college had not, over many years, built up a strong relationship with a large number of organizations. The coastguard unit could not operate independently of HM Coastguard, similarly the other rescue services without the support of the national and local organizations, and the social service units can only function if they are closely involved with voluntary and state organizations. The close links with all these have not come overnight. It has been a long and sometimes painfully slow process of convincing such organizations that young people have the ability to undertake the responsibilities. While student enthusiasm is always obvious, it takes patience, persistence, and the grasping of every opportunity to translate this into an acceptance that they are also capable of making unexpectedly worth-while contributions in many areas of local community life. However, having gained the confidence of any organization, it is rarely lost.

The most accessible of these outside organizations have been the voluntary ones. By their very nature, help of any sort tends to be welcomed, and they have always responded positively to approaches. Once contact has been established, it can rapidly mature into close cooperation, to the mutual benefit of both sides. There are further advantages that accrue: reputations are established, which can be of vital importance when local and national organizations have to be approached, and further requests for assistance often pour in. In the past year alone, the college has been able to involve students in the running of cub and scout groups in a local village, to provide a small team to give illustrated talks to local schools on water safety, and to organize evening entertainments for a holiday home for the elderly.

Defining CASS

While the main emphasis has been on the outside community, it is important (and perhaps more relevant to other schools) to consider the college's attitude to internal service. The IBO provides no help in defining what is meant by 'Service' in its documentation on CASS, other than stating that it 'does not mean exclusively social service but can include environmental and international projects', and this lack of clarity led to considerable and sometimes heated debates about what was, and what was not, a legitimate service commitment for the students. The purists argued in favour of some commitment where only those outside the college benefited (and the ultra-purist even insisted that such commitments had to involve face-to-face contact, thereby calling into question the validity of the rescue services and conjuring up scenarios of members of the public being pushed over cliffs to ensure that all students had contact!). However, in the end it proved useful and the college was able to agree on a definition of Service which, in its practical implementation, clearly allows flexibility in the range of activities while remaining prescriptive: 'Service should be a responsibility undertaken with the prime purpose of benefiting the community; the need should be real and not artificial; it should be of educational value to the individual.' In the college context, the nature of the service was most likely to encompass social, rescue, or environmental aspects, but it did allow groups and individual students to involve themselves with service-related activities meeting CASS requirements – such as the maintenance of the sailing boats, the running of departmental libraries, and the production of the college newspaper. This is obviously an area that can be exploited more fully in schools where outside responsibilities are limited or where the age-range is greater than that found in a purely IB school, and the possibility always exists that such initiatives can be further expanded to include the outside community.

Evaluation

The success of the whole programme at the college will be obvious to any observer – and can be confirmed in casual conversation with any student, or, if more scientific proof is required, by analysis of the self-evaluation reports made by students at regular intervals throughout the two years. These reports are based on what are believed to be the most important aspects of the programme, but the students are encouraged to think and comment more widely:

- ☐ In which ways has your programme enabled you to be of *service to others*?
- ☐ How much *face-to-face* contact does this involve with the community?
- ☐ In what ways does your programme involve you in *international issues* or contribute to your gaining *international understanding*?
- ☐ Do some parts of your programme encourage *originality, creativity, or critical thought*?
- ☐ Has your programme enabled you to become *physically fit* or to become fitter?

- ☐ What *skills and techniques* have you learned? How would you assess your skill levels in these areas?
- ☐ Are some parts of your programme especially *challenging*? How do you respond to these challenges?
- ☐ Do some parts of your programme encourage *individual or collective responsibility*? How are you able to react to this?
- ☐ Have you enjoyed your participation in the extra-academic programme?
- ☐ Do you have any comments you wish to draw to the attention of the organizers of specific activities – or any other comments you wish to make?

Their answers are always illuminating, and often surprisingly so. After some initial reticence arising from a concern about the confidentiality of their responses, the comments have become thoughtful, honest, and critical both of the individual student's own involvement and of perceived weaknesses in the programme as a whole (and this has proved particularly helpful in identifying potential problem areas and in initiating changes). However, most encouraging of all, it frequently has been the underlying sense of excitement they have felt in their involvement, as for instance in comments such as: 'The programme stretches my mind (and body) in so many different directions I didn't know I had!' or 'I want to talk about it all – writing is not expressive enough.'

Of course, there have been failures (some of massive proportions!) – not all ventures have flourished, and some have never got off the ground while others have withered and died as circumstances changed or simply from a lack of attention. The gardening analogy is apt: we are dealing with a tender plant that will only reach fruition if all the conditions are right and if it is cared for constantly. However, once the initial digging and planting are complete, and the programme has been introduced, it does take on a momentum of its own and rapidly establishes itself as part of the ethos of the institution. It may be necessary, every five years or so, to re-examine and review – the garden may not need redesigning, but it may well require some weeding, pruning, and transplanting. This all involves hard work and considerable commitment, but the fruits are well worth the labour.

There is one final aspect that deserves comment, despite its apparent insignificance: the programme is referred to as 'extra-academic' rather than 'extra-curricular'. It is part, therefore, of the total educational experience of the student and, as such, enjoys a status almost equal to the academic programme. The college recognizes its relevance to the process of educational development, as it is now also being recognized by the IBO, and increasingly so by universities, polytechnics, and employers. It is a welcome and very important change. Hopefully, this fact alone should ensure the emergence of extra-curricular activities from the murkier corners of school life to a more central position where the 'academic' and 'extra-academic' are inextricably bound together in an educational package designed and developed to benefit the whole individual.

Bibliography

International Baccalaureate Office (September 1989) *CASS Activities – Guidelines for IBO Schools*: Geneva

Part 4: The interaction between national and international education: each learning from the other

Introduction

Patricia L Jonietz

Ian Hill, Senior Private Secretary to the Minister for Education in Tasmania, explains how well the International Baccalaureate serves the needs of Australia's diverse national population.

> Approximately 3–5 million (22.4 per cent) of our population of 15.5 million were born overseas and 2.25 million (14.4 per cent) were born in non-Anglo-Saxon countries. A federal government multicultural policy seeks to preserve and respect other cultures while at the same time assimilating people of other ethnic origins into Australian society which is itself shaped by immigrant cultures. The IB may well be inviting and appropriate for some of this 'international' student population living permanently in Australia. The attraction of the IB to Australian education is not that it enables students to discuss world problems, to learn other languages, to read other literature, since these are possible with the local upper secondary school curricula. The uniqueness of the IB is that it is not about other parts of the world, it is other parts of the world. As an internationally derived and internationally examined diploma, it provides direct international experience. As more schools outside Europe offer the IB, the constantly evolving curricula and assessment procedures become less Euro-centred as they respond to what is being taught in other participating countries. Here is a wonderful opportunity to contribute to and benefit from a world curriculum and assessment network. (Hill 1990)

The IB is a popular example of the ability of an international idea to move across the international community. Recently, other educational topics have also begun to transfer ideas between and among nations. The use of the IB in a national school in Australia, the adoption of the ISA curriculum in a national school in Canada, the growth of a UWC campus in Africa, and the development of international links for national teacher training and programme development in computers, special needs, and gifted and talented education are all examples of this move towards international sharing and communication.

Pearce is concerned with the cultural misunderstanding on all sides which can result when individuals enter the international school system. Using admissions interviews, Pearce constructs three models of national systems to train teachers and families to recognize the implicit values in other systems. Though the parents' schemata of their national educational systems proved to be inaccurate, these are put forward as commonly held and influential attitudes. The origin and nature of the proposed schemata are considered, and some examples of parents' comments are shown. The parent information is better understood with an understanding of the national model. The usefulness of this approach to schools is discussed.

Parsons offers in a school in Tanzania a British national education exam – Integrated Humanities. He explains why this is appropriate, how it is implemented, and why it is successful. He goes further to describe the way one national education system can learn from the international education experience.

Turner was the GCSE Chief Examiner who travelled to Tanzania and directed the in-service training for the teachers in the international school. He also had an opportunity to visit the students and to accompany them on their community service work. This experience gives him a special insight into the way an international population adapts a national curriculum and uses the local community as a learning laboratory to see the common international problems of man.

Hansen describes the international move from segregation to integration of special needs students through the example of one national school system. However, the decade of the 70s saw special needs emerge as an important topic for many nations. Civil rights and non-discriminatory practices forced many nations to devise a programme of revision of services and opportunities for special needs students. The Danish experience with 'Schools For All' is a model for all to view with interest.

Hedvall gives a description of the Schoolproject/NORDNET 2000 which proposes education that is a joint venture among teachers, pupils, and parents. The project crosses national boundaries and hopes for international participation. It is based on introducing and employing technology in education to maximize all financial resources and integrate school and home in the educational system.

Caccamo and Henley went outside their country to research models of post-secondary education. Using the suggestions from other nations and trying to avoid their problems, they developed for their community a programme for students making the transition from secondary school to work. They present the programme design and implementation as well as a review of the present state of development.

Freeman discusses the needs of highly able children in general, and then with regard to provision and attitudes from three cultural perspectives which vary considerably. In the West, though there is often enough money, there is often inadequate provision. Eastern Europe, the area which used to be Communist, makes generally better provision for its most gifted children, though it is hampered by some backward attitudes. The Developing World has the problems of poverty, including children who have to work for a living, so that getting children to school and keeping them there is a challenge. Suggestions are offered to improve administration and teaching approaches with concern for local circumstances, especially in the poorer parts of the world. These involve the application of psychology to styles of teaching.

16. Understanding national education systems to facilitate transition in international schools

Richard Pearce

The problem

A perennial problem in international schools is the 'culture shock' suffered when children enter from other educational systems. The discontinuity which they experience is made up of very many elements; some reflecting general cultural differences, and others related to the differences in the aims and the methods of schools. One of the major duties of an admissions officer is to understand and communicate the nature of the differences, so that children, parents, and teachers are all forewarned.

Clearly, there are too many variables for one person to know, let alone communicate. In the words of C A W Manning, Professor of International Relations at the University of London:

> Understanding of the other man, then, especially if he is a foreigner, must always be imperfect, always a matter of degree. A lifetime is not long enough for acquiring all the knowledge with which one should wish to have begun. (1964)

I have set out to make a series of generalizations about national systems which will offer an accessible model to explain at least some of the fundamental differences in national educational systems for the benefit of all parties in international education. If I thought that a taxonomy of education systems could be both simple enough for the amateur and precise enough for the professional, it would probably be based upon the analytical structure set out by Holmes (1984), but it is only my intention to offer a tool, not a complete theoretical structure.

Origins of the model

However carefully we prepare printed explanatory materials, the major impressions of school, students, and parents are most often formed at an initial face-to-face interview. Parents at interview may see things which reveal their expectations. They may mention significant national targets, such as Italian *Maturita* or Spanish *BUP*; they may refer to institutions like American cheerleaders or Japanese uniforms; or they may exhibit values such as a deep concern for discipline or academic competitiveness.

Over many interviews, these indicators repeatedly fall into a number of patterns which demonstrate fairly coherent attitudes towards schooling and which at first I began to relate to the economic and social norms of each country. A second look showed that on the one hand there may be strong similarities between attitudes in several countries, and on the other hand some countries may contain more than one attitude. An attempt to relate them in detail to the countries concerned shows that the families' views are poor caricatures of their national systems, and that they are not distributed along strongly national lines. Although these views are consistent enough to be valuable, their nature needs further study.

Notional not national systems

In explaining our school to foreigners at interviews, we cannot afford to be subjective. In order to avoid our own narrowly national perceptions, we are bound to use objective, academic, statistical information such as the proportion of students attending university or the amount of time usually spent on homework. Newly-arrived parents often have difficulties in comparing even these objective norms with their own, and present us with a view based on their own experiences and memories, to which they have a personal, subjective allegiance. For example, from the English, with the intimacy of fellow nationals, we hear observations such as: 'Everyone I know took their A levels'; 'I was always taught . . .'; 'Boarding school taught me to stand on my own two feet'; 'I'm just looking for a good school.' Their all-important picture of education is based not upon their academic knowledge of comparative education but upon their perception of education, however this has been acquired.

It is evident that they do not simply acquire their expectations through their own experience of school, important though this may be, because their subjective statements are often inaccurate. A typical error is to overestimate the rate of university entry in the home country, owing partly to national pride, partly to optimism for one's children, and partly to having an advantaged background. It will be worth some comment later on how and why families' expectations deviate from what their country actually provides. For the moment, the essential point is that these mental models or schemata are more valuable than the truth in so far as they represent perceptions of education, for it is by our perceptions that we take decisions, often in the guise of 'common sense' (good) or 'prejudice' (bad).

The power of the schemata

In dealing with perceptions, we are operating in a complex and intractable area. As Gramsci (1975) wrote, 'Education is a struggle against folklore.' During 1989–90, events in Eastern Europe have shown us how resistant the folklore of human values is to the reforming forces of State-legislated political education. On the other hand, we put great trust in the body of received opinion which we call 'common sense', although by definition this is only common to a limited community. Writing of the English system Crispin Jones (1985) says, 'The one feature that is very clear in the present system is the persistence of attitudes, institutions, and organizational arrangements despite efforts to change the system.' Our perceptions are conditioned by the 'mental states' which Holmes (1984) lists as the most intractable determinant of an educational system.

It is my contention that these 'mental states' are the main force shaping the child's views on education, through conversations with their parents. 'What did you learn at school today?' 'You can't go out until you have finished your homework.' 'I'll write a note to the teacher to say you were sick.' 'I was always taught that . . .' 'That's not neat enough.' 'What was the highest grade for that project?' 'You can have a bicycle if you pass.' 'All they seem to do is play all day.' All these comments convey value judgments on the child's experience. The parents' view in its turn was acquired by them as children in the light of their parents' approval or disapproval of their schooling.

The influence of school

The relative effect of home and school on learning in a number of developed countries has been examined by Postlethwaite (1975), who suggests that with the exception of foreign languages the level of achievement is chiefly determined by influences from the home. In developing countries, the major determinant is in general the school, but work by Moegiadi and Elley (1979) shows that in urban areas of Indonesia the economic status and interest of the home correlates closely with school success. The section of the community with high status, in which the home is the most influential, is the one likely to be represented at international schools. For an expatriate family, finding the outside world much less coherent than their own, the parental effect will be even stronger.

In adolescence, the child will learn to resist the dominance of this influence, but during the early stages of schooling it is challenged only by the surrogate parent who stands in front of the class. As time goes by, the child's schema will change through daily exposure to peers and teachers at school, but the parent's schema is less accessible, less malleable, and more likely to come into conflict with the child and the school. In some cases, as in communities which are historically alienated from their social surroundings, the parents may win a tug-of-war between the reality of values at home and the triviality of values in the outside world, isolating the child from the school's influence.

The relation of the schemata to national norms

If these schemata are widely shared, we should find them closely linked (either as cause or as effect) with much of social or political life. If, for example, the family are typical members of a homogeneous and democratic country, it may well be that the schema of education to which they and the majority subscribe will have been enacted by their government in response to democratic forces, and will appear as a national system. As we have seen, though, in many countries the legislation may reflect either a more progressive or a more conservative view than that of our sample parents, and in any case the views of parents relate to personal school experience which is naturally a generation out of date. Again, in countries such as the UK, there may be more than one educational tradition, which in England gives rise to two distinct schools systems: public and private.

On the other hand, those who attend international schools are unlikely to be typical members of any national society. The French Lycée Charles de Gaulle in London, for example, brings about 94 per cent of its pupils to the level of the Baccalaureate General, as against national figures for the age cohort of 24 per cent. It commonly happens that a family emigrates because they belong to a persecuted or underprivileged minority group whose world-picture will be anomalous. Dissidence and alienation are frequent causes – or consequences – of expatriate life, a point which applies as much to teachers as to parents at international schools.

The diversity of cases

International schools are diverse and have a wide range of constituent families. A classification produced by Matthews (1989) after Ponisch (1987) differentiates satisfactorily between 11 types of international school. My concern is in general with those families for whom the curriculum or the national ethos of the new school differs from their previous experience. In some cases, there will also be a language barrier, and much of the past research has been done by second language teachers, often with the primary aim of improving language. In certain particularly difficult cases, the family has already made an international move in the past, and problems of adjustment have been ignored or resolved in some irrational way which is obstructive and extremely hard to alter.

Constructing the models

We have to have some frame of reference to construct a model of the cultural operation of an educational system. It could be said that types of curricula are the major variable, for they determine the landmarks such as public examinations and graduation requirements. However, they are not necessarily the most obvious variable to the pupils and the family as they intuitively form their schemata. The approach which I think is most useful is to look at what each country asks its schools to do.

Essentially, the three models start from the parents' questions: 'What does the schooling offer my child?' 'What must he or she do and what benefit can he or she gain?' Since the major concern is the child's economic and social targets, the schema will be built upon the economic, political, and social/religious values of their country.

The use to which education is put in a given community is in general a compromise between desire to give as much education as possible and the need to select and prepare citizens appropriately for productive life. I offer three models, showing different compromises between the two forces.

Finally, a word of caution. There is a risk that a summary of comparative education in a few hundred words could be taken for a complete and authoritative instrument for the resolution of all cultural misunderstandings. A moment's thought of the range of individuals in a class in one's home country is a reminder of the variance to be expected from any sample of our species, and of the importance of stereotypes. I propose this elementary model solely as a mechanism for exploring problems. Any reasoned analysis of educational differences is likely to promote the feeling that all systems, including one's own, have a logical structure. This objectivity can itself be the beginning of mutual respect which is essential for handling the problems of cultural adjustment.

The three models

Education as a preparation of all citizens, giving equal opportunities

Where this is the major function of education, we can expect to find that:

- ☐ The country is prosperous, so children are not forced to go to work.
- ☐ Few students leave before 18 years old.
- ☐ There is no rush to take on adult roles.
- ☐ Schools are non-selective; that comes later.
- ☐ Opportunities are believed to be expanding in that country or worldwide.
- ☐ Pass marks are set at levels which the majority can attain.
- ☐ Remedial programmes are offered for those who fail to reach this level.
- ☐ There is an analytical approach to the learning process.
- ☐ Assessment concentrates on what is right; to the needs of the individual students rather than vice versa.
- ☐ Teachers feel that it is their duty to adapt to the needs of individual students rather than vice versa.
- ☐ It is often associated with Reformed Christianity in which the individual must be equipped to read the Bible, and the priest is the facilitator rather than the sole intercessor with God.
- ☐ The individual is expected to develop him or herself to a high level of achievement.
- ☐ Class teaching tends to be directed towards a satisfactory level of attainment rather than a competition in which only a small proportion can succeed.
- ☐ If there is competition in society, it is practised outside the classroom or after compulsory education.
- ☐ Education is seen as an intrinsically valuable process, so skipping a year is bad.
- ☐ There is no selection until college entry, and subject specialization and differentiation only occurs after that.

This schema is common in the USA and Scandinavia and is influential in Australia, but there are elements of this attitude at primary school level in many countries.

Lawton (1989) points out:

> There is a temptation in those societies (USA, Australia, and New Zealand since the economic problems associated with the oil price rises of the 1970s)

to retreat to more élitist, less egalitarian policies with an emphasis on vocational training rather than education for the majority.

The collectivism which permeates Japanese and other oriental, Buddhist-influenced systems is very different from Western egalitarianism but has a superficially similar anti-competitive influence.

Education as a way of selecting and training citizens appropriately in a society with a limited range of opportunities

The majority of developed countries follow this pattern, educating for the State as well as for the individual. In these cases, we can expect to find that:

- ☐ Selection and differentiation of course occurs within the years of schooling.
- ☐ Numerous students leave before 18 years old.
- ☐ 'Delayed reward' and late independence are found in a middle class.
- ☐ It is recognized that opportunities are limited.
- ☐ At some stage, pass marks are set at a severely divisive level.
- ☐ Assessment concentrates on what is wrong; negative incentives are used.
- ☐ The student must fulfil the requirements of the teacher not vice versa.
- ☐ The approach to the learning process is empirical rather than analytical.
- ☐ Remedial education may be bestowed as a benefaction rather than a right.
- ☐ Streams are offered leading to different levels and types of careers (of more or less unequal status).
- ☐ This is often associated with social hierarchies.
- ☐ This may be linked with hierarchical religions, in which the priests play a superior role to the laity.
- ☐ A range of social roles exists with varying expectations of education.
- ☐ Hard work is the route to (and is rewarded by) success.
- ☐ Although it appears to be a meritocracy, social factors give some families an unequal opportunity.

This perception dominates in France, Italy, Germany, Eastern European countries, and secondary (particularly independent) schools in the UK. The *juku* in Japan is a response to a special type of competitive demand discernible also in other Far Eastern countries. The tension between the primacy of the individual citizen in Model 1 and the needs of the state in Model 2 finds a range of different balance points, as Lawton's comment on the influence of economic conditions shows.

Education as a preparation and certification of students for the roles they will inevitably occupy

This attitude may be found in countries where opportunities are very few and restricted to those in a position to take them. Its characteristic features are:

- ☐ Selection before school starts.
- ☐ A short period of compulsory education or none.
- ☐ Early maturity is desirable.
- ☐ Little social mobility.

- ☐ School training may be formal rather than functional, possibly representing vestiges of a former colonial curriculum and society.
- ☐ Much more emphasis on memorizing than on skills.
- ☐ Students' duty to teachers is paramount.
- ☐ Learning is a duty, and failure to learn a crime; cognitive processes are not analysed, and remedial teaching is not expected.
- ☐ Strongly hierarchical society and religion.
- ☐ Education makes an individual aware of the role he or she is to play rather than changing him or her to fit it; the authority of office is unchallenged.
- ☐ Qualifications are thought more important than content or competence.
- ☐ Since the content of a course is not important, skipping a year is good, and cheating may be routine.

Naming examples is a delicate matter, but elements of this schema are found in many developing countries in former British and other colonial territories. Bypassing the educational process through cheating is not an important matter because the process is not necessary; it is only a ritual. I put this model forward not to pillory it, but to show the internal coherence of a pattern which has many aspects which would be thoroughly deviant in our own systems.

These models can be summarized as shown in Figure 16.1.

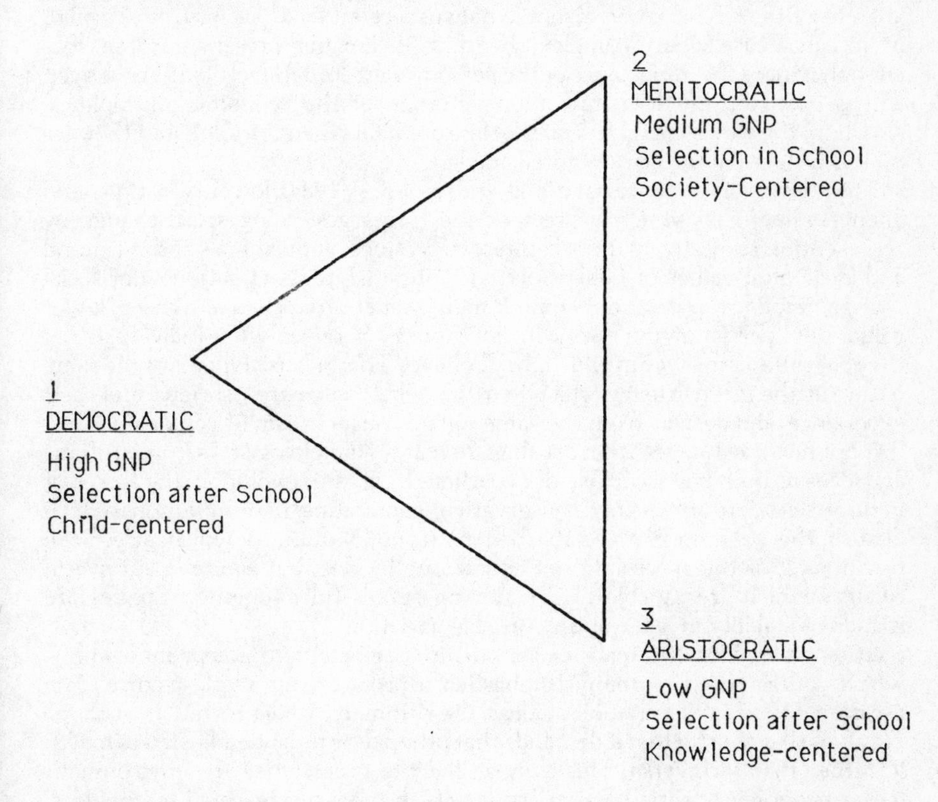

Figure 16.1 *Summary of three different models of the role of education in society*

The nature of the model

One explanation of these models, which have something in common with the child-centred, society-centred, and knowledge-centred modes of education, is that they are three phases in an historical sequence. On this interpretation, the schemata should be changing as they pass from generation to generation, and they should reveal some vestiges of the stages already passed through by that country. It is worth a digression to look at the process of educational evolution.

An illuminating account of the origins of education worldwide is given by LeVine and White (1986), who describe an 'agrarian' ancestor rather like Model 3. They do not put Models 1 and 2 in sequence though I suspect that some idealistic teachers would see 1 as 'progressive' and 2 as 'reactionary'. LeVine and White point out that change depends upon educational mobilization at both 'popular' (ie social opinion) and 'bureaucratic' (ie policy) levels.

The lines along which national educational systems develop are thoroughly reviewed by Boli, Ramirez, and Meyer (1985), who chart the influences which we can expect to direct change. They see the expansion of mass education in terms of two forces: central policy to increase state provision, and the local action to serve individual needs, as in the tension between federal and local democracy in the USA. Models 1 and 2 could depict two outcomes of this dialectic. Their analysis of the UK situation is somewhat suspect, and may suffer from a zeal to predict in a case where complexity forbids it. For our present purpose, it is enough to note the importance of the personal perceptual level of influence even if it is based on an inaccurate representation of the economic and political situation; the views of citizens may be less definable than the GNP, but they are no less influential for being unpredictable.

These levels of influence have links with Holmes' (1984) 'lower valuations' and 'higher valuations', which he sees as the forces governing social change by representing respectively the self-interested values of individuals and the moral and ideological values of public policy. Quoting Myrdal's (1944) view of social change, Holmes points out that '"high valuations" change while "lower valuations" persist giving rise to inconsistencies between what individuals say they believe and the way in which they behave.' This inconsistency is of the same nature as the inconsistency which I postulate between parents' views and their experience, and derives from the same innate conservatism of personal values.

If not historical stages what are the schemata? As a biologist, I see institutions and ideas as both being capable of evolution. In organic evolution, the forces of natural selection are mainly conservative, eliminating new mutations which disturb the coherence of established patterns. Mutations which affect the functioning of the species do not accrue one by one, but can only survive in clusters which are capable of functioning successfully together. Species are islands of stability in a sea of unworkable variation.

In terms of ideas, human conservatism is reluctant to accept innovations which conflict with so many established aspects of our world-picture. The occasional successful mutation of ideas, the Kuhnian paradigm-shift, is a change of values so powerful that it demands that other ideas must be adjusted to match it, rather than vice versa. This is most likely to occur when the environment (either economic or social) changes so as to favour the survival of different ideas. But as in the evolution of life-forms, a schema may contain illogical, nonfunctional vestiges of what was once logical, especially if the logic if these vestiges is seldom tested against the environment of real life.

Patterns of education do, however, change, most often by the invasion of a different population of ideas. LeVine and White point out that in copying a new model it is possible to by-pass the steps by which that model arose, a phenomenon named the 'late development effect' by Dore (1976). This would upset any historical sequence which we might otherwise expect to discover.

We can see, then, that popular perceptions of education are highly influential yet resistant to change. As the British education writer John Rae (1989) recently observed: 'There was a time when people in Britain did not think (the connection between education and the future of our society) mattered much; schooling was a rite of passage for the individual, not a means to an end for the country.' My thesis is that these two views are typical, that they coexist today, that it is unnecessary to see them as part of a deterministic sequence of events, and that they must be recognized and respected since they govern the expectations which we will encounter in an international school.

How schools can learn from parents

Since parents' comments on schools are to be seen as subjective, we can learn about their values from their conversations. If a family claims that a child had to work hard in the home country, there are several conclusions we can draw from that claim. First, that hard work is seen as a virtue. Second, that they mention it because it is perceived as a variable; they consider that there are schools – either at home or in the new country – where hard work is not the rule. Third, in mentioning it at all they are claiming the right to negotiate the child's future course of education.

It doesn't matter whether the country's students do work harder, nor how 'hard work' is defined or measured. We are concerned with the schema or world-picture which exists in the minds of the families and guides their judgement. It is clearly important for teachers to have pictures in their minds of these schemata, whether they are dealing with children or parents.

At this point, I would like to offer as illustrations some examples of parents' questions from initial interviews at the International School of London. These are glibly put in the form of a rather ambiguous phrase-book, but the interpretations should not be taken too literally. Textual analysis of the conversations alone is not enough to provide a print-out of the parents' conversation.

Some issues are not mentioned because the family is not aware of them; for example, remedial facilities may be non-existent or uniform unknown in their home system. Those matters which are discussed may well be the variables which most clearly distinguish good from bad in their home country's system. Yet, other variables are not mentioned because they are not known to vary. This was brought home to me in the early days of our English-system international school. An American teacher used to ask each term what figure denoted 'passing grade', and each term she would get a vague answer and some curious looks. Eventually, we asked what she meant by 'passing grade', which she patiently explained, together with the significance in qualifying a student for promotion.

In Britain, there is no parallel, since promotion is almost automatic and pass/fail assessments are only made in public examinations graded by external examiners. Once we agreed on the functions of our assessments, the way of expressing the grade fell into place.

Phrases used by parents	Possible interpretations (in UK terms)
We have heard of your famous school and have been told it is the best in London.	In our country, prestige is important./Don't take me literally, I am just being polite./We are here to negotiate./We only know one kind of education (to be understood from any inappropriate remark)
I have here a full set of transcripts, awards, and prize certificates from the last school, the best in the neighbourhood.	Our child is good; are you good enough?/We expect clear public awards for merit./We expect competitive distinction from our child and don't want any setback; the last school was a suitable competitive arena.
Brilliant, intelligent	Brilliance does not affect school success./This is an auction, not an analysis.
Any sort of complaints about the previous school system even if it was their own.	I have a critical attitude to life./I want to please you./My child failed at home but may achieve your lower requirements.
In our country, mathematics is very advanced.	We don't take your school as seriously as our own./Qualifications are more important than the teaching process./Don't patronize me./Maths matters more than humanities to me./Probably true.
One daughter wants to be a doctor, the other an engineer.	In our country, the parents do the choosing, not the school or the children./If we pay, we expect you to comply with our wishes./We need security./We belong to the élite (frequently sub-group doctor/lawyer). We come from a persecuted group in countries where the law has given protection to the persecuted.

He or she is very intelligent but playful.	He or she is immature and quite possibly evading recognition of his or her limitations./I don't recognize variation in cognitive ability.
We don't want him or her to lose a year.	Our country is the real world./Your schools are just like ours but maybe not as good.
We don't mind if he or she loses a year.	We take education very seriously./ Your school's qualification is better than ours./We had problems finding a place.
Is your school recognized by the Ministry of Education?	Our country is bureaucratic (and may value certificates above learning)./In our country private schools are of variable quality.
Can they start tomorrow?	In my country, decisions are made by the parents not the school./I am too busy to be involved./My wife/ husband handles education.
I want a private school not a public school.	I've heard comprehensive schools are just as good./I belong to the élite./I expect special attention.
She or he was at a mission school.	Don't associate us with the local system (eg Asian in Africa)./We belong to the élite./We are willing to adapt (eg Japan)
At the last school, my child had some friends but found most children too immature.	Probably only child and likely to prefer teachers to peers./Parents not concerned about fitting in then or now./Raised in Model2/3 but moved to 1.
I was never any good at . . .	I have learned not to worry about . . ./The targets for my children are not academic.
I am not so worried about the girl.	No comment

The impact of a new educational system may be felt in a variety of different ways, such as:

- ☐ Differences in language.
- ☐ Differences in past knowledge.
- ☐ Differences in classroom activities.
- ☐ Differences in school institutions.
- ☐ Attitudes to authority.

Using the models – teachers

The practising international school teacher may now be growing impatient with an account of a well-known problem which offers no solution. Marx said, in the words quoted on his tomb, 'The philosophers have only interpreted the world in various ways. The point, however, is to change it.' This attempt at a description of educational expectations in terms of the schemata lodged in the imaginations of the parties to education will justify itself to teachers if it can help them make changes in international education.

The most immediately accessible parties are the teachers, who are chosen by the school from various backgrounds, inducted into policies and precedents of the school, and should be guided by the colleagues in the professional conventions established there. At the International School of London, I have offered these models in outline to a generation of new staff as part of their induction programme, but their effectiveness is not easily measured. From my own experience, I can say, however, that the analysis was forced on my surprisingly and seemingly arbitrary remarks in conversations with parents, children, and foreign colleagues, and these surprises are now much easier to understand and less frequent.

Using the models – children

Children are also open to influences as they come to school five or six days a week. However, their degree of adaptability varies greatly during the years of schooling, according to the following factors:

- ☐ Relative importance of content and skills.
- ☐ Different balance of responsibility between teacher and pupil.
- ☐ Nature of pupil's duty – moral or pragmatic.
- ☐ Different conventions of approval/disapproval.
- ☐ Divergent signals from teachers, peers, parents.

A large proportion of these differences relate to specific cultures rather than to the worldwide variables dealt with by our models. The whole subject of what constitutes culture and how it operates in schools could – and does – fill a large number of books. There is also ample evidence that knowing about other cultures does not necessarily produce sympathy or sensitivity to them. In the words of C A W Manning (1964),

> To become "good" with foreigners is a question of becoming progressively better. And this, as has already been implied, may involve an element of moral and emotional self-mastery for which a merely academic preparation may be no preparation at all. All that a lecture can provide is a theoretical acquintance with some of the disabilities to be overcome.

An admirable practical aid is the handbook *Languages and Cultures in English-language-based International Schools* by Sandra Meakin (ECIS 1987) which contains a particularly valuable article on cultural adjustment at school, illuminating many problems and especially those encountered by EFL/ESL teachers.

In the early years of socialization, the children may be learning their norms of social expectation, and it may be just as infant bilinguals learn to be objective about the application of words to objects, so transferred children will learn a degree of objectivity towards conventions of behaviour. This is very different from learning a rationale of behaviour, and students may need to be fairly senior before they can use a theoretical model to help them understand why schools vary from country to country.

Students may in fact benefit most from these models through the effect on the teachers. All teachers pride themselves on the ability to communicate – it is our *raison d'être* in the age of computers – and their effectiveness may be improved by these models.

The impressionability of students also differs according to whether their home country enforced its norms in a moralistic or a pragmatic way. We should take care that in avoiding imposing our norms with a heavy hand we do not leave students without guidance. A well-intentioned cultural relativism which fails to offer a clear set of principles may lead to a state of anomia, a serious problem among Japanese children on their return from overseas.

Using the models – parents

The effect of the models on teachers may also be the most fruitful way of helping parents. Parents, as we have seen, are some way removed from the activities of school, and often have a very short time to establish an understanding with teachers, in circumstances which they may perceive as stressful and even hostile. I have not yet offered these models as a learning aid to parents, but they may be useful in a carefully organized process of familiarization. Here I see their use not as a portrait of the school's functioning, but as a device to help the family think functionally about education.

The conventions adopted by any international school must be in many ways an arbitrary yet dynamic comparison. The aim of these models is to ease the newcomer's acceptance of the conventions, but it should not be a passive acceptance. In a responsible international school, all the parties to the process should be encouraged to feel that they have a part to play in forming that compromise.

Bibliography

Boli, J, Ramirez, F O and Meyer, J W (1985) Explaining the origins and expansion of mass education *Comparative Education Review* **29** (2), 145–170

Dore, R (1976) *The Diploma Disease: Education, Qualification, and Development* Allen and Unwin: London, England

Gramsci, A (1975) *Quaderni del Carcere* (ed V Gerratana) Einaudi: Torino, Italy

Holmes, B (1984) Paradigm shifts in comparative education *Comparative Education* **28** (4), 504–604

Jones, C (1985) in *Equality and Freedom in Education* Allen and Unwin: London, England

Lawton, D (1989) *Education, Culture, and the National Curriculum* Hodder and Stoughton: London

LeVine, R A and White, M I (1986) *Human Conditons: The Cultural Basis of Educational Development* Routledge Kegan Paul: New York

Manning, C A W (1964) The knowledge needed for international understanding *The Yearbook for Education* Evans: London

Matthews, M (1989) The scale of international understanding *International Schools Journal* **17**, 7–18

Moegiadi, M C and Elley, W B (1979) Evaluation of achievement in the Indonesian education system *Evaluation in Education: International Progress* **2** (4), 281–351
Myrdal, G (1944) *An American Dilemma: The Negro Problem and Modern Democracy* Harper: New York
Ponisch, A (1987) *Special needs and the International Baccalaureate* MSc dissertation, Department of Educational Studies, Oxford University
Postlethwaite, T N (1975) *Educational Policy and International Assessment* McCutchan: Berkeley, California
Rae, J (1989) *Too Little, Too Late?* Collins: London

17. Midlands Examining Group Integrated Humanities: global humanities for the 14–16 age-range

David Parsons

Introduction

The Midlands Examining Group's (MEG) GCSE Integrated Humanities (IH) offers an international school the opportunity to implement a truly global education for the 14–16 age-range. The school can decide the content, and the five organizing ideas encourage investigation of local, national, and international issues while the nine essential skills help provide a firm educational base in the social sciences. Assessment is based on the production of work for a portfolio which is marked using a simple-to-use criteria referencing system. At the International School of Tanganyika, we began using the syllabus as a core subject in 1987. Three years later we have sufficient experience to report on the merits and drawbacks of a national educational plan adapted to the international school.

Syllabus

The requirements of the syllabus are simple. Over two years, students have to complete a minimum of ten assignments either in written form, on tape, or floppy disk. These are assessed by the class teacher on a 1–7 scale and moderated by a colleague. Nine skills are covered within three domains: Understanding and Communication; Enquiry; Interpretation and Evaluation of Evidence; Organizing Ideas; Continuity and Change; Freedom and Constraint; Conflict and Cooperation; Equality and Inequality; and a school choice, which in our case is Community and Environment.

Before we began teaching the course, the MEG Chief Examiner for Integrated Humanities, John Turner, came out to Tanzania to help us shape our content outline and to provide practice in marking scripts. Having seen the work from schools in England and having accurately marked samples, we felt more confident of being able to go it alone here in Africa. Since then, in fact, John Turner has provided on-going feedback on our performance and sent further examples of the work from schools in the English Midlands.

We prepare units as pairs of teachers or sometimes as a group of five. For each unit, we design an assignment which will both provide understanding of a particular issue, and at the same time will develop two or three of the course skills. The students are usually advised on how to structure their work, and they go ahead to complete the task. The assignments are assessed, and the class teacher's scores are checked by a colleague. This is necessary since there is no final exam. Samples of our work are further moderated by a panel of teachers in England who adjust the totals in order to equalize the grades for all the centres involved in the scheme.

During the production of assignments, it is acceptable for students to hand in drafts for initial assessment. This allows us the chance to explain how they might improve their work, indicate areas that have been given insufficient coverage, or perhaps go over key ideas and skill development again. This is a major advantage of IH, and one not shared by a majority of the GCSE exams which have a greater emphasis on final examinations. The IH assessment should be part of the on-going process of skill development.

Sample unit

The best way to illustrate the teaching process is to explain one unit in some detail. By September 1989, more and more media attention was being given to news coming out of Eastern Europe. It was clear that radical changes could occur, although the time-span was uncertain. Colleague Sue Perry and I felt that our 11th grade students should have a firm understanding of what was happening. Apart from the possible scale of the change, there were so many fundamental political concepts involved in any discussion of the Soviet Union and Eastern Europe.

By the beginning of October, the unit had been designed and presented, and the students were totally engaged in the tasks we had set them. I have rarely seen a class so absorbed and motivated – their interest constantly being reinforced by the latest news of speeches or governmental changes. We had asked them in groups of three or four to play the roles of Eastern European politicians, Soviet Government representatives, participants from major interest groups, or members of new political movements. Since our students were familiar with the annual student Model United Nations held in various locations around the world, we were going to hold a Model United Nations-style Assembly which would discuss the calls for change in Eastern Europe and the growing independence movement in the Soviet Union. At that time, only Poland had a new governing body, hence we felt it necessary to allow 'unofficial' groups to share the platform to ensure a balance of arguments and viewpoints as well as to stimulate lively debates.

We first outlined the historical background to the issues within the Eastern Bloc. To help students compose their speeches, we gave out packs containing relevant information: newspaper clippings, articles from journals, and textbook extracts. Undoubtedly, one of the most useful resources was the BBC World Newsbrief videos which provide a round-up of major international news each month.

The Assembly in mid-October was lively with students forcefully and on the whole accurately portraying the various viewpoints. Like the Model UN, the Assembly was designed so that opening speeches were followed by resolutions for debate. This ensured that everyone had a chance to speak. We fitted the method of role-playing to the requirements of the course by asking the students to write out their opening speeches, explaining their 'personal' ideas in great depth. This allowed us to assess individual knowledge and understanding of key terms and concepts, as well as the ability to communicate in a coherent and organized manner: two of the nine skills developed and formally assessed within the course.

One student, speaking as a representative of the German Democratic Republic argued:

> What is happening to socialism? Already we can sense that forces are trying to destabilize socialism in the DDR. To be replaced by capitalism of course. This is not what we want. We want to stay an independent country. We must defend socialism from the long arm of the West; defend our own ideas and points of view.
>
> Countries like Hungary have already been taken over by the West. In 1969, the DDR made an agreement with Hungary stating that neither country could let the other country's citizens pass into the West. Today, that agreement has been broken by Hungary. Hungary has let thousands of DDR citizens pass through to Austria towards Germany. Hungary has shown its worst and can no longer be said to be part of the Eastern Bloc.
>
> Our point has always been not to give in to the false lure of the West. To show them that they are of no need to us. We are in no need of help. I am sure that the representatives of Czechoslovakia and Rumania agree with us when we say that *peristroika* and *glasnost* are causing clear disturbances in the welfare of our people . . .

This example is representative of the level reached by a majority of our students. The entire speech covered two pages of typed A4 paper. We gave scores of 6/7 for the understanding of concepts, terms, and ideas, and 5/7 for communicating in a coherent, organized, and detailed fashion.

Additional unit content

Table 17.1 illustrates other units covered by various teachers. It shows examples of topics, the methods of study, and the skills developed and assessed. The topics reflect what we considered to be some of the more important issues with which we expected our students to be familiar. One argument in favour of the integrated approach to learning emphasizes how the real world cannot be divided at school-level into distinct subject disciplines. One argument against the integrated approach is that the course content is a hotchpotch of unrelated topics.

Additional benefits

We have had the opportunity to link social service work and community education projects into IH. One group of our students accompanied youngsters from a local school for polio victims to Mikumi National Park Fieldcentre. The

Table 17.1 *Examples of units covered in the Integrated Humanities GCSE course at the International School of Tanganyika*

Issue	*Method of learning assessed*	*Skills*
The role of women in rural Tanzania	Fieldwork in local villages	Report with data analysis
Deforestation	Guest speaker from Ministry, fieldwork	Report of problem with solution
Development of Dar es Salaam during colonialism and since independence	Fieldwork, mapwork, analysis of diagrams on housing and population	Report of growth and zoning
Refugees	Study videos, news reports, guest speakers, interviews with refugees, effect on lives, articles from NGIOs, role playing	Written work explaining circumstances
Apartheid	Booklets of history of Apartheid, videos, news articles	Interpretation, evaluation of evidence and recognition of bias
Aid	Textbooks and visit to cooperative	Report appropriate aid for Tanzania
Superpower relations	Textbooks, videos, news articles, role playing	Speeches in role, report on background emphasizing terms and concepts

goal was not so much to admire the animals but to live together for a weekend away from the city. Our students acted as hosts and provided some educational experiences. Other groups have visited Kindwitwi Leprosarium working on a building project. In both examples, students were prepared beforehand and asked to produce written assignments linked to what they had learned from their class discussions and weekend visits. During the course, students also produce two 'Special Studies' which provide the chance for research in depth into an area of particular interest. They design the research method, collect the data, and analyse it. We have a huge range of possibilities for local study: everything from poaching to Aid projects, welfare, environmental issues, and culture. Some students prefer to enquire into an aspect of their home country while others look at global concerns or international relations. Our aims have been to further both local and international understanding, to raise cultural awareness, to encourage collaborative learning, and to ensure that essential learning skills are developed.

Disadvantages

Certainly the requirement that ten assignments minimum be included in the portfolio is demanding on students' time. They need to write six to ten pages in order to achieve the higher marks. The teachers then have to mark it all carefully. With groups of 20, that means a minimum of 200 assignments over the two years. An additional demand on teacher time, although beneficial to the student, is the greater degree of individual instruction necessary. Since the teachers also design the course in addition to supplying the assessment, a high degree of commitment and team spirit are essential.

From the first assignment, the work is assessed at the final GCSE standard, and it tends to be the case that the early work scores low marks. As skills develop in the second year, higher marks are achieved. The result is that the early assignments lower the overall total. To some extent, this can be rectified by allowing students to improve certain pieces once they have grasped the methods. How much of a drawback this is depends on whether the course is seen in terms of final marks gained or in the level of improvement in the students since the beginning of the course. Final grades do compare favourably with other core subjects offered within the school.

The students tell us that they value the coverage of the issues and find the resources stimulating, but they do not enjoy having to complete so much course work, particularly when it is in addition to the internal assessment demands from all other subjects. I think this comment is partly related to their inexperience in organizing their study time and partly related to the school's need to restructure the school day to provide more self-study time. What is certain is that essential learning skills are developed in the areas of communication, research, evaluation of evidence, and recognition of bias. Our students gain an extensive knowledge of current affairs and are able to express their opinions in an informed and confident way.

Conclusion

By 1994, the British National Curriculum will begin to affect the content and assessment of most GCSEs. Integrated Humanities, if it does survive, which it may given the requirement that all students must study history and geography up to the age of 16 years, will have to be modified to meet state requirements. This may make it less attractive to the international schools. Yet, the essential features could be used to produce an 'International IH' syllabus available through the University of Cambridge Local Examinations Syndicate IGCSE subjects. A 50 per cent final assessment using open-ended questions plus a requirement of five course-work assignments would allow international schools to provide a course that promotes international understanding. IGCSE Economy now covers environmental and developmental issues but not current political concepts, major political changes, human rights issues, arms reduction, or the United Nations. A twin course to Natural Economy is perhaps needed which integrates international elements of politics, history, sociology, and geography.

18. Integrated humanities in the international school experience

John Turner

One of the main aims of the Integrated Humanities syllabus is to permit teachers maximum flexibility in course design and teaching styles, while offering an assessment approach which places minimal constraints upon freedom. The syllabus thus allows schools to teach its broadest themes through the specific contexts which they feel are most appropriate to their individual needs. Whatever the context, each piece of student work is assessed for its quality in terms of Understanding and Communication, Enquiry and Interpretation, and Evaluation.

This makes the syllabus particularly attractive to international schools, because it offers far more flexibility to tune the teaching programme to the needs of the students and also to the needs of the location of the school. In my visits to Dar es Salaam to work with the teachers at the international school, what struck me most was the commitment of the whole school teaching staff, not only to covering a range of international political, social, and environmental issues but also specifically to studying Tanzanian contexts. Thus, such issues as urban development and social change could be studied by first-hand contact with examples within Tanzania. I accompanied some students who were engaged in a community project in the rehabilitation unit of a local hospital where they worked with children who were victims of polio.

This kind of work not only allows teaching to be responsive to local circumstances but to current developments (such as the unpredictable changes in Eastern Europe during 1990), but also is able to place students from various parts of the developed world right into the middle of quite difficult and challenging situations in their host country.

As a means of motivating students to learn and as a mechanism for reducing the isolation that can occur for international schools, the Integrated Humanities syllabus can offer a way for creative and committed teachers to follow their personal intentions without having to compromise because of the inflexible assessment requirements so common in many other syllabuses within GCSE. The current Integrated Humanities GCSE will continue, with only slight amendment, until 1994 and probably until 1996. This gives ample opportunity for the investigation of the international school GCSE experience and adoption of the International GCSE if there is sufficient demand.

19. Integration/segregation – a major shift in international attitudes

Ole Hansen, with illustrations by Allan Stochholm

Introduction

The world keeps on getting smaller. The technological developments in areas like telecommunications which began with the astronauts' visit to the moon mean that international currents now have an immediacy for the individual that they never had before.

Systems change, ideologies fall, and borders open. New democracies rise, and we can follow the process as it happens through the media. We can no longer shut our doors in the belief that what is happening elsewhere in the world is not our concern.

Everywhere in the West, people are beginning to re-examine the so-called 'welfare model'. This is taking the form of a re-examination of the *way* we have built up welfare systems. To a degree, this is an ideological process corresponding to the ideological process being experienced in other orographic areas, but with a different content. In our part of the world, the debate centres on guardianship versus personal freedom and is strengthened by decentralization and a return of possibilities to primary countries – a tendency which is extremely strong in the Nordic countries. But what happens in Denmark and other Nordic countries is also influenced by broader, international currents.

The World Health Organization (WHO) puts forth a set of values which play a significant role in the development of schools in some parts of the world. The key words: *unity*, *equality*, and *independence* originate with the WHO and influence international thinking. When school systems are built, we listen to each other. The developments in Denmark, for example, are influenced by developments in America. The debate preceding the adoption of the American Federal law referring to 'mainstreaming' of special needs students marked, perhaps, the starting point for the Danish integration process.

Educational reform in Denmark

In 1969, a unanimous Danish Parliament ratified a school reform which in principle expressed Danish society's wish to *abandon* the set of philosophies which considered the handicapped from the point of view of *special* interests and

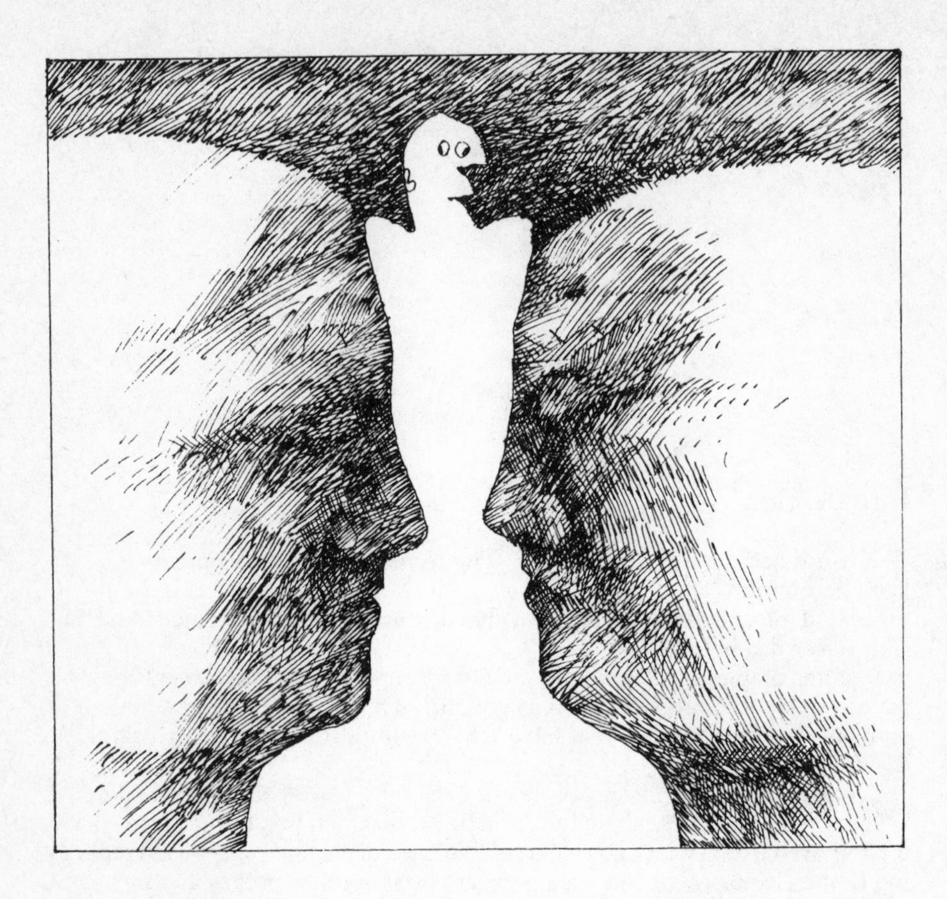

Figure 19.1

special treatment. This school reform was termed 'The 9-point Programme', and it stated among other things that 'teaching of handicapped children must take place as near to the children's homes as possible.' Prior to this reform, we had witnessed – both in Denmark, in the other Nordic countries, and internationally – a development characterized by society's special provision solutions for the handicapped. The adoption of The 9-point Programme marked a landslide shift of attitudes from segregation to integration. This became particularly evident in all western countries during the following two decades.

Phase 1: working for segregation

Internationally, the categories and the special treatment of handicapped students at special schools and in school classes for the handicapped had been growing during the sixties. For every category of handicap, there would appear a special school system, and categorizing partisans argued that with their sophisticated instrumentation they could distinguish and distribute the handicapped in groups and sub-groups. The marvels of test philosophies were discussed at great length and with great seriousness, and the labelling of students assumed a significant importance in their assessment.

In most western nations, within the framework of the regular school a number of categories emerged which aimed at the pupils' individual handicaps, and special classes and groups were formed, each having their specialized function: blind, deaf, mentally retarded, and emotionally disturbed. Problems were solved by referring pupils who invited novel approaches for special teaching at special locations:

- ☐ Pupils with reading difficulties were referred to remedial reading classes.
- ☐ Pupils with hearing problems were referred to hearing impaired classes.
- ☐ Pupils with visual handicaps were sent to schools for the blind.
- ☐ Mentally retarded pupils were referred to schools for the mentally disabled.

The various groups of 'deviating' pupils were further sub-divided, and the teaching offered became even more specialized. Frequently, the groups were sub-divided while the teaching offered was not. Over-protection prevailed and controlled the development.

This was most clearly seen in the case of the mentally retarded. Systems for them were established which ran parallel to the 'normal community' where the retarded pupils were offered alternative hospital facilities, social activities, and nursing. This period displayed the methodology of the segregating experts. Facets of an individual's personality were frequently spotlighted and erroneously emphasized as the ultimate discriminating factor. A rigorous correlation between diagnosis and location was the infallible remedy of those days. And this barred the regular school from developing a pedagogical day in which all children could share in the same teaching.

Teachability – non-teachability

Along with other international systems, we found ourselves in a period of Danish school history where the *segregation philosophy* determined society's teaching offers for the handicapped. The dividing lines between teachability and non-teachability were discussed with great intensity.

A large proportion of the schoolchildren received no teaching at that time; and if they did, the special day schools would frequently be a two- to three-hour drive away from home; or, alternatively, at an institution far away from family and familiar environments. International human rights declarations which penetrated the Danish attitude, and it may even be said all the Nordic countries' attitudes, reflect the influence of the UN's declarations to the effect that handicapped individuals are entitled to receive teaching. Internationally, towards the end of the sixties, these activities were extremely intense, and the major shift in attitude from *segregation* to *integration* took place at the end of 1969.

Phase two – working for integration

In reality, it may be argued that *segregation* and *integration* are two sides of the same thing. Like the two faces of a coin – each with its own motif. Integration is another word for normalization. In this view, integration activates our value sets and attitudes and enables us to realize the strengths of being different. Integration is not a drive to normalize, but it means that systems and services must be arranged so as to ensure that the special needs of the individual may be satisfied under the most appropriate conditions – as close to the individual's home base as at all possible. Integration is the approach which may be applied when a society or community wishes to instil in a new generation of pupils such democratic concepts as versatility and pluralism. Integration presupposes that special rules are dismantled and that the standard system is enhanced to cover all the individual's needs.

Normalization

From an educational point of view, integration is a method of ensuring that handicapped pupils have a right to education in the normal state school system, although not necessarily within the framework of the normal state school

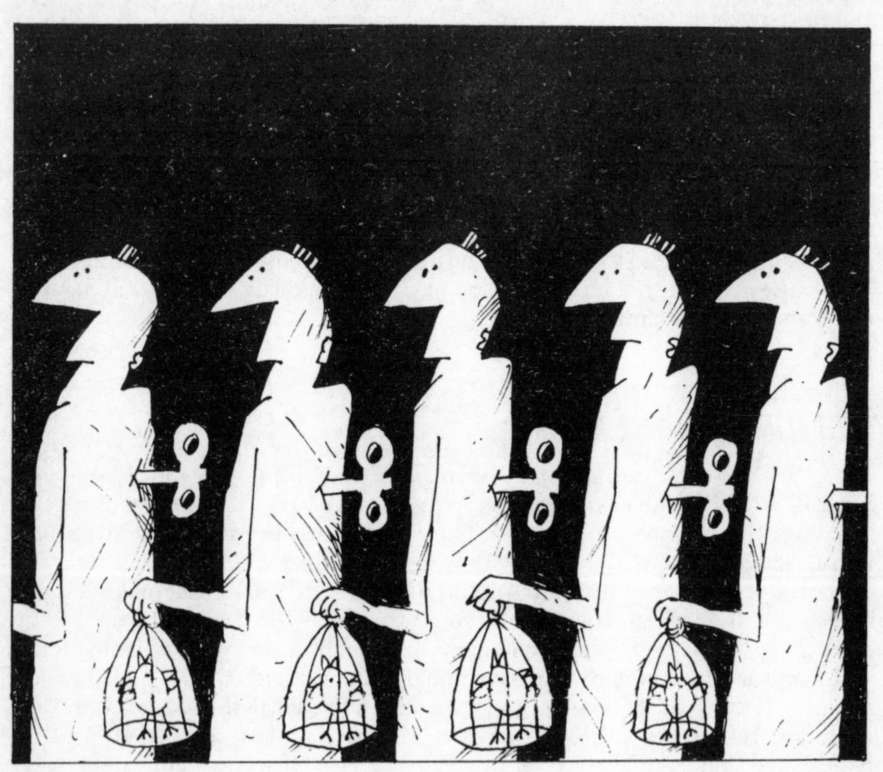

Figure 19.2

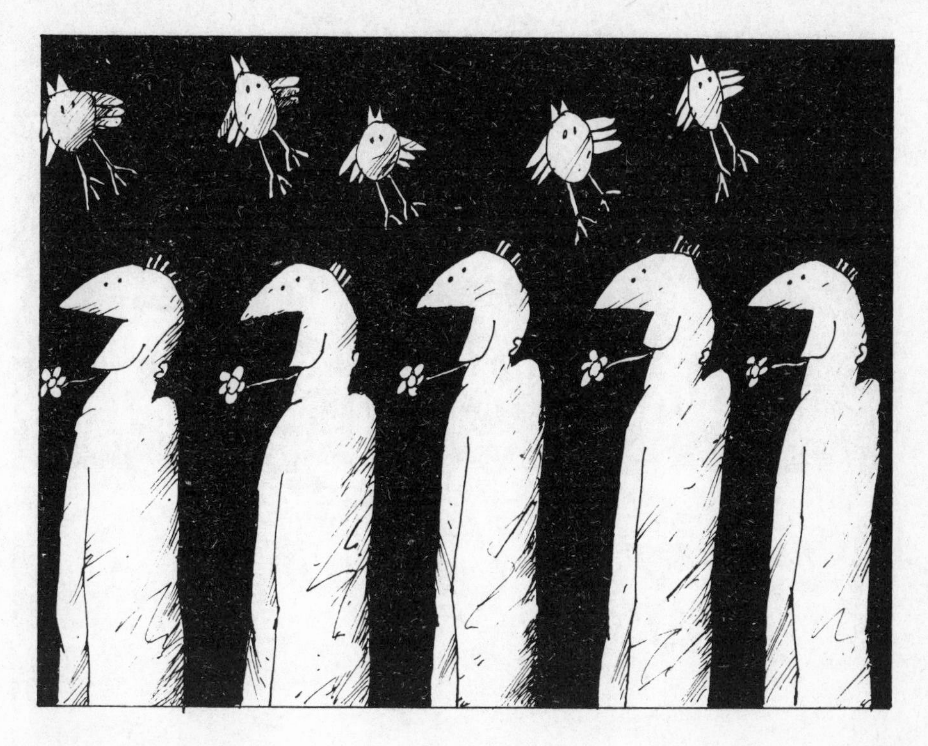

Figure 19.3

system as the individual's special needs may require special classes or special schools during short or long periods. Integration of the handicapped in the normal state school pursues the common Nordic education concept referred to as 'One School for All', which builds upon the following corner stones:

- ☐ *The concept of the comprehensive school*
  The comprehensive school concept means that pupils attend the same class for the entire ten-year school period.
- ☐ *The principle of class teachers*
  The same one teacher is assigned during the entire ten-year period to the task of ensuring that individual and social problems are solved optimally.
- ☐ *Educational/psychological service systems*
  The purpose is to ensure that the particular educational needs of all the pupils are satisfied by the school.

During the seventies, there were many so-called integration experiments in Denmark. These experiments were based on the principle that pupils were moved from special schools or special classes to regular school classes. Much of this development work contributed to changing the regular school's traditional view of what constitutes teaching. Teachers successfully took up the challenge of differentiation and theme-teaching and provided optimum offers for all pupils. New approaches to cooperation emerged, and both in teaching itself and

Figure 19.4

in the preparation phases, the underlying principle became the concept of themes. Teachers enhanced many other qualities of the regular school. Acceptance, understanding, and appreciation of the strengths of being different became basic concepts along with and in addition to compulsory education itself. The methods of the specialized educationalist became manageable instruments for the ordinary teacher and in ordinary teaching.

A number of these experiments failed. The pupils found themselves in isolation and were lonely, and some were returned to the special schools where they had come from. Over a period, this resulted in futile discussions between ordinary schools and special schools. There were many reasons for this stalemate situation, but a lot of experiments failed because the teachers found themselves alone with their problems.

The whole

Hindsight has taught us the lesson that integration fails when the handicapped pupil is not seen as part of the social whole. This means:

- ☐ When the focus is on the school only, without considering after-school life and the individual's needs for meaningful leisure time.

- ☐ When the focus is on the organization of education only, and not simultaneously on the content of education.
- ☐ When one preserves established and ingrained ideas as to what constitutes education and what does not.
- ☐ When the school in its organization and way of thinking is directed towards academic streaming and no alternative efforts are made to teach socially relevant subjects.

In the situation where the above considerations have been acknowledged and have been combined with an improved effort to enhance the awareness of special education with the individual teacher, integration has lived up to expectations.

Phase 3 – working against segregation

The 1990s are likely to be the period in international history where public education and teaching for the handicapped will work against segregation. Only in this way can we obtain real integration. Integration will arrive when:

- ☐ Children start school together.
- ☐ Nobody comes from a 'special' school or institution.

Figure 19.5

- ☐ The handicapping categories do not run the placement, but on the contrary direct the educational aims.
- ☐ Every teacher understands how to use his or her knowledge or how to obtain relevant help from experts in order to solve educational problems.

Particular roles – the pedagogical conflict

The success of the various educational tasks in a non-segregated educational system demands a lot from the way that the teacher regards his or her own role. Success means that the particular needs of the handicapped pupils should be met, and that teaching takes place when the pupil is an integrated part of the community of the class.

Two aspects are significant in this connection. The class teacher's wish to work with his or her pupils from the point of view of the whole, and the specialist teacher's need to target his or her pedagogic activities on the deficiencies and handicaps of the individual pupils. A pedagogical battlefield can develop in which the individual pupil may suddenly find him or herself in a 'vacuum of non-responsibility' because both teachers expect that the other teacher is in charge. The roles of the two teachers must form part of the whole and of shared experiences, the activities must be deliberately arranged to supplement each other, and knowledge of alternative methods must be introduced in the general educational strategies that dominate. This puts special demands on the educationalists.

The expert's working routine

School psychologists and other experts will also have to change their daily working routines. It will to a large extent be necessary to abandon the known evaluation instruments in order to make room for more dynamic interaction initiatives. The instrumentation of the experts is frequently tied to the characteristics of the individual. A detailed mapping of an individual's personality as a step towards preparing the individual/pupil for his or her confrontation with the school and its demands was a perfectly acceptable method. In the non-segregated system, the experts have to redefine their roles. Methods of analysis directed towards the responsiveness of the individual became uninteresting.

What is interesting is analysing tools which can help develop the options that are offered, and which can help organize these offers in such a manner that all pupils of a particular class level benefit optimally. At the same time, these tools ensure that the social and cultural activities stand out so as to enhance community and togetherness, thereby maintaining and developing the identity and self-esteem of each and every individual within a certain context.

The established professions related to the mechanisms of segregation will disappear, and a new educationalist personality will emerge with a thorough understanding of the interrelations and wholeness of a particular context. This development has already become evident in several situations. Today, professionally conscious school psychologists participate as equal collaborators in every day of schooling and contribute to the planning of the school's system changes.

Figure 19.6

The parents' commitment

The parents will play a more active role in the classes where segregation is obstructed, as the resources of the individual parent group will be emphasized in order that teaching should succeed. Acceptance, tolerance, and understanding must be notions that characterize class parent meetings. Openness, honesty, and confidence must be key-words when planning educational subject matter so that all the pupils of the class may profit optimally from the teaching.

Insufficient information may cause some parents to feel alarmed about the possibility that teaching may lack intensity and effectiveness when handicapped pupils are taught together with other pupils. However, this fear is unfounded as the situation is exactly the opposite. Children and classes that have difficult special pedagogical challenges as part of their everyday routines will reach the same goals as the other classes, and in addition so that they will learn something very important: better life quality through a feeling of togetherness, and respect for and understanding of other people's problems - qualities which parents around the world agree should be cornerstones for any grown-up generation.

The method: integration

Segregation and *integration* are not aims *per se*. They are methods used internationally to emphasize notions like versatililty and variety. Segregation and integration will become instruments to ensure that the next generation understands the elements of a democratic society.

Annotated bibliography

Emanuelsson, Ingemar (1988) The consequences of integration ideology *Nordisk Tidskrift fur Spesialpedagogikk* **66**, 1–8

It is emphasized that integration is first and foremost understood as a challenge to all who work in schools. Group values and norms which lead to a rejection of those who are different should be combated. Looked at in this way, integration must be regarded as a process of development. The author wants research within the area as he points out that otherwise there is a great risk that the causes of poor/unsuccessful integration will be laid back at the door of the handicapped.

Hansen, Jurgen and Mogens (1987) School psychology in a school for all *Skolepsykologi* **24**, 264–279

This article is concerned with the possibilities and significance of school psychology for the establishment of a school for all students. As this subject is regarded as extremely vital in many circles, it should be understood as an expression of the fact that many people see a positive connection between the two concepts, something which is not always obvious. In all the Nordic countries as well as in others where school psychology is a reality, there are undoubtedly many teachers, parents, or politicans who associate school psychology with classification, segregation, and rejection - in general, a system in opposition to the concept of school for all.

—— (1989) Theme *LEV* **38**, 21–59

This number of the journal of the National Association for the Welfare of the Mentally Handicapped is concerned with the return of responsibility for service for the handicapped to primary countries. This is illustrated by statements and examples taken from the experience of a school association in connection with the development of the school for all. The objectives for the development of primary schools within the primary country area can best be characterized as a wish for normalization.

—— (1989) *PU Journal* **91** (1), 3–53

This Nordic publication is dedicated to the theme of 'the rule of law and the right to ordinary services'. This is a significant contribution to the legal aspect of the integration process whose goal is 'society for all'. The question of special legislation in connection with reducing the role of the institution is also entered into. 'The most fundamental right is the right to be an inviolable human being on one's own premises.'

—— *PU Journal* **92** (2), 3–41

The placing of responsibility for service for the handicapped on primary countries is an expression of the developmental stage arrived at by the system in the process of integration. The WHO's set of values for health for all in the year 2000 is an ideological input in this analysis and problematization of service for the handicapped in the Nordic Countries and was carried out by an international group of politicians.

English summary is available from the editorial office of PU, Svinget 2, 8382 Hinnerup, Denmark; tel: 45 8698755; fax: 45 86985705

20. The Schoolproject and NORDNET 2000: a way to internationalize education through the classroom, the teacher, the pupil, and the parents

Jan Hedvall

Introduction

Education has always been successful when there exists an accordance between the 'age', the school, and the people. Today, we are experiencing severe problems in the educational field. Internationally, I do not know of any industrialized country not having 'school crises'. Is it strange? No! It is a sign of health and possibilities. The problem is: How do we, nationally or internationally, react to the symptoms of sickness? It is said that a Swedish politician recommended the replacement of all teachers in order to get a new school system. This describes in many ways how we seem to perceive teachers: they are a hindrance, and we are the cure. We do not need teachers if we have politicians and administrators. Do we even need pupils? Of course! Pupils are what we place in focus.

When I was educated in the forties and the fifties, the teacher was respected in the local society: he belonged to the élite even if he was a she. It was not because of his or her professionalism. No, it was because the teacher was the gatekeeper to a better society. Today, the teacher is neither the gatekeeper nor the professional. It seems as if they are not part of our future any longer. A teacher told me that he asked his pupils about computers, and they told him not to bother: 'Computers are something for the future and not for school.' Do not the school, the education system, and the future belong together – regardless of future multimedia advances and information technology? In each country, we are now changing curriculum, organization, financing system, and anything else in sight, and we are even trying to make the teacher a local resource without definition, but we are not changing the schools. In many countries, there are ongoing projects leading nowhere with administrative costs higher than operating costs. What is wrong? We have forgotten the teacher – the classroom teacher!

The result has been a relatively more isolated school, a lower status for the teacher, and deteriorated pay standards. Education and knowledge have the same value as before, but that value is less and less related to the school. All people demand intellectual space: education, knowledge, and future. Life in context framed by the situation of their lives, needs, and aspirations. Regarding information, economy, and social life, our lives are international today. The pupils are internationally orientated through culture, television, papers, parents, and holidays.

The national and international teachers know that the renewal of any education system needs a teacher who is a professional. The teachers should be locally established with the pupils and the parents but should also have the opportunity to exchange experience, knowledge and work with other teachers from their own country and from other countries. We wanted to create opportunities for Danish teachers to interchange ideas and experience with other Danish teachers, with other European teachers and with international teachers.

The Schoolproject

This is the background of *The Schoolproject* with which we have been working for approximately two years. We started with the focus on the teacher – the conveyor of culture, attitudes, and knowledge. A good teacher, if regarded and treated as a professional, realizes that he or she is a professional and becomes a more dedicated teacher. We planned NORDNET 2000, an international educational network used by teachers and later by pupils and parents, in order to develop and preserve a Nordic cultural identity in a united democratic Europe. NORDNET 2000 makes possible an international exchange of experiences among teachers, evaluation of methods, comparison of results, and sharing of products made by teachers and/or pupils.

Instead of beginning with a mandatory nationwide implementation, we started in the classroom. We found from international investigation that an international computer network is a costly thing (number of computers needed in education, the number of teachers involved, and the quantity of teacher training necessary to integrate computers actively in education) and must be cost-effective, active, and lasting. It is not cost-effective if the teachers do not use it. The local education authorities do not have the money for costly experiments.

That is why our training is concentrated on how to make the computer identifiable in the teaching profile of the teacher, a part of the teacher in the same way as a book, pencil and chalkboard are. Our training program is based on the ordinary teacher's seeming dread of the computer and the increasing complexity of classroom work. In our program, we engage teachers to teach other teachers. Our object is education not computer technologists. We have seen that this cost of training is so low compared to other methods of introduction that the cost of the computer is – so to speak – saved.

We know that individual teachers and pupils produce very good teaching materials which can be used by other classes and schools – even used in other countries. By building up local school computer bases connected to a regional base, and hopefully to international bases, we can begin to exchange experiences and products and at the same time save money. If we want the teacher to use the computer base, we have to start building it up from the classroom, where the user and producer of the material lives.

A tool is needed for connecting the teacher, the pupil, the school, and the home. We found a computer which almost everyone involved could afford and which could be used in connection with already present equipment in the schools and in the homes. Anyone can take part in the process if they want to. Introduction to the computer must be related to a variety of different individual interests among not only pupils but also teachers and parents, or they will very effectively eliminate the possibility of usage. Although we are using a 'social standard' not an industrial standard, our training will mean that the computer industry will later receive individuals able to use technology to solve problems.

After reviewing the many programs to be purchased from the international computer market, we started to develop educational programs together with our teachers and pupils. This was an approach used successfully in American school systems. We sought programs suitable for the teacher's purpose and daily school work. This has given us at least two advantages: 1. because of in-house development, a cheap program based on 2. known and accepted pedagogy. This makes it easier for the teacher to identify the appropriate situation in which to use the computer as an educational aid. Step by step, the teacher can formulate his or her own professional requirements.

When we introduce *The Schoolproject*, we inform all the teachers about the entire range of capabilities within the system. We have found that the teacher wants connections between the system and the classroom stated in a pedagogical context. They want the computer to be one among the many educational aids in the classroom. In a way, *The Schoolproject* is a tool that the teacher can use to develop his or her professional skills and continually strive towards a vision or goal, perhaps the vision that motivated him or her into becoming a teacher.

The Schoolproject has taken local authority interests into consideration too. Education is one side of the project, and administration and financing possibilities are the other. The present international trend towards decentralization of decision making is important for teachers, and presupposes a computer-based support system, but that (from our point of view) is not the same as an educational computer system. Teaching people to count is different from counting the costs of teaching.

An important task is to keep the feeling of 'belonging' alive among the teachers. Professionals know that they are 'together' as a unit when they can identify themselves as a group. We produce for that purpose a periodical with the same name as our Nordic Network, NORDNET 2000. In this paper, we publish articles by participants from all over Scandinavia, and would welcome articles from interested international teachers.

Conclusion

The Schoolproject is now working all over Scandinavia and establishing cooperation with teachers and others in many countries. Our approach to the teachers has proved to be very productive. We can see that a kind of international information 'life-style' is evolving among 'our' teachers. What is more important, they readily initiate the use of the computer when they see it to be appropriate and they look forward to communication possibilities.

We see as our next objective the further linkage of international teachers through NORDNET 2000, the development of better computer programs, and a more efficient distribution of our international periodical NORDNET 2000.

21. Transition of handicapped youth from school to the world of work: a model of international cooperation

James M Caccamo and Robert L Henley

Introduction

The successful transition of students with handicapping conditions from school to the world of adult living has been a major concern of the international special education community for many years. Around the world during the past ten years, there has been a dramatic change in planning for educational and related services provided to students with handicapping conditions. Internationally, emphasis has moved from segregation to integration of students with non-handicapped peers in the most normal setting possible and providing them a high quality education.

As a result, today's young people with disabilities have more experience with the non-handicapped world and are better prepared to enter the world of work and adult living. However, many young people with disabilities still need assistance with and preparation for this transition. The United States, Sweden, France, the United Kingdom, Denmark, and Canada are some of the countries that have identified in their curriculum planning the provision of transition assistance as a top priority within their educational systems.

Since 1983, the School District of Independence, Missouri has worked with the National Association of State Directors of Special Education in the United States and the Organization for Economic Cooperation and Development's Center on Educational Research and Innovations in Paris to gain a broader perspective of successful service delivery models in international curricula. This perspective has assisted us in developing within our own curriculum an innovative programme to assist the handicapped youth in the Independence, Missouri schools in making the transition from the school curriculum to the world of work.

Gathering background information

We visited the Individual Transition Planning programme in the United Kingdom and the Kurator system in Denmark, and also investigated the Liaison Officer programme in Sweden and the Cotorep programme in France. We studied programmes for transition in Belgium, Italy, Canada, Germany, and the

Netherlands. In addition, we investigated various programmes in the United States.

One amazing fact that kept recurring was the similarity of problems in each of the countries trying to resolve the issue of the transition of the handicapped youth from school to adult living. Some of the problems experienced internationally were the unemployment rate, national government policies (employment quotas), the size of the country, and the social services available to handicapped youth reaching adulthood.

In each of the programmes studied, there emerged common solutions. The most striking was that a successful transition programme required the efforts of a facilitator who demonstrated the following characteristics: experience with handicapped youth, good communication skills, a knowledge of services in the community, good case management skills, knowledge of various handicapping conditions, and good listening skills. The facilitator could not be a person who made decisions for handicapped youth but rather one who presented options for successful transition from school, guided the family and the youngster through the options, and developed a written plan once the student and family selected their options. The written transition plan helps to keep student, curriculum activities, and goals in focus.

Programme

In 1985, by blending the information that had been learned through international cooperation with our existing programme, the School District of Independence began the implementation of a School Transition programme. The programme's goal was to strengthen and coordinate the education, training, and related services that assist handicapped youth in the transition from school to competitive or supported employment, post-secondary education, vocational training, continuing education, or adult services. Within the school curriculum, the programme provides preparatory vocational training, job site developments within the community, and transitional support services for handicapped students to enable them to make in the least restrictive environment a successful transition from school to the world of work.

The programme is called STEEP SPAN, and its objectives and activities are similar to other programmes found around the world. The components of the programme are embodied in its name:

S – Skills
T – Training
E – Evaluation
E – Education
P – Placement SPAN

The objectives of our STEEP SPAN transitional programme are:

- ☐ To develop with the curriculum vocational evaluations.
- ☐ To offer inservice training to educators, businessmen, and community leaders about the curriculum changes and plans.
- ☐ To conduct curriculum revision to include entry level skills.

- ☐ To provide within the curriculum skills training, work behaviour, and personal/social adjustment.
- ☐ To provide experience-based community education.
- ☐ To develop a work-behaviour checklist.
- ☐ To develop follow-up transitional IEPs.
- ☐ To have an Advisory Board comprised of parents, students, and business representatives.
- ☐ To develop a handbook which identifies the community employment services available to students with handicapping conditions.
- ☐ To develop an interagency, direction service component for the successful transition of handicapped students from school to the world of work.

The programme began with 17 students and is currently serving 36 students. The project has served a total of 190 students over the past five years. One hundred and fifty-three students received complete services and 37 received only an evaluation.

Assessment

The STEEP SPAN evaluation component was established and became fully operational in the middle of the first year of the project. The assessment component is staffed by three staff members who work with students on an individual basis. In addition to extensive school-administered academic and vocational interest testing, life-skills and manipulative testing is also an integral part of the evaluation. The students are provided with paper and pencil tests as well as hands-on evaluation. The McCarron Dial and the MESA testing instruments are used. The students are also assessed in physical and mental aptitudes, vocational interest areas, daily living skills, cognitive-verbal skills, sensory-motor skills, best learning style, work habits, behaviours and emotional strengths and needs. When a student is referred for a vocational evaluation, the STEEP SPAN staff and the staff of the student's home school meet with the student and his or her parent(s) to explain why the assessment has been requested and what will happen during the process. Once the assessment is completed, the same 'team' is reassembled to discuss the results and the recommendations. A written report is developed for each student. This report then becomes the basis for the development of the individual transition educational programme.

We have found that many of the students show little knowledge of their vocational abilities and the vocational options available to them outside the school. The students in the programme appear to be very responsive to the vocational evaluation. They demonstrate a great deal of enthusiasm in learning their vocational interests, aptitudes, and abilities. The written report of the evaluation has been a significant tool in developing the student's Individual Transitional Programme (ITP) and is a primary source of information to the student's parents. The purpose of the ITP is to outline a specific individual transition programme to assist the student with successful transition from school to the world of work. We have developed a four-year, long-range transitional plan for each student in the programme. The team develops a folder for each student that clearly outlines the student's goals, objectives, test results, and work performance over the four years of high school.

ITP

The full-time Vocational Adjustment Coordinator works with the students, their families, and their employers as a part of the ITP to assist the student in achieving successful implementation of the transition. Each student's programme contains a work-study programme. First, the student spends a portion of the day in an academic component which covers various functionally orientated areas. The student might take maths, basic reading, social studies, or English classes that are practically (functionally) directed to learning those skills that are needed to become a functioning contributing member of society.

Second, the work component in the ITP is an on-the-job experience. The student learns work-related skills directed towards the actual job and to job-related areas: time on task, workplace social behaviour, and being on time for work. In addition to the work-study skills, the programme offers the student an opportunity to practise job interview skills and to learn other adult living skills, such as community involvement and recreational options.

Community outreach

Identifying job sites for the students in the programme has not been difficult. The Independence, Missouri Chamber of Commerce and local businesses have been very supportive of our efforts on behalf of handicapped students. The Vocational Adjustment Coordinator has developed a handbook with various job offerings. We have used the *Sorkin Directory* which lists all of the businesses and industries in the seven-county metropolitan area. This has been extremely helpful in locating prospective employers and has diminished the need for the handbook. In addition, we have worked with the Area Vocational Technical School and the Union Arts programme of the Greater Kansas City Building and Construction Trades Council to identify those employers and union training programmes open to our students. We currently have a list of all employment services provided in the Independence and Eastern Jackson County area. The staff has visited each of these agencies to determine what services are currently available to handicapped students and the level of support provided for handicapped students. There are many employers in the metropolitan area who are anxious to employ our students; those employers are generally pleased with the performance of our students and their work effort and accomplishments.

The School District of Independence has developed a transition booklet for students, parents, and employers. The intent of this booklet was to give the reader some basic information about transition and the STEEP SPAN project. We have disseminated over 250 booklets to parents, students, employers, and other school districts from around the nation.

Comparison with similar international programmes

Some of the barriers to successful transition identified internationally – such as unemployment rate, national government policies (ie employment quotas), the size of the community, and the social services available to handicapped students on reaching adulthood – have not been a problem. Perhaps, they were not a barrier to the programme development because we were able to adjust for them as a result of exploring the experiences of our European colleagues. The unemployment rate is such in our community that there are a sufficient number of entry-level jobs for our students. Government policies have in fact assisted the programme. The United States tax structure offers incentives to employers who hire handicapped workers.

While we have not experienced the barriers identified internationally, we did experience *some* barriers. There are identifiable barriers to successful transition in our community which may be present but not discussed in other international areas. These barriers are provincialism, transportation, and parent objection. The issue of provincialism comes into play through the other school districts and even through other vocational placement programmes in our own school district. Most of the 16 school districts in Jackson County provide some type of transitional services to their handicapped students. It is very difficult to get these districts to work together to serve the students from among all the districts. Each district wants to take care of their own. It is felt that this does hinder the successful transition of some students who might be better served if the districts cooperated more in evaluation, intervention, and placement.

Transportation is always a barrier. Independence and Eastern Jackson County are suburban and rural. There is little public transportation to allow students to get to jobs. Very many job sites are available but they are several miles away from the student, and the student has no means of transportation. It would be wonderful if in every metropolitan area there were public or private contracted transportation for these students to get to job sites. Finally, we have had three students who were placed on the job at an entry-level position either in food service or physical labour positions. The students were not successful in the placements because their parents felt that the assigned jobs were socially or educationally 'beneath' their youngsters. Even with parent counselling, these parents did not believe that their children should be in the particular job placement. Remember that the students had been assessed, trained, and identified as capable for the positions in which they were placed. Often, the parents were not openly negative about their youngster's employment and would, in fact, seem to support the employment while at a staffing meeting. It was their lack of day-to-day support in matters like transportation that contributed to the creation of unsuccessful student attitudes.

Evaluation

Like our international colleagues, we also found four areas which influence placement: pre-placement training, job coaching, mediating with the employer, and the relationship between the Vocational Adjustment Coordinator and the employer. Pre-placement training focuses on issues such as work ethics, workplace behaviour, work attitude, communication skills, and dress code. Many of our students had to be taught these items. We have a stimulated work environment in the programme that helps teach these skills in a more realistic setting. We have had community leaders and advisory board members come to our project and provide workshops for our students on clothing and clothing selection, workplace behaviour, work ethics, and how to get along on the job. The students have responded favourably to these efforts.

The job coach has been an invaluable support to many students and employers. A workplace is more likely to be successful when the coach can be there and 'ensure' that the job will be done. The job coach and/or the Vocational Adjustment Coordinator often work very hard at developing a close working relationship with the employer. We want the employers to know that we are there to be sure that the placement works. We are willing to help to mediate disputes and teach the students how to deal with those that arise in the workplace.

As with our international colleagues, our post-secondary experience with students has been rather limited to date. While we do some follow-up on the students, once they leave our school programme and graduate from high school our formal contact with them is limited. We have had several students attend post-secondary programmes at the community college in computer/data processing, real estate, and business. We have had several students attend the cosmetology school. Several students attended vocational trade schools in auto mechanics, clerical/business, and one in a para-legal training programme. While the preliminary data on the students would indicate success in post-secondary training, it is still too early to determine the successfulness of these programmes. The students who have attended a post-secondary programme have been diagnosed Learning Disabled or Learning Disabled/Behaviour Disordered. We know and hope to demonstrate that the post-secondary programme shows that students with special needs who have transition training can be more successful.

Summary

As a direct result of working with international colleagues, the School District of Independence began a programme within the secondary schools to assist handicapped students in making a successful transition from school to the world of adult living. We were able to learn from our colleagues and to benefit from their experiences. Information on their international work helped us to identify locally the barriers to transition and to indicate the characteristics that would aid the development of a successful programme. Armed with this information, the school district began a transition programme and has operated it for five years. The programme has been successful in placing students in suitable work sites and teaching them skills to be successful in the community.

22. International education of the highly able

Joan Freeman

In education, there is no escape from politics, nor for that matter from cultural influences. These truths become emphasized in the education of the highly able; in the same way that these exceptional individuals function at an extreme, so too do attitudes towards them. To consider international variations in the education of the gifted, enables some conclusions to be drawn about systems which appear to work well for them and which may be transferable to other countries. However, it is often difficult to extricate a nation's cultural outlook from its specific educational practices.

I am concentrating on three major cultural, rather than geographical, divisions in which there are relatively distinct forms of provision for the highly able. They overlap considerably, in that pockets of all kinds exist within each division, but any other division, such as into fluid and rigid societies, is at least as value-laden. These divisions are: first, the Western World – including Western Europe, North America, and Australasia; second, Eastern Europe – the countries that were Communist until 1989/90; and third, the Developing World – Africa, South America, and the Far East.

International concern for the gifted

In all societies, the reasons for concern about the highly able are dual – to serve the individuals in their personal fulfilment, and to serve the community. This special concern for the highly able is humane (at the very least) and will eventually increase knowledge to help enhance everybody's life, although a high intelligence is not necessarily the foundation of good leadership or superior morality. For example, a child with an exceptionally high IQ may have been brought up in an overly scholarly regimen, which could produce either a religious dictator, or an academic professor who lacks both social competence and the ability to cope with others' demands (Miller 1990). The highly able are neither more nor less moral than anyone else.

Experimental education for highly able children is increasing and the results are becoming more readily available to teachers, among whom concern for the gifted is growing steadily. However, as teachers in most of the world are only just beginning to accept the idea that gifted children do need special provision, this is often uneven and dependent on individual efforts.

There is a need to develop policies for the highly able on an international basis, but the greatest care must be taken in their preparation. They should make full use of the research knowledge we are accumulating, because opinions are merely opinions, and should always be seen as such. What is valued as high ability in one part of the world may not be seen as such in another – such as a trance state which is valued in Thailand, but may put the child in the hands of a clinical psychologist in the West.

Some international problem areas

There are two major, pervasive influences which often prevent the identification and development of gifted potential, and their effects are cumulative for each individual. The first is socioeconomic status – even in the relatively rich West and in the 1990s. The second is gender stereotyping, which slots boys and girls into areas of study that are not necessarily the most appropriate for their abilities. When children are nominated by parents or teachers, without testing, as gifted, this usually results in two boys being presented for every girl. The physically handicapped are often missed too, since giftedness which is not obvious or all-round can be difficult for teachers to spot and cope with.

In multicultural societies, children of non-majority cultures have to adapt to both home and school, and consequently may not fulfil the expectations for gifted pupils in the educational system. For example, the children's spoken language and self-expression may be considerably better in their home language, but to find this out requires efforts by teachers towards close communication with parents, probably including home visits. This consideration also applies to children born in inner cities who may have limited school language ability but excellent 'street language', causing them to be relatively non-communicative in the classroom. It applies also to the children's performance on nationally standardized tests of ability. The culture in which children feel comfortable can even be set to work against achievement at school, in the simplest sense of 'them and us'. This often occurs in an educational system which is imposed from above, without adequate concern for the real needs of the recipients.

Acceleration is not uncommon for gifted children worldwide, as it is the easiest way a school can manage them. Alternatively, a school may just have one fast stream or even one teacher working faster with a bright group, most frequently for mathematics. This is a form of acceleration 'without tears', avoiding the frequently accompanying problems of this move, such as immaturity relative to others in the class, difficult peer relations, or small physical size, when one child is very much younger in the teaching group. Acceleration may also be offered in certain subjects for individual children, if the school can cope with its timetabling. In some countries, there are specialist teachers to provide guidance for the education of the gifted.

Research evidence indicates the importance of both material and cultural provision if children's abilities are to be developed to an exceptionally high level. I have been following up both gifted and control children in Britain since 1974:

all the 210 children, their families and schools were visited and questioned. The children's emotional adjustment was found to be independent of their measured IQs. However, their scholastic achievements were significantly affected by the provision of learning materials and tuition, as well as by the family culture. The follow-up results have reaffirmed the message from the original study – that gifted children need adequate material and teaching provision to realise their potential at both school and home. Relationships between teachers and pupils were also seen to affect the pupils' self-concepts and thus their achievements. Some children's gifts appeared to have been abused, in the sense that their education was intensely focused on examinations to the detriment of their creative side, so that some had taken examination success alone as the source of their self-esteem (Freeman 1991).

The Western World

Most children's physical needs are being met in the Western World. Indeed, the common aim of free compulsory education for all children, continuing with the availability of further education throughout people's lives, has been almost accomplished. This means that energy has been freed to refocus on improving educational opportunities. Although national resources and outlook are varied, there is a considerable commonality of approach to educational research and development, built on the scientific and philosophical tradition which spread from the 'old world' of Western Europe to the 'new worlds' of North America and Australasia. However, more subtle differences in outlooks between the thrusting new and the complacent old are apparent in what they offer the highly able.

In Europe, as the political edifices of many previously Communist countries crumbled, thousands of bright young people seeking a better life have streamed into the western democracies. They bring with them different attitudes to the education of the highly able, and a few are even bringing world-class teaching expertise in subjects such as sports, gymnastics, singing, ballet, circus, and mathematics.

The style of interest they bring is different too. Eastern Europe has generally been more concerned with the practicalities of teaching and outcome, whereas the West has a more prolific output of theory. At its extreme, the difference seems to be like that between the training of young gymnasts on a trampoline and the production of academic research papers which conclude that we need more research. Yet, because of these recent political changes, the extra money and provision which have been put into the promotion of competitive excellence may now be redirected within Eastern countries, so that the two halves of Europe may eventually become more balanced in top-level achievements.

Historically, Europe has had hundreds of years of selection in education, which still lives in its collective memory, and to a small extent in reality. Although this was originally by social status and money, the Middle Ages saw the beginnings of selection by ability for some boys. Present-day British grammar schools, German gymnasium, and French lycées, are schools which emerged from the 15th century, to provide academic tuition, originally in preparation for clerical and church positions.

Selection by ability gripped the whole of Britain in 1945, when every child in the country was tested at 11 years-old for entry to the grammar schools – the Eleven Plus exam. It succeeded in providing bright, working-class children with the opportunity to go to previously middle-class schools, but failed to make allowance for individual development, and has almost entirely been abandoned. Among other problems, there was much incorrect placement, as well as wide variation in the number of grammar school places between education authorities. In the 1990s most British children, like their counterparts on the European continent and in the rest of the Western World, attend comprehensive, all-ability, neighbourhood schools. The difference is that in Britain and the USA, about 7 per cent of children go to private schools.

Nevertheless, many comprehensive schools throughout the Western World are still internally selective, having fast streams or tracks, or other forms of division of the children for different levels of tuition. Younger children may be sorted in class by more subtle and flexible distribution into groups, identified by the teacher's estimate of their abilities.

Western attitudes to high ability

In most Western countries, the training of teachers for guiding the learning of gifted children is patchy. It is possible, for example, to take a doctorate in teaching gifted children in a few parts of the USA, but in Western Europe it would be difficult to find even a teaching diploma which provided that kind of instruction. However, in Munich, a new college for teachers of the gifted is due to open in 1992, and a new postgraduate course is about to start in Switzerland. There is a little input on the subject at initial training level, but short in-service courses are growing everywhere.

For most Western teachers, the spectre of élitism, whether of wealth or ability, is their major apprehension. They do not like categorizing children, and have serious doubts about the validity of psychological tests of ability. Also, they often feel that giving more time and money to the already gifted would take resources from those who have more obvious needs, such as the handicapped. There is still a long way to go before the majority of teachers in the West become convinced that gifted children need special attention, and are prepared to give it to them.

However, in its individualistic way, the West engenders voluntary groups who exist to make good what they see as gaps in provision. Most countries have at least one association for the gifted, run by parents, indeed, many have several (often competing) associations. In fact, the amount of interest in a country could be judged by counting up the number of these parent associations. These usually run out-of-school sessions for the children and their siblings, as well as summer schools and weekend conferences in special subjects. Although they may also investigate what facilities are available and give help to individuals, their overall aim is the greater recognition of gifted children and the encouragement of appropriate provision for them within normal schools. Mensa is an international non-scientific association, largely social, to which people can belong by passing a test, set by the association. The European Council for High Ability (ECHA), based in Bonn, Germany, is the only association of psychologists and educators which uses evidence rather than opinion, and which crosses all European national boundaries.

There are hundreds of privately funded national competitions and activity centres for the gifted in the West. Many countries have a Young Scientist of the Year, Young Engineer, Young Musician, etc. International competitions include the Mathematics Olympiad and Foreign Language Competitions. In many countries, local education authorities and individual schools may receive financial help from industry for specific projects, such as scientific field trips or collective creativity on a technical project.

School provision

There are very few special schools for the gifted in the West and these are normally for the teaching of the arts – music, fine art, dance and drama – though in the USA, a school for 'rapid learners' was set up as long ago as 1868. Some very selective private schools could be said to be schools for the intellectually gifted, though their curriculum is rarely different from that of other schools. Because western education is generally not centralized, most decisions being made by local authorities, provision for the gifted in normal schools is very variable in quality and quantity. However, this is often supplemented by weekend and summer courses, which are either inexpensive or without cost to parents. In addition, there are often good links to help the gifted between schools and organizations, such as museums, laboratories, industry, and theatres. In the USA and Canada, particularly good links exist with courses in higher education, so that bright pupils may either attend special courses and gain credits or go to university at an early age. In these countries, as in Australasia, national governments have enacted laws to provide for the gifted – a situation not yet existing in Europe.

However, in many western schools falling rolls and the tightening of educational purse-strings, have narrowed the curriculum. There is also some disillusionment among the young as to the value of working hard for examinations. Counselling and guiding the highly able, which might counteract this feeling and help where they are vulnerable, is not widely available in Europe, and at present there are no signs of its growth. It is only some parents' organizations, primarily in Great Britain, Germany, and The Netherlands, which offer that help. Nor is there adequate training of teachers in the understanding and skills they need to teach very bright children; in this respect, Europeans can learn much from Canada and the United States, where counsellors in schools are usual.

Encouraging creativity is also a problem, and here the European outlook is more set in tradition than that of North America, so that it often allows talent to slip away unnoticed. Teachers are still distracted from recognizing high-level potential by out-of-date notions of appearance and culture. Sometimes, the most creative European youngsters have to find out by themselves how to overcome the barriers of their social constraints. Nor are most European educational systems set up to encourage creativity in general communities. European education needs to teach in a more creative, open-minded way in all lessons.

The lowering of economic and educational boundaries for the countries of the

European Community (EC) in 1992, is likely to provide further opportunities for the highly able. Although the dominant language will remain English, the internationalisation of education has meant an increase in foreign language learning, for which the EC is financing the Lingua project, not restricted to member nations. There are also other communication initiatives, such as money for student exchanges on courses in higher education. The European Council for High Ability (ECHA) is supporting communication between the West German foreign language competition and others in Britain and France, as well as their expansion.

Eastern Europe

Education has been an integral part of society in Communist theory and practice. Although all teaching is ultimately concerned with producing the 'right' attitudes in the taught, Soviet education has done so openly and specifically; the goals were clear and relatively inflexible to change. Consequently, highly able children who were able to 'fit-in' stood a greater chance of being outstandingly successful, whereas in the West, there are so many ways in which a child can find its way through the system that a great variety of outcomes is always possible. This can be seen, for example, in the outstanding performances of Soviet athletes, trained from childhood for that role.

There are over 12 million children at school in the Soviet Union, in a system which has experienced only relatively small modifications since Lenin outlined its aims in 1917. The changes that have occurred were designed to make it more effective – such as improving vocational guidance, the recent introduction of more modern teaching aids, and, most well known, the institution of special schools for talented children in Khrushchev's educational reforms of the late 1950s (Dunstan 1988). This last was brought about by the intense international technological competition of the time, particularly in space programmes, and also by the poor economic growth of the Soviet Union (though the full extent of this has not become clear until recently).

The special schools are either boarding (mathematics and physics), or day (language schools, which taught all subjects but sometimes entirely in a foreign language). In addition, special education for the highly able is offered in the neighbourhood comprehensive (all-comer) schools, in the form of elective courses (options) taken in addition to the basic curriculum. Choosing them wisely can make a positive difference to a pupil's chances of getting to university, though their provision can be determined by such matters as the teachers' workload. In general, academic specialization is delayed as long as possible, usually until adolescence.

Education in the Soviet Union appears to provide an example of how it should be done – a model of equal access to opportunity, which even includes the highly able. Children from all backgrounds can be selected for special schools, which cater for their specific educational needs, and the country can be seen to benefit thereby. Girls too appear to be given the same education as boys in the sciences. But the truth is less inspiring: the Western European concept of a liberal education which teaches pupils to think for themselves was as alien to Peter the Great as to Stalin.

Education Russian-style begins in kindergarten, where the children learn revolutionary songs. At the primary school, the way they learn each subject is designed to make a specific contribution to political education. Science lays the foundation for a materialistic view of the world and foreign languages provide access to the works of 'brotherly communist and workers' parties' (Tomiak 1984). History lessons in particular (as in many other countries) provide the 'evidence' to show how the system in power is right and other systems based on capitalism are morally wrong and so must fail while socialism triumphs. However, all history textbooks are currently being rewritten, as part of *glasnost*.

Since the 1930s, the Soviet Union's aim has been to 'polytechnize' the curriculum, though this has only been partially successful. To do this, the more abstract aspects of the curriculum have been diminished, in favour of the more practical, especially in maths and science. Real-life skills which would be linked to productivity in the farms and factories, were to be enhanced so that the children would be best served by practising their manual skills there. But teachers, parents, and pupils all objected. The more able pupils did not see themselves as entering the world of manual work, and their aspirations did not fit in with the current state plans. In the Soviet Union, as in so many other countries, highly able pupils aim to stay in education and end up as professionals in physics, engineering, medicine, etc.

The specialist schools for the highly able were set up in the 1930s as centres of excellence in languages, sport and music, but took a new turn in the 1960s. The Russians then started what in the United States were later called 'Magnet' schools. Ordinary schools were made specialist in a particular subject area to provide 'profound' study, where excellence was considered to be needed by the state, most particularly in science, mathematics and computer technology. To achieve this, the schools were allowed to break their original all-comer intake and to select entrants. Matthews (in Tomiak 1984) estimates that there are about 290 of such schools, and if one adds the Olympiad movement and the widespread enrichment courses provided in ordinary schools, Russian provision for the gifted seems generous.

However, all the way through the setting up of the present Soviet system, the expressed doubts – familiar in international educational circles – about keeping balance in the children's development, and whether and how to select in any way, did bring about some compromises. For example, there are no separate classes for the gifted in comprehensive schools, as there are in the USA, but instead, differentiation in education takes place both during and after normal school. By 1973, it was said that 54 per cent of pupils were taking the extra options, and differentiated teaching for the highly able has now been accepted on these terms for many years. About 3 per cent of secondary schools (around 1,500) are special schools for the highly able, but as they are small, they probably cater for only about 2 per cent of the school population.

However, girls, unless they are lucky, are still in a decidedly less good position than boys to flex their gifts (Hansson and Liden 1984). The Soviet Union is a vast tract of the earth, and some of it is still functioning in centuries-old ways. In parts of Soviet Central Asia, for example, girls are still sold as brides at the age of 13, and the price drops with the extent of education she has had. Even in the cities of European Russia, gender stereotyping has kept the schoolgirls sewing, while the boys do metalwork; nor do girls apply proportionately to the science schools, as they believe that boys are better at science. And when they grow up, it is now well recognized that Russian machismo keeps women at both the workplace and the kitchen sink. Soviet education for women still has a long way to go.

Additionally, opportunities for bright children from farms and workers' collectives, where 70 per cent of the children live, are not good. The options system, for example, must have a minimum number of children to operate, which is difficult in the smaller rural school. Also because special schools are usually set in the centres of cities, some have only a 6 per cent intake of workers' children, a figure halved by the age of 16. Their pupils are far more likely to come from the intelligentsia and white-collar workers (see Dunstan 1988 for specific figures); somehow their parents are better able to get their children in, whether they were talented or not. This can be seen in the tiny numbers going on from the language schools to study language at university, though their chances of entering higher education at all are improved by having been at those schools. One reason for the situation is that the children did not have to pass any aptitude test to enter them.

Soviet criticism of specialist education in similar to that given to the selective gymnasia and grammar schools of Western Europe - that they are overly academic in a world which is turning more and more towards vocational matters. Yet, in tune with the West, there seems to be an overall decline in university applications in the Soviet Union, which may be a reflection of the greater pull of vocational training, away from theory. The options system, though, does provide enormous opportunity for young people to excel in subject areas which are seen to be useful to society, such as aircraft construction or fashion design. The differences in the shortage of resources available to fuel special education tends to be of labour and materials in Eastern Europe and funds for this purpose in the West.

The most recent and approved 1986–90 plan of the Soviet Academy of Pedagogical Sciences promotes differentiated teaching in accordance with the pupil's abilities. It recommends that the basic school curriculum be altered for the highly able, so that they can study subjects in greater depth, from a wider viewpoint, and with more concern for the future application of this knowledge. This should be particularly available for the senior years, and it should be aided by specialist literature, specific assignments, and a more creative approach. Language schools have been increased in number, and in line with *perestroika* (the restructuring of Soviet society) a National Centre on Creative Giftedness has been formed by the Soviet Academy of Pedagogical Sciences. This is for research into high ability learning and into appropriate teaching methods, with heavy emphasis on creativity in all its facets (Matyushkin 1990). There are constant interchanges between Soviet and foreign schoolchildren, and the future for the highly able in Russia looks promising.

The Developing World

The Developing World is more dependent than other parts on the productive power of human resources; in most of it, however, basic educational provision is limited, if not missing altogether. Brazil, for example, has 20 per cent total illiteracy, 50 per cent of children not finishing their fourth year of primary school, and 41 per cent living in extreme poverty. Unfortunately, when the need for health and welfare is urgent, the education of the most highly able children, possessing the talents most needed for their country's future prosperity, is pushed aside as irrelevant.

In parts of the People's Republic of China, however, a great deal of research and provision for their ablest has been offered. Several big cities, such as Shanghai, have Children's Palaces that act as sieves to find bright, motivated children. Whole classes attend to try out the lavish provision for learning – everything from computers to bicycles. If children are keen to come, they will be allowed back to make progress in their chosen area; the keener they are, the more teaching they are given, but those who lack interest are not allowed back. The standards reached by the children who want to learn are world-class, but this kind of provision is not available to the vast majority of children. There is nationwide research, in progress for over quarter of a century, going on into the attributes of Chinese gifted children, who appear to have similar ways of thought and behaviour to gifted children in other countries (Zha Zi-xiu 1990).

In the Developing World, there are two major psychological reasons for failing to provide for the highly able. First, insecurity encourages short-term patching-up solutions, because who knows what drought and wars the future may bring. The result is that when scarce resources are spread too thinly, the results are also thin, so that, for example, expensive foreign experts have to be brought in because there are not enough homegrown ones. And there does not seem to be a shortcut, in that the promotion of high-level ability and skills takes at least a generation to be effective.

Secondly, even more than lack of money, probably the greatest difference between attitudes and provision for the highly able in the Developing World and the more industrialized parts respectively, is that of cultural outlook. This may even specifically prohibit new ways of confronting local problems, thus inhibiting production and achievements, and keeping the country poor and backward.

Any child living in a shanty town, obliged to forage for a livelihood from the early years, is simply not open to gifted-level development. Girls especially are often obliged to take on an extra load of domestic work at home, and are in charge of younger siblings for many hours, even at night when their parents are out at work. In poor areas, parents are not able to help the children educationally, as they themselves cannot read and write, but they usually do what they can.

A typical school serving such an area has very few resources, certainly no complex, up-to-date teaching materials for children who are often part-time attenders, if they come at all. Sometimes, in order to fit in those who want to come, they have to operate a shift system, each group being taught for a few hours a day. Classes tend to have wide age-ranges, which makes teaching difficult and as teachers are usually badly paid, their turnover is high, so that individual care is very difficult to provide. Lessons have to be basic for most of the children – reading, writing and arithmetic. An important part of educating such very poor children is feeding them, and governments sometimes try to do this through the schools with free food and milk. For some children, this is the prime incentive to come to school.

The first action must be to assess and mobilise all teaching resources to their greatest advantage, because the tools for teaching, such as books and technology, may be poor. The effort has to be entirely practical and seen to work, both for the teachers and administrators, who may have very different cultural approaches. For example, recent surveys of attitudes towards education for the gifted among teachers and administrators in the Asia/Pacific region showed that these were different from North American teacher attitudes (Roldan 1986; Gallagher *et al.* 1983).

Most Asian teachers felt that government support and funding for this work are vital, compared with the USA, where teachers were more inclined to seek private support. The Asians were also against the separation of gifted children for their education, seeking to make better use of the facilities they already had before paying for more – although they well recognised the limitations of insufficient equipment. Americans were much more concerned with administration, whereas Asian teachers were relatively disinterested, being decidedly more child-orientated. In fact, the highest ranked aim of Asian teachers – to exercise their pupils' individual talents using enrichment and personal attention – was the lowest ranking aim among the American teachers. Asian teachers saw their greatest problem as one of specific teacher training, closely followed by general disinterest and lack of awareness of the subject. What most would appreciate is the impetus and knowledge they could gain from meeting others with interest and experience in this area of education, which is difficult in this widespread region. Perhaps surprisingly, they did not complain about a lack of materials, as teachers in the Western World commonly do. The policy makers who were questioned were unanimous in their support of special education for the gifted, the most frequent reason for this being that it is for the good of the whole community.

No matter how poor a nation, there is nearly always the possibility of finding some way of nurturing the hearts and minds of its brightest children, those who are capable of breaking through cultural and economic boundaries to reach out for what the rest of the world has to offer, while keeping the best of their own ways. The Developing World does not need more scholars of the old-fashioned type, absorbing information to reproduce in examinations. Rather, the need is for native problem solvers, set in an understanding of that culture; it is for creative people who understand the past and can apply its lessons to future changes.

Yet in order to focus scarce educational attention on those who can give that service, children of high potential have to be identified. There is a variety of means for this, such as tests restandardized to national norms or practical demonstrations by the children of their potential to develop to a high degree. Combined teacher/parent identification is extremely valuable in a cultural context, although it has often been criticized in Western terms. The education that the selected children would receive would, of course, have to be appropriate to the objectives.

Three major considerations are worth looking at:

1. Cross-cultural coordination: provision within a culture should be coordinated with what is going on in other cultures. Too intense a focus on the local meaning can increase, rather than decrease the limited vision which people have for solving their familiar problems.

2. Presentation of teaching materials: this should be sufficiently attractive to assure that it is acceptable and is in fact used. Excellent teaching material lies gathering dust all over the world, because it does not seem worth the teacher's while to learn how to apply it. The material should also be seen to be working, to give encouragement to teachers, at least in the interim. Feedback from pupils is valuable for this, preferably in the form of demonstration. The preparation of teaching ideas and practice which is designed for a particular setting, should involve both teachers and parents at all stages of gathering information and the ideas into action. It is more time-consuming, but always worth while to have everyone concerned working together.
3. Communication: it is vital for the success of any procedure that it be part of a greater national whole. Others within the same country may be working along similar lines, and it makes sense to coordinate ideas and experience. It also gives added strength to those who are moving into new and sometimes unpopular areas of education, that they do not feel isolated. However, to get these people together requires money, which may be very difficult to obtain in developing countries.

In the end, real help has to come from the top, from the government for its own children. Yet it is possible to help children in poor circumstances to realize their abilities by using applied psychology in teaching, the single most important difference from what usually happens is one of style. Taking a pre-packaged educational programme off the shelf is not the answer, because the teacher has to adapt the package approach to the facts of the children's lives in that locality. For example, applied psychology means improving motivation by taking genuine account in daily lessons of the children's (rather than the teacher's) concerns and values. One problem which such children may have in common is that in coping with their everyday obligations, they have difficulty in thinking and planning ahead; this impairs their developing feelings of control over their lives, as well as their development as all-round people.

Conclusions

Every country has limited resources and is concerned to know how best to use them; this question of management is politically influenced. It is especially so with regard to the education of the highly able, because of the apparent contradiction between aiming for excellence and aiming for equality, so that the needs of the gifted minority may seem to be in competition with mass interest. The choice is essentially threefold:

1. Whether to offer an undifferentiated education to all; or
2. Whether to pre-select some children for a deeper and broader education; or
3. Whether to provide equality of access to those who want it.

Politically too, policy decision making in education is becoming increasingly professionalized, where advisors such as university professors of economics or statisticians, are gaining greater access to power. They operate in policy institutes, think-tanks, and universities – producing, among other things, national education policies. Sometimes, though, the outcomes are closer to ideology than to a holistic concern for the children whom the policies affect.

Educating the gifted as all-round people, who are to make the most of their abilities while retaining balance in their lives, is not dissimilar from the normal educational aims for all children. Their different needs lie essentially in the intensity of their learning abilities, especially in their greater facility for speed and depth of learning. This calls for differences of teaching style, as well as for competent, imaginative teachers, who should also be aware of their pupils' emotional development. Such matters as self-confidence, perceptual difficulties and personal relationships, are as important as the mastery of skills and knowledge.

What is true for the gifted is basically true for all children, but the gifted are different because of their exceptional abilities; they have special vulnerabilities and special strengths. In all countries, it is important for them to be recognized for what they are, because work which is pitched at the level of the national average may restrict the ablest. However, in many countries, the overriding problem seems to be the poorly organized system of educational provision; research evidence has shown that both material and cultural provision are vital for the development of abilities to an exceptionally high level (Freeman 1985).

But whatever the educational system, there are always some children, however packed with potential, who fail to take advantage of it because something has gone wrong. This could be as little as a long-running disagreement with an important teacher, or as big as being born in a poor area where obstetric facilities are poor and birth injury causes you to be spastic and thus unrecognized as potentially able. Maybe much of the future for the highly able lies outside educational establishments, with the world of commerce and industry, rather than in the learning and reproducing that so much of our present education appears to demand. Already, work experience is helping gifted youngsters to see beyond traditional school- and gender-orientated choices of study.

Specialist education for the highly able is not a priority in poor countries, though the argument for training a potential leadership élite holds some sway. In Kenya, for example, a highly selective school, endowed by Jomo Kenyatta, is giving children something like an expensive English private school education, including Shakespeare and Latin. The argument for that choice of subjects is that it trains the mind – and has been seen to work. Nevertheless, experimental work towards an appropriate education for highly able children is gaining momentum. Results are filtering through to teachers internationally, even though in many parts of the world, they are only just beginning to recognize such pupils' special needs. As awareness grows, so does provision, even if it is often dependent on individual efforts and local conditions.

The teacher's dilemma is to be concerned with basic learning, while allowing for individual differences in its acquisition, and the gifted particularly need flexibility in their teaching. Some countries turn to relatively structured teaching programmes – a defined procedure with a stated outcome, to be accomplished within a given span of time, closely followed by an evaluation to see the extent to which the aim has been fulfilled. As a European, I am wary of the implied rigidity of that approach for the highly able, feeling that a deep appreciation of history, geography and mathematics does not depend on structured lessons, but more probably on a good caring teacher and mental freedom to explore. That older approach plants children in a nourishing ground of stimulation and information, and waters them well with encouragement. However, the composition of that compost includes both the manifest curriculum and the hidden one, the kind which comes through the unrecognized pressures and expectations of the social context. Both have to be carefully balanced if the teaching is to be effective.

Encouragement of creativity, however, is a problem. The barrier is often tradition, which may allow talents to be overlooked, distracting attention from high-level potential by received notions of appearance and behaviour. Sometimes, creative youngsters have to find out by themselves how to overcome the barriers of their social constraints. Nor are most educational systems set up to encourage creativity, which requires teaching itself to be creative and open-ended, and in all lessons. To work well together towards these goals calls for the involvement of the brightest minds – minds which are flexible enough to be alert to problems and solutions which may not yet even have been recognized.

What we need is a model educational policy for the highly able, which each country could adapt and modify for use. It must include the evidence that already exists, and such conclusions as could logically be drawn from them, with some input from the experiences of both teachers and parents. This basic policy should not only be for children, but ideally take a life-span approach, from infancy to old age – an aspect on which very little research has been published. Indeed, a pertinent factor in the search for highly able individuals in the western workplace, unlike the Developing World, is the increasing average age of many populations. Europe especially is experiencing a shortage of young people. Since it takes many years and costs a great deal of money to train new personnel, it is becoming more usual to look among older high achievers in the workplace, and at women.

The most able have a need for *consistent* challenge, and there are myriad ways in which it can be provided, using the resources we already possess. There is recognizable if slow progress towards this. Here are just two examples of new and workable ideas, which are applicable worldwide:

1. Open learning centres could be provided in school or community buildings, outside school hours, with equipment and teachers available for all who want to use it, ie without selection. These centres would also act as a learning support for regular teachers. They should be well coordinated both with other educational services and with industry, and not simply act as places for teachers to offload their problems.
2. Team-teaching around a theme, where teachers reinforce their work by coordinating their approach, covering the many generated aspects of the theme. An example could be the wheel, bringing in the physics of movement, aesthetics, the philosophy of the acceptance of new ideas etc. Nursery practice actually provides a model for this global approach, because little children cannot work in a linear learning pattern, only in a differentiated, wider way.

Internationally, in recent years, there has been a significant growth of interdependence in economic and political matters, which has also promoted genuine cooperation in social and cultural policies. Though there are very many well-meaning people struggling to help the highly able, in the end, real help has to come from the top – from each government for its own children. But in places where education does not have a high priority, the daily battle must continue primarily at ground level with the daily efforts of teachers and parents.

Bibliography

Dunstan, J (1988) Gifted youngsters and special schools. In Riordan, J (ed) *Soviet Education, The Gifted and the Handicapped* Routledge: London

Freeman, J (1985) A pedagogy for the gifted. In Freeman, J (ed) *The Psychology of Gifted Children* John Wiley and Sons: Chichester

Freeman, J (1990) The education of the highly able. In Jones, N (ed) *Special Educational Needs Review* Vol. 3. Falmer Press: Basingstoke

Freeman, J (1991) *Where do Gifted Children Go?* Cassel: London

Gallagher, J J, Weiss, P, Oglesby, K and Thomas, T (1983) *The Status of Gifted/Talented Children's Education: United States Survey of Needs, Practices, and Policies* National/State Leadership Training Institute: Los Angeles

Hansson, C and Liden, L (1984) *Moscow Women* Allison and Busby: London

Mathews, M (1984) *Education in the Soviet Union* Allen and Unwin: London

Matyushkin, A (1990) Gifted and talented children: the nature of giftedness, screening, development *European Journal for High Ability* **1** (0), 72–75

Miller, A (1990) *The Untouched Key; Tracing Childhood Trauma in Creativity and Destructiveness* Virago: London

Roldan, A (1984) Report on a survey of gifted education based on the Fifth World Conference in Manilla. In Cropley, A J, Urban, K U, Wagner, H and Wieczerkowski, W (eds) *Giftedness: A Continuing Worldwide Challenge* Trillium Press: New York

Tomiak, J J (1986) The dilemmas of Soviet Education in the 1980s. In Tomiak, J J (ed) *Soviet Education in the 1980s* Macmillan: London

Zha, Z (1990) Analogical reasoning of supernormal and normal children *European Journal for High Ability* **1** (0), 11–14

Part 5: Future issues in international education

Introduction

Patricia L Jonietz

Earlham College in the United States is a small liberal arts undergraduate college which serves here as an example of the ECIS-affiliated colleges and universities. In his 1988–89 President's report, Richard Wood looks ahead to what the new century may mean to colleges and universities, especially those interested in international education:

> Tomorrow's leader will need to be a broad thinker who can explore vistas with courage. Tomorrow's leadership skills include vision, experimentation, empathy, and negotiation. Globalization will be ubiquitous in the next decades. Travel has changed the world in ways unimaginable at the turn of the last century. The ability to communicate instantly to and from any spot on the earth and in space together with advances in rapid air and land transportation have enabled a major portion of the planet to experience a shared life. National interests are by necessity being supplanted by international consciousness. John Rosenblum, Dean of the University of Virginia's Darden Business School, indicates that future leaders will be required to think in ways which will enable them to understand and transcend international differences. 'The global manager is someone who has the ability to manage new situations, to manage ambiguity, to manage complexity. These are the same words that describe the person who can deal with the new technology or the demographic diversity in this country.' At Earlham, we believe that intercultural education strengthens students' capacity for moral leadership by increasing the range of reasons for acting – by including in that range the needs and concerns of people different from ourselves.

The topic of 'Future Think' is one which affects all participants in international education and international schools. Perhaps those best able to describe the future are those most intimately involved with the past. Joe Blaney, Bernard Ivaldi, Gray Mattern, and Robert Blackburn represent all the past interlocking threads of the history of contemporary international education. All have long backgrounds as thinkers, writers, and doers in international schools: Blaney, formerly Director of the International School in Geneva, currently Head of the United Nations School in New York; Ivaldi, associated with UNIS in Geneva and IBO, serves now as President of ISA; Mattern after years with European

Council of International Schools; and Blackburn, a typical 'third culture' product coming from Ireland to England and then to UWC, IBO, and other international organizations. Each speaks from a life-long commitment to education and a special devotion to international education and international schools.

Blaney says that in a world society which is global and has interests, concerns, and needs (along with its major problems) transcending national boundaries, national systems of education are rapidly becoming obsolete. Yet, there are no models of international systems to guide them towards what they could become. The IB and certain examination schemes – the Cambridge Syndicate being a good example – are components of international systems, but only components. He sees in the existence of a small but excellent group of bona fide international schools, the potential for the beginnings of an international school system. He says that the initiative should be seized to exploit this potential fully, creatively, and effectively.

Ivaldi describes the essential innovative, cultural, economic, and social forces which are in the future and must be faced by the International Schools Association and all international schools.

Mattern posits what he believes should be the chief curricular elements of an international education. These ideas were originally expressed in the opening address at the ECIS Annual Conference in 1989. In science and maths, he is concerned with teaching means not content. In foreign languages, he feels the common requirement of mastery of two languages does not help us to achieve the goal of internationalism although it may help move some towards biculturalism. The choice of which language to study also deserves attention and for non-English speakers one language must be English. In social sciences and humanities, he cites the special problem international schools have in finding an unbiased teaching perspective. He asserts strongly that international schools must explore values as central to their educational mission, and he cites five discrete areas of principle, common to all cultures, which should and can be examined.

Blackburn, in the autumn of 1989, agreed to be interviewed by me on the subject of international education. Although he best represented the generation of men who created so much of what we now describe as 'international education', his focus was on the future. He was excited by the growth of the IB in national schools and the future possibilities of international education in Eastern Europe and the Third World. In a chapter of future think, it seems appropriate to include his personal statement.

23. The international school system

Joseph J Blaney

Rationale

While there are entities known as international schools and an approach to teaching and learning called international education, there does not yet exist an international school system.

The world has already become transnational and multicultural. Economically, scientifically, technologically, and financially it is interdependent and interwoven. Even government is being perceived more in terms of transnational imperatives – witness the coming of age of the UN and developments in Eastern and Western Europe. Educational systems rooted mainly in national concerns and constrained by national ideologies, cannot educate young people to live meaningfully (happily and effectively) in a world society which is global, whose interests, concerns, and needs – along with its major problems – transcend national boundaries. These national systems of education are rapidly becoming obsolete, yet there are no models of international systems to guide them towards what they could become. The IB and certain examination schemes – the Cambridge Syndicate being a good example – are components of international systems, but only components. We have in the existence of a small but excellent group of bona fide international schools, the potential for the beginnings of an international school system. The initiative should be seized to exploit this potential fully, creatively, and effectively.

Definition

An international school system will be non-prescriptive in that its membership will be strictly voluntary, based on shared needs, purposes, and philosophy. It will be a system in the literal sense:

> A set or assemblage of things connected, associated or interdependent, so as to form a complex unity; a whole composed of parts in orderly arrangement according to some schemes or plan; an organized scheme or plan of action, especially one of a complex or comprehensive kind; an orderly or regular method of procedure.

Therefore an international schools system, while non-prescriptive in its membership, will meet the criteria of a system.

Needs

The shared needs are to provide students of international families with a programme of studies and a set of examinations which are continuous, consistent, and uninterrupted as they move about the world when the careers of their parents require periodic transfers from one location to another. A secondary, and in the long term more important, need is to establish and maintain schools which can serve as urgently needed examples to host country educational systems; models of what the education of children and young people ought to be in order to be relevant to the world in which they exist. The schools which are part of the international system will serve as a resource for the demonstration of curricular and pedagogical strategies and techniques, which differ from those of host countries, and as training centres for interested host country education officials and teachers. Clearly, a tenet underlying the creation of an international school system is that national or state systems of education, however rigorous they may be, no longer mirror world society which has been transformed. The major needs that should be met – which ought to be the framework of contemporary schooling – overreach national, cultural, and ethnic boundaries. Central among these needs are the preservation of peace, protection of the environment, elimination of poverty, famine and disease, development of the earth and its resources, control of population growth, and exploration of the seas and outer space. Just as there is universal recognition of the requirement for international political, scientific, and economic structures, there must evolve a parallel recognition of the requirement for an educational structure and system to prepare the young in every country to live effectively in the world as it has become and to contribute to its well-being in meaningful ways. The international education system proposed here meets these needs. Therefore, it represents in its philosophy, purposes, programmes, and practices what national systems must become to make possible the effective education of all the world's children and young people.

Characteristics

The common elements of an international school system are those characteristics or attributes which define it and differentiate it from national systems. The common elements are found within the following categories:

- ☐ philosophy;
- ☐ mission or purpose (goals);
- ☐ curriculum;
- ☐ staffing and enrolment policies;
- ☐ pension, medical, and other staff benefit schemes; and
- ☐ comparable compensation practices.

If these are indeed shared elements – that is to say, if all of the schools in the international school system are alike in these categories – then the movement of students within the system is assured (and greatly enhanced with respect to staff who require motivation to move about as well as portable pension and medical schemes and comparable salaries).

Along with the basic elements shared by the member schools, there should be coordinated, cooperative, and collaborative approaches to:

- ☐ The development of curriculum and curriculum resource materials.
- ☐ The formation and in-service training of teaching staff and administration.
- ☐ The conduct of field research.
- ☐ The establishment of policies and practices which enhance the attainment of system goals.

In addition, here are a few considerations regarding the common elements of the international school system.

Philosophy

The international school system's programme and practices testify to its fundamental values, beliefs, and commitments. These have been well formulated by UNESCO:

- ☐ Recognition and respect for the worth of different cultures and nations.
- ☐ Awareness of the interdependence of all living things, peoples, and nations.
- ☐ The necessity of international understanding, cooperation, tolerance, solidarity, and peace.
- ☐ Respect for universal human rights and fundamental freedoms.
- ☐ Respect for and preservation of the natural environment.
- ☐ Commitment to a more equal sharing of the earth's resources among all of the peoples of the world.
- ☐ Elimination of poverty, hunger, and disease wherever they may exist.
- ☐ Peaceful, cooperative uses of science and technology towards the betterment of global society.

From the above philosophical framework, arise the *purposes* or *goals* of an international school system. The purposes and goals are classified instructionally in much the same ways as those of national or state systems:

- ☐ linguistic, literary, and communicative;
- ☐ mathematical;
- ☐ scientific and technological;
- ☐ aesthetic and creative;
- ☐ moral and ethical;
- ☐ human and social;
- ☐ social service; and
- ☐ health and recreation.

However, the details differ in significant ways from the details of teaching and learning in national or state systems inasmuch as the international school system serves internationally mobile communities of children temporarily residing in a foreign location, and eventually moving to another. They also serve local children who wish to benefit from an international education. The international school system seeks to develop students with:

1. A global view with respect to political, economic, social, technological, and ecological matters because they have learned why and how the implications and ramifications of these matters cross all political and geographic boundaries.
2. A commitment, in demonstrable ways, to the preservation of peace and order in human affairs and to the protection of the natural environment as a global resource.
3. The knowledge, skills, sensitivity, and desire to live and work successfully with others from totally different national or cultural backgrounds.

Curriculum

The curriculum of the international school system is its single most important feature because it manifests the philosophy and achieves the purposes set forth above, both of which are different in large measure, if not in kind, from the philosophies or purposes of national or state systems. The curriculum – more than having an international student body and/or faculty, more than acquiring proficiency in other languages – sets the international school system apart. The development of a comprehensive K–12 curriculum should be the first objective of those schools which agree to establish the international school system. The International Baccalaureate already provides a common exiting curriculum (grades 11 and 12), although its own evolution continues. The IB is both international in character and academically rigorous in content. It leads to the acquisition of a credential recognized by universities around the world. Therefore, it can serve very well the purposes of the proposed international school system. For the remainder of the curriculum (K–10), work done by several schools under the coordination of the International Schools Association may serve as the basis for a curriculum in the middle years. As for the rest of the curriculum for an international school, it remains to be designed.

In so far as possible, the curriculum ought to be developed by the founding schools of the system, involving to the extent practicable, the staff of those schools. This work should be supported by several universities with established reputations in international education. Technology such as fax machines and computer electronic mail will greatly facilitate inter-school cooperation and collaboration in the design and establishment of the curriculum. A careful review ought to be made of the curriculum extant in international as well as national schools, to draw upon the best and most appropriate of what has already been done. The instructional language should be English, with the study of other languages, including mother-tongue instruction, being a chief characteristic of the schools in the international system. The schools within the international system, because they will share a common philosophy and curriculum, should adopt a common structure for organizing the studies of children between 5 and 18 years of age.

Staffing and enrolment

Staff should be carefully recruited so as to represent, without an unreasonable financial burden being placed upon the schools, the major culture areas of the world and as many nationalities as feasible. This will help assure internationality among intellectual traditions and pedagogical approaches; it will also provide the students with a variety of racial, ethnic, and national role models. Both sexes should be equally represented among the teaching and administrative cadres of the schools. Credentials required should be those required for individuals for the position being filled by that individual in his or her own nation or state, pending the establishment of a new credential system more appropriate to the nature and purposes of the international school system.

Enrolment must be open to all students regardless of race, nationality, ethnic culture, or religion. The students should, like the general population, represent various ability levels. The only students not eligible would be those with mental, emotional, physical, or behavioural problems the schools are neither staffed nor equipped to deal with. As with the faculty, an effort should be made to draw students from all major culture areas and nationalities. Strong financial aid programmes should be available to prevent the schools from being economically élitist. Students in the system should transfer automatically from one school to another within the system, whenever circumstances require, with the same ease that students transfer from one school to another within a national or state system.

Pension, medical, and other benefit schemes for faculty and staff

One of the hallmarks of the international school system will be the movement of teaching and administrative staff from school to school within the system. This will generally result in a broadened, enriched experience for these persons which, in turn, should strengthen the teaching and leadership of the schools in ways not possible with personnel who rarely move, or with personnel entering and leaving the system from unlike schools operating according to other systems. In order to facilitate transfer of staff, opening career development possibilities of the sort not now readily available, it will be essential to have portable pension and medical benefit schemes. A commitment on the part of each school in the system to participate in common pension and medical programmes should be an absolute requirement for membership of the school in the system.

Compensation

Similarly, compensation structures (salary and vacation allowance) will need to be standardized so as to be comparable for each position, allowing for differences in the cost of living from place to place. (Other differences such as hardship due to extreme weather conditions or geographic remoteness can also be provided for without unduly affecting overall comparability.)

Perceived benefits of an international school system

Obviously, the establishment of an international school system will have the most immediate effect on families of the international community. Transfers of diplomats, international civil servants, and businessmen will be eased and, perhaps, encouraged by the existence of such a system. As noted above, children will be accepted automatically as they move from one school to another within the system, moving essentially within the same programme of studies and organizational structure.

There has been increasing resistance to being transferred on the part of persons in international organizations, usually for family reasons – the foremost being concern about the schooling of the children. Therefore, the organizations in which these persons are employed will also benefit as a consequence of less disruptive movement of their personnel.

The second major beneficiary of an international school system will be the international schools themselves. Becoming a part of a larger whole will mitigate to a very great extent their isolation – both real and perceived. It will make more easily available to these schools opportunities in staffing, and in programme and staff development, and on a more cost-effective basis. It may also help to stabilize their enrolments over time, as a result of the encouragement and ease of student transfers.

More importantly, over the long term, the design and establishment of an international school system should have a pervasive impact on education generally, and in particular on the national systems of the countries in which the international school system is represented by a school or schools. Some developing nations are looking for alternatives to the educational systems they operate. Likewise, in a number of industrialized nations as well (the United States and the United Kingdom being good examples), comprehensive reappraisals of the relevance and effectiveness of their educational systems has revealed the need for fundamental change. In both instances, the international school system would be a vital source of new ideas about curriculum and about teaching and learning. The international schools would play a vital role in a non-threatening way, creating partnerships and alliances with education ministries, schools of education, and local schools alike. The tremendous interest found among national and state systems in 'education with a global perspective' is evidence of awareness of serious shortcomings in the way children and young people are being educated. National and state systems were set up to respond to issues, needs, and challenges which have changed significantly over the years. To that extent, these systems are a reflection of a world which no longer exists. The bona fide international schools, on the other hand, do mirror the world as it is evolving: they do so not yet perfectly nor completely, but certainly much more closely than do other schools. They are, in a very real sense, the forward edge of elementary and secondary education in the world today: in their philosophy, in their purposes, in their programme, and in their practices.

Problems and constraints

Establishing an international school system will necessitate overcoming a number of problems which constrain us. There are at least three sets of these:

1. The rapid turnover of board members, administrators, parents, children, and, less often, teaching staff make it extremely difficult to launch and maintain initiatives of this magnitude. A way must be found to sustain interest, commitment, and energy over time after those who begin the task have left.
2. Change inevitably generates resistance in organizations and in individuals. Change on this scale will certainly be met by significant resistance. Schools may fear excessive standardization and/or bureaucracy, or loss of autonomy. There may be concerns about funding various aspects of setting up the system – eg how much financing will be needed and how will it be raised? If part of this funding is to come from the schools, how can the cost be equitably apportioned? Will a disproportionate burden be placed on the founding schools?
3. A number of the schools which might see themselves as candidates for membership in the international school system are more expatriate than international in character. Certain of these schools are large and influential. There is some potential for obstructionism on their part when they perceive the cost of membership as the loss of their national colouration – be it American, French, British, Japanese etc – or, if remaining outside the system, perceiving the system as a threat to their continued well-being.

These problems and constraints, along with others not identified above, will need to be squarely confronted and resolved. It is essential to acknowledge at the outset that the difficulties involved in establishing an international school system are likely to be formidable. Not to do so would be to foster unrealistic expectations, which, in turn, could lead to frustration and discouragement. The 'architecture' of a project of this scale and significance is a large undertaking not to be underestimated. At the same time, the benefits to be derived are also hugely important and worth while.

24. The year 2000 is tomorrow: where is international education going?

Bernard Ivaldi

Introduction

The policy of international education must determine the objectives of the International Schools Association's activities, the essential values which guide the organization. The general trends which will be presented here do not define a new policy, but on the contrary are in keeping with the continuation of our Association's activities. If these objectives must be affirmed, it is primarily to avoid losing sight of them in the whirlwind of change. As everyone knows, school structures, programmes, systems, teaching methods, teacher-training, and classroom life cannot be altered overnight. This statement is therefore directed at all those who wish to have an idea of ISA's major plans and its main choices.

Since the beginning of the 1960s, reforms, modifications and pedagogical experiences have multiplied. Change for the sake of change, not at all. The democratization of studies, the upswing of programmes and methods, and the introduction of computers, responded to the transformations of population, society, the economy and the professions, to the evolution of children and adolescents, and to change in families' educational aspirations. Scarcely more than ten years separates us from the year 2000. In terms of educational policy, this is both a little and a great deal: a little because children of primary school age will be in the middle years of schooling in the year 2000; and a great deal when one thinks of the energies which will be invested between now and then in the daily operation of our schools and in essential innovation, because cultural, economic, and social innovations follow each other. Some people forecast real social changes for the ten years to come; profound alterations demanding fresh adaptations by our schools. It is clear that in future we will not be able to base our hopes either on simple and expeditious solutions or on new structural reforms. Henceforth, change will become the rule. In our schools, as elsewhere, innovation will become part of the routine.

Innovation

It is important, therefore, to encourage creative energy and to direct this change according to two major axes:

1. Continually to improve the daily operation of the school system, and to ensure the best possile qualify of life, in order to promote learning for all.
2. Constantly to direct energies and resources towards the aims of the teaching system, such as they are defined in the objectives of the International Schools Association.

In order not to get lost in the diversity of situations and concerns particular to each establishment, let us confine ourselves to the perspectives which affect the majority of students and those who work in the school systems, by tackling five major subjects.

Democratizing access to knowledge

For several decades, our schools have endeavoured to battle against backwardness and scholastic failure and to fight social inequalities in education. A school's fundamental mission is to facilitate and therefore to democratize access to knowledge, to information, to education. Today, more than ever before, it is apparent that economic development and democratic life take place through a high level of education for all.

In this perspective, we will particularly emphasize strictly pedagogical measures: individualization and differentiation enhanced by teaching in all schools and in all disciplines; adaptation to this end of teaching methods and evaluation practices (which must become less selective and more formative); management of space and school timetables; diversification of pedagogical aids leading to their integration as far as possible into classroom work.

Educating for a pluralist and open society

Insistence on the acquisition of knowledge must not make us forget the school's educative mission, in the broad sense, of preparation for life in a complex multicultural society undergoing a process of rapid change and opening up to the world. It must, indeed, contribute towards developing tolerance with respect to minorities, immigrants, and refugees, to promoting openness towards other cultures, to the equality of men and women, democratic participation in political life, solidarity with the less fortunate, integration of the handicapped, respect for the environment, the defence of human rights, and the refusal of all kinds of discrimination.

To reinforce such values and attitudes, in respect of each person's personality and beliefs, is not an easy task. It is not enough to affirm their importance in the abstract; one must also put them into practice in classes and in schools. In this area, one cannot proceed 'scholastically' by means of lessons and exercises; rather, teachers must be encouraged to take time, time for reflection on and discussion of sociological matters.

Regaining the unity of general culture

Today, we live in a society in immediate communication and interdependence with the whole world.

Science is not only the instrument of reason and progress. It also raises questions and concerns with genetic experiments, major ecological hazards, excessive armament, and the computerization of daily life.

The development of education is founded on a blind faith in knowledge. But when knowledge is in a state of crisis, so is a school. How do we tackle this situation? Nothing obliges us, in education, to follow blindly the explosion of knowledge on the encyclopaedic model, nor to make programmes heavy under the pretext of modernizing them.

We need to concern ourselves with the coherence of the whole: to rethink the general culture taught in our schools, to bring out the essential learning and know-how appropriate to each discipline, to give more importance to transverse skills (reasoning, capacity for analysing, synthesis, and communication) and to give individuals the means of maintaining a critical distance when faced with science and technical subjects. We must increasingly keep our balance and reaffirm the importance of knowledge and experience while calling on all aspects of the personality.

Diversifying the forms of access to learning

The school has for a long time been the only institutional form of education. Nowadays, audio-visual equipment, computing, and telematics are changing the facts of this situation. The school must appropriate the new technologies, integrate them into daily pedagogical activities, and in particular make computers a tool, the use of which is to be judiciously controlled.

The school must today allow everyone to learn how to learn. The formula is common to all, but putting it into action demands, from the primary school onwards, the application of different media, different technologies, and different approaches for the acquisition of knowledge.

Energizing the operation of the school system

An educational policy can come into effect through the total adherence of all participants (teacher, parents, and pupils). It is important that everything which can be is decentralized in the management of resources and the realization of common objectives.

We must strengthen the identity of institutions, make colleagues aware of their responsibilities, encourage the taking of initiative, especially in the pedagogical domain, while keeping a steady course, common rules, and a control on the essentials. This inevitably happens by a strengthening of continuous staff training. The most appealing and generous ideas are worth nothing if those who are able to realize them do not invest in them their energy and whole heart.

Conclusion

In touching on these themes, I have confined myself to the bare essentials. Each one of us, in our schools, must accept a long-term understanding, obliging us to take up numerous challenges. I hope that these trends will allow us to mobilize our energies and set the debate in motion.

25. Random ruminations on the curriculum of the international school

W G Mattern

If I had a pound for every essay that has been made at defining international education, I would surely be a good deal richer than I am now. If I had read them all, however, I am not sure that I would be much farther along towards a comprehensive definition: what constitutes or should constitute an international education remains a complex and controversial matter. Much more research and experimentation are undoubtedly required, but needed even more are greater imagination and bolder outreach. In this paper, there is certainly no final list of ingredients, no fully specified recipe. But a few personal observations may contribute thereto.

First let me recall what I wrote in a recent article in the *International Schools Journal* (Autumn 1988):

> We must . . . stop thinking of 'internationalism' as a merely cosmetic appliqué to attract more numbers to what remains essentially the same old school. Internationalism is more than a mix of student nationalities and languages and cultures and religions, no matter how well stirred . . . . It is more than a market strategy, to be manipulated for the gaze of the public. We must stop playing with the bits and pieces coincidental to our heterogeneous collection [of students and teachers] and face up to the fact that is and of itself [that collection] may constitute an international *school*, but not at all necessarily an international education. The two concepts are not inextricably intertwined . . . [and because we have one it does not ineluctably follow that we must have the other.]

The article then goes on to say that:

> We must discover . . . a way to use the riches of our heterogeneity to create an educational programme genuinely different from that available in any domestic setting, an eclectic synthesis drawn from the best that is known about teaching and learning from wherever in the world it may be found. We must become a truly discrete branch of the profession, committed to the identification of those elements which are basic to the concept and practice of global citizenship, and skilled in the art and science of transmitting them to those for whose education we are responsible.

What I should like to do then, is to explore further 'those elements which are basic to the concept and practice of global citizenship'.

The work of others, to be sure, has gone before. The ideas of Alex Peterson came to be embodied in the philosophy and practice of the International Baccalaureate scheme: the International Schools Association developed an international curriculum for the middle years of schooling; and there is a brave and imaginative, if as yet incomplete, International GCSE programme of the University of Cambridge Local Examination Syndicate. Less visible, but no less earnest efforts are currently being pursued by scores of organizations around the world, all equally dedicated to the ideological task of providing an educational experience which will yield true global perspectives. All of the above activities deserve attention: they provide valuable insights and in many cases practical programmes worthy of the serious consideration of anyone interested in international education. But there are still, in my view, enormous and deeply significant omissions, some blatant misconceptions, and even here and there some downright nonsense. Let me be specific.

To start at the easy end, I sense little disagreement in any of the curricular schemes with the proposition that all students should be taught to be numerate and should have some science. There may be quarrels about what level of competence in mathematics constitutes numeracy and what the ingredients thereof should be, but such squabbles are for the most part among mathematicians and are not for sensible people to get involved in. Much of the same can be said about science. From the point of view of the internationalist, Newton's laws apply equally in the Gambia and Kingston-upon-Thames (though whether we shall be able to continue to be so glib once we have colonized Mars is perhaps moot). Additionally, the procedures for manipulating numbers usefully are the same around the world, as our binary computers beautifully illustrate wherever we plug them in – that is, of course, if we have the right plugs to connect them to the mains, the right voltage, and disk contents undamaged by security checks.

To be sure, the tools by which we teach mathematics and science need some more thinking about. I would suggest that as internationalists we can do better than teach addition and subtraction to Peruvian children in terms of pounds and pence, and that Jordanian students are not likely to be riveted by heat exchange problems centring on igloos in northern Alaska. But, even with the heterogeneous lot in most international schools, it would seem that we are at least missing an opportunity to broaden horizons when the cultural reference base is left solely up to the textbook publisher. I am aware, of course, of the practical problems, but I am also aware that these become genuine and highly significant educational problems for the internationalist. We must do some more thinking about them. At the moment, there is a good deal of message in the media, and too often not the one we should wish to convey.

But of all the areas of the traditional curriculum that have received the attention of the internationalist, language seems to have generated some of the greatest heat, if not yet much light. Indeed, I would go so far as to say it has spawned some of the most arrant nonsense in this whole dubious field of curriculum planning – including the sort of statement one international educationist made not long ago, to the effect that if you did not really know another language you just could not think. That would come as grievous news to the likes of such monolinguists as Plato, Abraham Lincoln, and William Shakespeare.

At the same time, the issue of language learning has certainly given us some of our most sacred cows. Consider bilingualism, for example, not a firm fixture in the credo of many schemes for international education. The underlying rationale seems to be the truism that a knowledge of the language of another culture provides the key to understanding and appreciating that culture. Perhaps so, but it is not a fact of much practical significance for those plotting school curricula. If bilingual education – and bicultural exposure – could start at the moment of participation, then there might be some relevance. But when the study of another language (even if integrated across the curriculum) is started at the early adolescent stage of formal education, as is usually the case, true bilingualism is hardly ever the result and biculturalism will surely be lagging far, far behind. Yet, it is the latter that is said to be the real point of the exercise. The acquisition of language skills in themselves, of no matter how high an order, may be impressive, good for business, excellent mental discipline, and a pleasant social emollient, but it is not *per se* the same thing as the acquisition of another culture.

We must not delude ourselves here. Those Asiatic businessmen, for example, whose skills in English so impress us do extraordinarily well in the passage of commerce – and it could be argued that commercial clout is an effective prelude to cultural influence. But bicultural they are surely not, nor would claim to be. Indeed, how many people with skills in a language other than their native tongue such as to be regarded as 'totally fluent', can say with hand on heart that they have thereby achieved true access to another culture? More so than they would have had without language fluency, yes; some measure of appreciation and understanding that they would probably not have acquired – or, more accurately, would not have been in a position to acquire – without language skills. But will anyone ever be able to stand wholly comfortably in the shoes of someone of a culture different from one's own? To claim so must surely be to misunderstand what culture really is!

Perhaps more to the point at issue, however, is the question of just what is so international about a bilingual or for that matter a bicultural person? If one is Anglo-French, that does not help much with understanding how Poles feel, or what life is like in Burma, or what is on the mind of the man in the street in Swaziland. Might there not in fact be a kind of anti-internationalist parochialism (not to mention a certain whiff of smug insular arrogance) in laying claim to an international perspective because one has mastered two Western European languages? Not one European plus Arabic or Urdu or Mandarin Chinese – any of the great regional languages and cultural repositories – but just, say Spanish and Portuguese? That would certainly make one bilingual – and would, by the way, satisfy the letter of the language requirement for the IB diploma and Cambridge's International Certificate of Education. But it must be obvious that it would scarcely satisfy the spirit of either. If we must – for practical reasons, let us say – talk about a student's acquiring a command (a more ambiguous, but probably for that reason a more apt word than 'fluency') of two languages only, then surely it must be the case that for the curriculum planner in the international school the choice of *which* two ought not to be resolved exclusively, as happens presently in many institutions, on such considerations as geographical proximity, literary values, ease of acquisition, or just good old current chic. Moreover, let us not lose sight of the fact that no matter what two languages we are talking about, a person would obviously be better off, better qualified as an internationalist, being trilingual or quadrilingual or as multilingual as a Danube riverboat captain: short of omnilingualism, we are still, it may be said, dealing with degrees of parochialism.

If bilingualism is not itself, then, the definitive hallmark of an international education, there are still some further things that need to be said about language in the international curriculum. If we accept a humbler role for foreign language – a key to the front door of another culture, or even just the servant's entrance, but surely not free passage to the entire structure; if our expectations are both less and fewer, then surely competence in another language is something to be desired, a beginning not an end. But the choice of *which* additional language remains important.

For those who are English-speakers, the alternative, the second language, must surely be one of the great regional tongues – or arguably the language of a student's future home, place of business, or spouse, though to choose any of such at age ten is a fairly daunting responsibility. For those who are not English-speakers, however, the choice by this last decade of the century can only be English. I know any anglophone must be suspect in making that statement, and I shall not defend it here except to say that all considerations of demography and economics, politics and statistics, even linguistics and aesthetics, must lead the unbiased to that conclusion. Omnilingualism for all people is an impossibility; one language in *common* for all people (though never all people speaking but one language) might well be a goal to pin to the heart of every true internationalist.

And one more word only about language: I have been referring above to verbal language, but there are, of course, other kinds of language – though what I have in mind are usually called, in curricular terms, the arts. Music, all of the visual arts (including architecture), dance – all of these are in truth ways of communicating, and probably more readily accessible to those who do not share a common verbal language than the medium of words. Moreover, because of their affective content, they can more persuasively and comprehensively address cultural differences and comparisons and cross-cultural issues. For the international school even more so than for domestic institutions, the arts, far from being frills offer an enormously rich if yet largely untapped and unexplored means of bridging the chasms of importance, close to the heart of those things which people really care about most. There is much creative work yet to be done in this part of the teaching programme.

And now we come at last to the social sciences and the humanities. Here, by common agreement, is the area of the curriculum which most obviously can carry the great bulk of the assignment to convey global perspective and all the other messages about economic and social and political interdependency and the imperative of peace. And for that reason it has received chief attention from those working to internationalize the educational experience of students. Much of that work, indeed, has been done on the domestic front, targeted on young people attending schools in national systems, because there is now a very sizeable home market for educational materials focusing on global issues. It is now practical – and in some areas profitable – to spend time and money and the brains that can be bought therewith on producing such materials, for education for global citizenship has become a good business, because it is big business. When idealism and the profit motive coincide, the combination is unbeatable!

Problems do remain, however, for those in the heterogeneous international schools. Though much of value has been done by some extremely able people, almost all of that which is publicly available has its root in the national systems, from which in fact arise the difficulties. There is, for example, the presumption of homogeneity and a given perspective in the student consumer of these materials. The teacher in the international schools can make no such presumption. If, for example, it is one of the tasks of domestically orientated materials to combat a set of prejudices reliably characteristic of a particular culture, the international school has no one set of prejudices to deal with and there is surely nothing reliably characteristic of the students except their very diversity. Who, for example, are 'the barbarians' to young Soolong from Shanghai, and who are they to young Sarah from Seattle sitting alongside? Who are the 'infidels' to Master Albert from Abington, brought up in the traditions of the chapel, and who are they to his neighbour Ali from Ankara, raised in the shadow of the mosque? Clearly, the perspectives with which one starts are of crucial importance to the understanding of any message.

But there is a further problem for those in the heterogeneous schools which aspire to offer a truly international education. It has to do again with perspective, but this time, that of the institution rather than the students. And by that fact, the difficulty becomes more complex and serious, affecting all those areas of study in which human culture, in its broadest sense, is involved. I call it the Atlas problem, recalling the Hellenic Titan who must have a place to stand in order that he may bear the world on his shoulders.

In the relative homogeneity of most national schools, a teacher may in general rely on the similarity of the cultural backgrounds of the majority of students in the classroom and that those backgrounds will be characteristic of the particular national setting. Even if there are some students of dissimilar origins, they will usually be in a minority, and while the good teacher will certainly try to be sensitive to and respect their differences, it is after all to be expected that acculturation to the characteristic majority beliefs and perceptions will occur, consciously or unconsciously, planned or unplanned, in and out of the classroom. It may even be seen to be part of the teacher's job to assist his or her charges to become good Americans or true Brits or whatever – perhaps (it is to be hoped) with global perspective, but nonetheless proper citizens of the country.

But the teacher in the international school surely has no such responsibility. Here the classroom is significantly different, in that in all probability there is no majority nationality, but only greater or lesser minorities. Moreover, the teacher, far from being expected to acculturate students into the appropriate pattern characteristic of the school's setting, is proscribed from doing so. On the contrary, the professional assignment is to avoid all national biases, to speak and behave and teach as an internationalist only. And just how does one *do* that? Who is offering a training programme in *that* kind of teaching? Where does one find appropriate textual materials? Where does Atlas stand?

The hard fact of the matter is that there are no well-defined, comprehensive answers to such questions and the dilemma they imply – yet. There are only partial answers, inadequate and imperfect. We see yet as in a glass darkly.

Fortunately, however, that is not the same as being totally blind, and international schools need not act as if it is. They can surely do better than just fumbling around with that unending celebration of national days, or those wear-your-own national costume, bring-your-own national food festivals that really do not put much to the test except the efficacy of the antacid tablets. The mix-and-stir approach to international education may be diverting and fun and occasionally even instructive, but finally it must be admitted that it is at best only a beginning. For there is a critical difference between having information, even a great deal of information, about cultures and beliefs dissimilar to one's own, and having an understanding and appreciation of them.

So deal one must with the Atlas problem, that awful paradox with which all who have thought deeply about the concept of international education have always wrestled, very few with any success. At its heart lies a word which, except in its mathematical sense, has been banished from most of the institutions purporting to give such an education: the word is *values*. It is banished because schools do not want to display bias. They do not want to imply, unless something can be held up to some universally accepted (and thus 'objective') measuring rod, anything is better than, worth more than, in any sense exceeds in value anything else. They behave in this way not simply because they wish to avoid wounding the sensibilities of students deriving from different cultural systems. Their behaviour arises rather from a philosophical conviction that, to the true internationalist, all cultures are of equal worth and anything inherent in any of them, any concept or belief or practice, is of the same value as that comparable concept or belief or practice characteristic of any other culture. And so schools do not talk about values at all – except perhaps as artefacts to be described, their lineaments committed to memory and stored away with all the rest of the unsorted baggage the soi-disant educated person is supposed to tote around. Thus, from schools which consider themselves enlightened, even daring, children can come away knowing something about the historical Jesus, Abraham, David, and Solomon, Muhammad, the Gautama Buddha, and maybe even a few bowdlerized Confucian sayings, though probably not much of any of the great ethical thinkers from Aeschylus to Zoroaster (and not forgetting Charles Schultz). But the point of the exercise will not have been to examine the ethical content, only to come to know about the historical phenomena, like tectonic movements or the Napoleonic Wars or who won the Battle of Bull Run. There will have been nothing about the ethics, about values, because the epistemology of the internationalists forbids it.

And from thence arises the dreadful, ironic, sad paradox: those persons and institutions who are committed to the moral proposition that all men are created equal and have equal and inalienable rights to the opportunities afforded by human existence – they are the ones who by that very commitment are muzzled from the statement of their convictions and the tough-minded exploration of the means by which to achieve universal realization. In practice, in the vast majority of international schools, teachers do not allow themselves anything nearer an examination of values than what may be implied by the handbook of institutional rules, and perhaps occasionally something about the safe pieties of the UN Charter ilk.

I would suggest it is time and overdue for an amendment of life: a place must be found for Atlas to stand. The foundation stones exist, in fact, in many places: there are certain values, whether derived from religious or mythic origins or strictly practical tradition, whether expressed in the language of theology or that of the secular forum, which are and have been common to every civilization past and present. No violence can be done to any culture-based sensibilities when these values are explored in our schools.

To wit, every ethical system holds firmly to the importance of truth-telling and proscribes deceit. The value is essential to the conduct of human affairs as organized in the third grade and on the entire planet – and both should be used to illustrate the point. It is at the heart of mathematics; there can be no science without it; history which lies is worse than a waste of time – and all those points need to be made as well.

Similarly, every society, every ethical system teaches the importance of some kind or degree of respect for the rights of others and specifically proscribes the expropriation of those rights. From thence proceed the curbs of law and custom on bodily harm to another, theft in all its forms, and individual or corporate violence. The fundamental principle is as essential in the sandbox as in the affairs of nations – and its application to both needs to be talked about and explored.

Perhaps less obvious but still of critical importance is the value which every society and ethical system places, in order to ensure the fulfillment of the preceding principles, on valid premises, contracts, and laws. The good ordering of all relations between people relies on a respect for and observance of this value, whether we are talking about the tacit contract between teachers and their students or much celebrated treaties among nations – and both need to be deeply considered.

Nor is it inappropriate, in this era in which virtually every nation on earth lays public claim to being a democracy (though some of them seem to be rather peculiar versions thereof) to explore with students the philosophical and ethical bases of such systems of societal ordering. The relationship between authority and those over whom authority is exercised – its variety of forms, its limits and controls, its basis in written or traditional contract – all of these are potentially fruitful grounds for consideration, whether the model be the school, community, or a specific political entity. And it is particularly worth while to explore the matter of the balance between, on the one hand, the rights and responsibilities of the individual, and, on the other, those of the societal group, however defined – and marvellously illuminating it can be to see how the balance can change depending on the definition of that societal group. Is this not what history, in the international school, should really be all about?

Finally, I could hope there might be some schools and teachers bold enough to ask their students to explore one further element in a system of values which, if not totally universal, certainly has very good credentials. It is that factor in relations between people which moves beyond the legalistic, mechanistic, systematic, logical and purely intellective – which, indeed, transforms them into *human* relations. It is that which the Greeks called *agape*, which Confucius referred to as the need for respect and benevolence, which both Jews and Christians enjoined on men as 'Love thy neighbour as thyself', which Kant embodied in his insistence that human beings owe one another both love and respect; and which has in our own time come to underpin virtually all of the great documents dealing with the affairs of nations, in which the common condition and mutual responsibility for one's fellow members of the race are taken as essentials of the social fabric.

I believe, indeed, that there can finally be no meaningful or effective teaching about internationalism which shuns the matter of values. Schools are deluding themselves and cruelly depriving their students if, no matter what the rest of the curriculum, they fail to give young people such a firm place on which to stand. A sense of values is needed to inform both all the rest of their studies and their life purposes as well. Without it, they may be clever, knowledgeable, even wondrously creative, but they will never become citizens of the world nor give it their gifts as should those who have known a true international education.

26. A philosophy of international education – an interview with Robert Blackburn, Deputy Director of the International Baccalaureate Office, London, 25/9/89

Patricia L Jonietz

How does one become a specialist in international education?

My own background is that I was one of the founding members of the Atlantic College in Wales. I went down there as Deputy Headmaster for seven years. Then, when Lord Mountbatten was appointed the President of United World Colleges, he invited me to come up to London and work for him setting up the International Secretariat of the United World Colleges in London House, just down the road. So I worked for Lord Mountbatten until just before he was assassinated. Prince Charles had taken over, and I had worked for the United World Colleges for quite a long time when I was invited by the then President to move over to the International Baccalaureate Office. In fact, my connection with the IB goes back to the earliest days in Atlantic College. As you probably know Atlantic College was one of a group of pioneering schools that was in the beginning of the IB.

There is some debate as to who founded the IB. I think it was John Kennedy who said that success has many fathers, and many people are maintaining that they founded the IB. In fact, it arose out of the academic and international needs of a group of schools: the International School of Geneva, the UN School in New York, and Atlantic College were really the pioneers of that whole business. They wanted an international curriculum at upper secondary level, and they also wanted an international examination for university entrance with something like universal validity.

How did you perceive that as different from the national system from which you came?

First of all, they are meeting different needs. The problems for international schools with nationalities from 30, 40, or more countries were that they were in fact using the curriculum and examinations from particular countries (quite often the American or British systems) which were designed for particularly and entirely legitimate national needs but were quite inappropriate in the international context. So, the IB was designed really to see if it could meet the needs of the internationally mobile student. That was the original thing.

Of course, there were many other differences, I think, from national systems. One was our emphasis on all students doing at least one foreign language, with the emphasis on world literature as an important component of what we describe as Language 'A' – Language 'A' being broadly speaking the mother tongue of the student. The assumption being that if a student had been educated overseas for a number of years, very often in an English medium school – for example, a Swedish student in an English-speaking school in Tanzania in East Africa – that student could often reach the stage where his or her English was often better than the mother tongue. Of course, this was a disadvantage if the student wished to return to higher education in Sweden. So both for cultural and practical reasons, we insisted and still do that the first requirement of the IB was a knowledge of their own mother tongue, language and literature. On the assumption, and this is an important matter, I think, in the philosophy of the IB about the nature of internationalism and international education. We would maintain, I think, that internationalism and international education does not mean a denial of one's own culture, one's own background, and one's own language. Indeed, that is a kind of substructure which must be found with internationalism as the top storey. Also there is a very practical reason with students going back to European universities, Scandinavia, France, Germany and so on, they really did need a knowledge of their own tongue and a particular qualification in it. There are some real differences from national programmes.

Having said that, the question still remains, how international is the IB? We are not happy with this. We feel the content of many of our programmes is not international enough, and one of the big debates that is going on in the IB at the moment is how to make the curriculum more genuinely international, not just cosmetically international. There are certain things that you can do about that: introduce new subjects as options in the diploma which we think contribute more directly to the international purposes of the organization. There is the new programme in Environmental Studies which Colin Jenkins pioneered. That is becoming very popular. I am concerned with a new programme on the history and culture of Islam. We felt in the spectrum of the IB curriculum there was really nothing about the whole history, culture, and civilization of Islam, which is important to the growing number of schools in the East doing the IB and to the rest of the IB schools. Here is a major part of human experience and a major part of the contemporary political world.

What do we do in terms of curriculum development? When a new idea comes along, we get the idea, we process it, we talk to outside experts, and then we set up a pilot scheme of a small group of interested schools (like we did with Environmental Studies and as we are doing with the History and Culture of Islam). In fact there are four schools in the pilot scheme – two in the Islamic world and two outside; if that experiment is a success, then the whole programme becomes on general offer to all IB schools.

Do you make a distinction between an international school and an international education?

There are many international schools which have been set up to serve the mobile community which do not, it seems to me, provide very much in terms of international education. They are merely based on the American system of education or indeed the British system.

Or a German or a French?

Absolutely, absolutely. It seems to me that those schools overseas (overseas from the UK) very often lose an opportunity, although these schools were the first group to look to the IB for alternatives. There is a very interesting development in the IB now, that is a growing number of national schools, state schools in particular systems, are looking to the IB not so much as an alternative to the national curriculum but as a kind of supplement to it. Let me give you some examples. Well, the major example of course is in North America, particularly in the United States, where now there are 160 IB schools in the US and in Canada. Most of these, not all, are public (state) high schools. They have looked to the IB. Now, why?

First of all, I think that they like the links with an international organization. They like the idea of external assessment which is objective. And, of course, if you read any account of American secondary education over the last ten years, going back to *A Nation at Risk*, what are they saying? We must improve the standards of English. We must add foreign language. We must have mathematics continuing through secondary education. We must place emphasis on academic rigour and so on. When you have said that, you have said something like the IB.

In the case of European countries, it is interesting indeed, and something we never anticipated. In the Netherlands, for example, there are now 11 IB schools, three of those are international (like the International School of Amsterdam), and seven of them are Dutch state schools nominated by the Ministry of Education in Holland as IB centres teaching the IB usually in English and a mix of English and Dutch. The same thing has happened in Scandinavia. If you take Norway, four of the leading gymnasiums in Norway (Oslo, Bergen, Stavanger, and Trondheim) are now IB centres offering to Norwegian kids a programme in English as the language of instruction, but an international programme leading to an international qualification. The Norwegian kid wanting to enter the London School of Economics, or I dare say to MIT either, will find it now very much easier to do this on the basis of the IB qualification rather than the Norwegian national exam.

Do you think this is why the International Schools Association is piloting their middle school curriculum in state schools in Europe and Canada?

I think it is the same need at a different level. There has been a debate in IBO which has gone on for many years and is not totally resolved yet about whether IBO should get involved in what you describe accurately as a middle school curriculum or what we would describe as a pre-IB curriculum.

ISA does not like the term 'pre-IB'

No, of course and there is a reason for that. They feel that they are catering to a much larger range of students than just future IB candidates, but in our terminology what we are interested in is a pre-IB curriculum. There are two schools of thought about that. One, we were set up to provide a university matriculation, and there is a lot to be done still: internationalize the curriculum; there is a major and continuing task to be done in improving recognition agreements although the IB is now pretty well recognized world wide; and we have just completed a major task in improving our examination organization. So that arguments ran, that we should concentrate on doing more effectively what the organization was set up to do. On the other hand, we also recognize that international education does not begin at 16+. That there is, of course, a backwash effect of the curricula down into the secondary school and that there is a real need for what we would describe as a pre-IB curriculum. So, we have encouraged ISA and the IGCSE in Cambridge, but we have not got administratively, financially, or operationally involved in this ourselves.

Is the 'backwash' effect you mention not only what is taught but also how to teach in the earlier years?

Absolutely, the needs of the exam determine how students think and communicate and also the methods of assessment. It is quite interesting, and it is a real and growing need in IB schools. If you go to meetings of the heads of IB schools, this will always be a major item on the agenda. What can we do for an international middle school curriculum which will provide an appropriate base for the IB or whatever?

Many, especially British overseas schools, got very excited about the IGCSE. My impression is that there are questions now being asked about that, particularly about the 'I' bit. How international is the IGCSE? I believe all the examiners are British? How international is that? The ISA began and is still run by a group of very high-minded idealists. There is still that sort of feeling about the group, although it is changing to some extent because the work that had been produced by ISA in designing the curricula over the last few years is a marked improvement over anything which has gone before.

Are the United World Colleges at a similar place in development?

There is a philosophic element and they would claim a philosophic justification to UWC which other schools do not have or perhaps need. So if you take any IB school from the UN New York to the International School in Dar es Salaam, both excellent schools, these were set up to meet actual, practical, and local needs. The UWC were not set up for any practical need but to further a particular educational and international philosophy that educational barriers can be broken down and that internationalism can be made effective at the 18+ age. There is a different motive between the UWC and many of the other schools. In terms of curriculum in the UWC, they have played a major part in assisting the development of the IB and certainly in the early days of the IB the UWC were, I suppose, one of the more significant groups of schools in the project in terms of number of diploma candidates. This is radically changing because there are over 400 schools in the IB, our growth rate is over 25 per cent a year. The role of UWC within the IB is a good deal less dominant perhaps than six or seven years ago.

The two organizations are of course totally separate: constitutionally, administratively, and financially they are separate bodies. This is a confusion people often make overseas that they are the same body or linked and they are not. Having said that, of course there has been a great deal of cooperation between both organizations and still is between the IB and the UWC and many of us have played a role in both organizations. There are special links. Many of the same links are between ECIS and ISA and the other regional organizations. I think myself this is healthy and the degree of cooperation is important. So often, regional organizations tend to exist in their own little field doing exactly the same thing as someone over here.

May I ask you to return to the topic of languages, do you think that language teaching and learning are an essential part of international education?

I find it very difficult to think of international education at this level which did not make the teaching of foreign language (at least one foreign language) an essential feature for all the obvious reasons: a tool of communication, an introduction into ideas and literature. It is interesting that in the European context we are under very considerable pressure from European colleagues not to do one foreign language but two. We will resist that because it is not viable in our terms.

The European Community School require three and also content teaching in a second language. Is that important?

I would have thought so. This linkage with European colleagues is developing and will become more important. The European Commission is quite interested in looking into what are the educational implications of '1992'? Should there in fact be some common qualification as a means of easing transfer between secondary education in one community country to another? Of course, there are only two bodies in the field: the IBO and the European Baccalaureate. The EC Commission has agreed that they will host a conference to seek advice and information from all organizations (including other nations) with experience in international education that would be relevant to '1992' developments in Europe.

Where would you begin future research in international education?

In IBO terms, we would put that money (and we would like a big grant thank you) into improving our curriculum. In national terms, we have very little resources to actually design and improve our curriculum. Over the last few years, we have been putting any resources we had into improving our assessment process. But we have that to a respectable standard and can look College Board in the eye now, perhaps even more than that. We can certainly look IGCSE in the eye. We have looked into the production of our assessment, the rationale, the variety of assessment we use and so on. But we would like to see now much more emphasis on improving the curriculum.

By improving I do not mean the level of physics or chemistry. They all go back to Harvard and Nuffield in any case. We would like to see a very serious attempt made to do what I mentioned earlier. And that is, not in a cosmetic sense but in a real sense, to make the international experience which our students have more real. This is easy to say and in fact very difficult to do when you get down to the philosophic bedrock of what you are trying to do. That is our highest priority.

After a lifetime in the field, can you personally define international education?

If you had asked me 20 years ago, I would have been very quick to give you a definition without any problems. I find it much more complicated now, because I have become more aware of the difficulties and the opportunities. I would have said the real purpose of international education is both positive and negative. The negative aspect is that it must be used to break down barriers. Education must be used as a tool to break down the barriers of race, religion, and class which separate our students. I do not think this is a matter of idealism any longer. This seems to me a matter of fact.

If our students, our children, our grandchildren are going to be given an education which remotely prepares them for the world in which they are going to have to live then they must have a knowledge of other people's cultures. It strikes me very much when I look at my grandchildren, partly Ugandan and partly English; it seems to me that one of the purposes of international education is not only to break down barriers which is a negative thing but also a much more positive thing.

It is so difficult to define. I would put it, I think, that the purpose of international education is to teach our kids how to welcome diversity not just tolerate it: diversity in language, diversity in culture, and diversity in race seem to me one of the few desirable aspects of the human condition, and yet, most educational systems ignore the possibility or in some cases work flatly against it. I would have thought that those seem to me to be the two aspects, speaking quickly off the cuff, that appeal to me. I want to say you really do see this in IB schools. Diversity is not something to be tucked away in somebody else's backgarden but is welcome. Whether I go to an IB school in East Africa or the north of Italy or wherever, I do see students who are getting this kind of experience.

What is the effect of the IB? How has it impacted on national school systems?

Our first task would be to improve the curriculum, and the second task now would be a serious research project into the nature of the IB experience: how it affected subsequent careers and academic choices of IB students. We have started that to some extent based in our Geneva office with Phil Thomas who started a research project, but, a shortage of funds prevented its development. If you look at the IB this May, we must have 13,000 students taking our examinations, and my guess is that we have about 22,000 students following IB courses worldwide. We do not know a number of things. We do not know the exact numbers, we do not know what happens to these students, to what forms of higher education they go, and still less do we know, and this is an essential question, what has been the nature of the experience. We all have our ideas, I would not arrange an IB meeting now without arranging a panel of present and former IB students.

I have my own view of what the experience has done to these kids, but we must get some research started on this. It is a major task and we have not started it yet.

Who do people see and what do people investigate who want to understand international schools and international education? What resources are available?

It is interesting that at this level there is remarkably little done in this area. It is all about post-war and comparative education, but comparatively little except Peterson's book, *Schools Across Frontiers*. If you really want to know, I would get together a half a dozen students and talk to them: one present student, one from three years ago, and one from ten years ago, and talk to them to compare the changes in their perspectives and experiences. The kinds of things I hear and we hear are: 'The IB experience is very challenging.' 'It was very difficult.' 'We had a very heavy workload.' 'In American schools, we had to give up quite a lot in the case of social activity to cope with the IB.' 'We are so glad that we were forced to learn another language.' Nine times out of ten, the former IB students remember best the 4,000 word extended essay describing their personal research which they say is the thing they dreaded most and is the thing they remember best.

Roberts Blackburn died 16 July 1990 at his home in Norway. He was on holiday, but he was working. The office of his mind rarely took a holiday.

Primo Levi, an Italian chemist and writer who also rarely closed the office of his mind for holiday, poses in his work two questions, 'If not this way, *how*? And, if not now, *when*?' Robert Blackburn spent his life not only encouraging all of us to discover *how* to make international education relevant but also challenging all of us to make the *when* of international education now.

This volume represents the work of many who profited from his encouragement and accepted his challenge.

Biographical notes on contributors

Robert Blackburn (Chapters 2 and 26) graduated with honours from Trinity College where an interest in modern history led him to a teaching position at the Merchant Taylors School. In 1962, he became the first Deputy Headmaster of the United World College of the Atlantic at St Donat's Castle in Wales. At the invitation of Lord Mountbatten, he moved in 1969 to the UWC International Council to help with the development of the project. In 1979, he joined the IBO as Deputy Director General with special responsibility for IB development in the UK, Africa, and the Middle East, along with relationships with governmental and international organizations. After long committee work with the UN, IBO, and European Association of Teachers, he became a member of the EC Working Party Conference on European/International Education. Robert Blackburn died in July 1990.

Joseph J Blaney (Chapter 23) is an American who earned history degrees from Iona College and Fordham University and a Doctorate in Educational Management and Policy Studies from the State University of New York. He is the Director of the United Nations International School in New York City and was at one time the Director General of the International School of Geneva in Switzerland. He has held local and state positions in the New York State education system and has been involved in international education for the past 15 years. He served as consultant to the European Council of International Schools (London), the State Department of Overseas Schools (Washington, DC), and the United Nations in New York. He has been an advisor to international schools in Athens, Budapest, Dusseldorf, Geneva, Hamburg, Paris, Rome, and the Regional Centre (Vienna) serving 12 international schools in Eastern European capitals. As a UN advisor, he established international schools in Baghdad and Hanoi.

James M Caccamo (Chapter 21) has a distinguished 25-year career as a teacher, administrator, and author in speech and hearing science, mental retardation, and learning disabilities. Since 1973, he has been at the University of Missouri in Kansas City both teaching in psychology and supervising students in the area of speech and hearing science. Additionally since 1980, he has been the Assistant to the Superintendent for Special Programs in the School District of Independence, Missouri. His responsibilities include programme management, supervision, special education programme development, and special project development. He had extensive professional affiliations both in the United States and the United Kingdom through his administrative participation in the 1987 and 1989 World Conference on Special Education.

Maurice W Carder (Chapter 13) lives and works in Vienna at the Vienna International School where he is Head of the ESL Department. He is keen to demystify the whole area of bilingualism and language learning, seeing it as a natural process for children in international schools, while at the same time recognizing the importance of making monolingual teachers and administrators more aware of promoting this valuable personal asset. He has been working on the IB Bilingualism and Language Testing Project, a thoroughly worthwhile venture which will give greater recognition to bilingualism for all students taking the IB exam. He is chairman of the ECIS-ESL Committee (recently renamed 'ESL and Mother-tongue Committee'). He and his wife bring up their children bilingually.

Malcolm Davis (Chapters 7 and 14) is Director of Studies at Vienna International School. He serves on the Curriculum Planning Committee for the International Schools Association. An experienced international school teacher, he is currently engaged in producing a resource book to aid in the teaching of Islamic history.

Caroline Ellwood (Chapters 7 and 14) is Head of the Middle School at Vienna International School. She was recently selected as a BP Education Fellow at Keble College, Oxford. An experienced international school teacher, she is currently engaged in producing a resource book to aid in the teaching of Islamic history.

Joan Freeman (Chapter 22) is the author of a considerable body of internationally published research and presentations on the development of high abilities, an arena in which she has been working for more than 25 years. She received her doctorate in Child Psychology from the University of Manchester, England, and has been honoured with Fellowship of the British Psychological Society. She has been elected as first President of the European Council for High Ability (ECHA).

Deon Glover (Chapter 15) was born and educated in South Africa before moving to Swaziland where he became involved with the founding of Waterford/Kamhlaba School which has since become part of the United World Colleges. He now teaches geography and environmental systems at UWC Atlantic and is also Vice Principal with specific responsibility for the development and implementation of the extra-academic programme.

Ole Hansen (Chapter 19) was born in Denmark in 1944 and graduated from teacher-training college. He holds a Master's degree in psychology and pedagogics. He is a member of the EC Working Group on Educational Integration of Disabled Children, ILSMH's Educational Committee, and project leader of HELIOS Local Model Activity 1, School Integration. He is also editor of the Nordic periodical *PU-Bladet* which focuses on mental retardation.

Jan Hedvall (Chapter 20) is a Swedish economist who has worked as a professional in the national and international educational area for many years. He is now working as a national and international consultant on the use of the computer as an educational aid.

Robert Henley (Chapter 21) has, since 1975, combined consulting and college instruction with being Superintendent of the Independence School District in Missouri. From this position as author, speaker, and administrator, he has fostered the growth of innovative programmes with local, national, and international focus. In 1987, he was selected as one of the 100 Outstanding Educators in the United States, and in 1988, he was one of seven educators to receive the School Administrator Award by the Alliance for Arts Education. In addition to local and state-wide programmes in early childhood, pre-school, daycare, science and maths, gifted and talented, and arts education, Dr Henley was instrumental in organizing in Missouri, with the assistance of OECD and British and American School Administrators, the World Conference on Special Education in 1987 and 1989. His interest in global and international education can be seen in a well-established teacher and student exchange programme held yearly between Independence, Missouri and Buckinghamshire, England.

Alex Horsley (Chapter 12) has, since 1985, been headmaster at Atlanta International School, an independent organization run by an international board of trustees. Forty-five per cent of the student body is American and the remainder represent 48 nationalities. It is a completely bilingual programme with three language tracks: English–French, English–German, and English–Spanish. Educated in England (BA Hull, PGCE London, and MA Oxon), his interest in bilingual education grew out of his training in modern languages. Prior to Atlanta, he taught languages in New Zealand, India, and England, served as a department chairman at schools in England and the United States, and as headmaster at the Friends School in Mullica Hills, New Jersey.

Bernard Ivaldi (Chapter 24) moved from being secondary school division head at the United Nations International School in New York to become the Director of the French–American International School in San Francisco, an IB school since his arrival in 1976. He is now Superintendent of the International School of Geneva and current president of the International Schools Association. He has written about both the IB and the ISA and their place in international education.

Patricia Jonietz (Introductions and Chapter 26) has completed work on a research project in international schools. With postgraduate degrees in both communication and special education, she has taught in secondary schools and university programmes in the United States and in Europe. Formerly the coordinator of a special education programme in a large international school, she currently works as a consultant for families in transition within the international community.

James Keson (Chapter 6) has been associated with Copenhagen International School since 1969. Appointed Headmaster in 1978, he has been active in the ECIS Accreditation programme and has had the opportunity to investigate various styles and philosophies of education in current practice. He has recently written on the subject of international education in Europe within the European Community schools as well as in ECIS affiliated schools.

Jeff Koopman (Chapter 10) was born in Bandung, Indonesia. He studied biology at the University of Nijmegen in the Netherlands. Since 1974, he has been on the staff of Jeanne d'Arc College in Maastricht. In 1984 when the International Department came into existence, he moved to that staff and began teaching biology in the IGCSE and the IB. He is now Coordinator of both the IGCSE and the International Department.

W G Mattern (Chapter 25) retired after 25 years in independent education in the United States, during almost all of which he served as headmaster of two boys' boarding schools. In 1974, he was tempted out of retirement to be Executive Secretary of the European Council of International Schools and established its headquarters outside London. During the next 15 years, ECIS grew enormously in members and available support services. Dr Mattern retired again in 1989 and was named ECIS Executive Secretary Emeritus. He continues his active interest in international education, writing and speaking at professional meetings, and consulting with individual schools.

David Parsons (Chapter 17) is the IB Coordinator/Head of External Examinations at the International School of Tanganyika in Dar es Salaam, Tanzania. While teaching in Exeter, Devon, England in the early eighties, he became interested in World Studies and Integrated Humanities as a method of teaching global education to students. During five years in Tanzania, he has played a major part in the develpment of GCSE Integrated Humanities as a core subject in Grades 10 and 11.

John Paterson (Chapter 4), born in Ceylon (now Sri Lanka), was educated in England. After graduating from King's College, the University of London in 1940, he served in the Royal Artillery till 1946 when he began teaching in England and later South Africa till 1956. Between 1957 and 1982, he served as a headmaster in Zimbabwe, Switzerland, and England. In 1988, he retired after six years as Co Director of the College du Leman International School. During a long association with the European Council of International Schools, he served as a member of the Board for eleven years, Treasurer for eight and Chairman for two. In 1973, he was elected an Honorary Member.

Richard Pearce (Chapter 16) was born in 1940, educated at the City of London School and Trinity Hall, Cambridge, and has taught at independent schools in England and in the USA. Since 1977, he has been Director of Admissions at the International School of London. He has written on English Education with particular reference to the problems and perceptions of mobile students.

Gerard Renaud (Chapter 1) was born in France and studied at Besançon and Paris-Sorbonne. He taught philosophy, art, and classics in France, in Africa until 1957, and at the University of Geneva where he was actively involved with the development of the International Schools Association. He was the co-founder of the International Baccalaureate Organization and served as director of IBO-Geneva till 1976 and as Director General till 1983. He is currently Pedagogical Consultant to the IBO and the ISA.

John Sadler (Chapter 5) is a Senior Examination Development Officer at the University of Cambridge Local Examination Syndicate (UCLES). His main areas of responsibility are the International General Certificate of Secondary Education (IGCSE) and the Module Bank System (MBS). Prior to joining UCLES in 1986, he taught Chemistry and was a Chief Examiner for O'level and 16+ level Chemistry. He has written a number of books.

David Brooke Sutcliffe (Chapter 3) graduated from Cambridge University and began teaching modern languages at Salem School in Germany and at Gordonstoun School. This association with Kurt Hahn and his philosophy of education led to his 20-year involvement with UWC of the Atlantic in Wales. After 13 years as headmaster, he helped found the new UWC campus in Italy and became its headmaster. He served as Vice President of the Executive Committee of the International Baccalaureate Office. He has written for many publications the history, philosophy, and growth of the United World Colleges movement.

Arturo Tosi (Chapter 11) came to England from Italy in 1976 as Coordinator of the European Community Project on Bilingual Education. He has taught at Oxford Polytechnic and the Universities of Sussex, and London. He has also conducted research on bilingualism and bilingual education in several European countries, Canada, and Australia. From 1987–90, he was Coordinator of the Bilingualism and Language Testing Project at the Institute of Education, University of London.

John Turner (Chapter 18), an advisor with a United Kingdom local education authority, was formerly Chief Examiner for Integrated Humanities GCSE. His background is in teaching sociology and humanities, but, more recently, he has been organizing, leading, and contributing to active workshops and conferences for teachers on course design and teaching methods.

Michael Waldron (Chapter 9) has been living in Brussels for nine years and works for the Council of the European Economic Community. He is married and has three children, the second of whom, Hannah, has Down's Syndrome. He is a founding member and current president of Brussels Support for the Handicapped, an advocacy organization for multinational families in the Brussels area. BRUSH has a nominal membership fee and publishes a regular newsletter as well as sponsoring meetings and conferences of general interest to the international special education community.

Bibliography and further reading

Articles, periodicals, and working papers

Belle-Isle, Robert (1986) Learning for a new humanism *International Schools Journal* European Council of International Schools: Petersfield, England **11**, 27–30

Bennett, Gordon (1982) Internationalism under Siege *International Schools Journal* The European Council of International Schools: Petersfield, England **3**, 7–16

Bergen Jr, Thomas (1986) Teaching for international understanding *International Schools Journal* European Council of International Schools: Petersfield, England **11**, 31–36

Bradby, E Hugh (1987) *Access to Higher Education in the UK from International Schools: The Problems of Examinations* MSC, Oxford University

Briggs, Lord A S A (1981) Crossing boundaries: education for a changing world *International Schools Journal* European Council of International Schools: Petersfield, England **2**, 39–46

Bruce, Michael J (1987) International schools for international people *Phi Delta Kappan* **68** (9), 707–708

Douglas, J Elizabeth (1980) *Supranational Schooling in a European Context With Special Reference to the European School* Research submitted for a Diploma in Education, Oxford University

Droppert, Alida Joan (1984) *A Study of Administrators', Teachers', and Parents' Perceptions of the Role of an International School Administrator* A dissertation, Michigan State University Department of Educational Administration and Curriculum PhD

Droppert, Alida J and Bale, Rupert M W (1985) International school administration: constraints and stresses *International Schools Journal* European Council of International Schools: Petersfield, England **10**, 45–56

Enloe, Walter (1985) From Hiroshima: the need for a global perspective in international education *International Schools Journal* European Council of International Schools: Petersfield, England **10**, 17–26

Foreman, Martha M (1983) Learning difficulties and the bilingual/multilingual international school student *International Schools Journal* European Council of International Schools: Petersfield, England **6**, 59–76

Fox, Elizabeth (1985) International schools and the International Baccalaureate *Harvard Educational Review* The President and Fellows of Harvard College: Cambridge, Massachusetts **55** (1), 53–68

Geller, Charles (1981) International education: some thoughts on what it is and what it might be *International Schools Journal* European Council of International Schools, Petersfield, England **1**, 21–26

Goodman, Dorothy B (1985) Transcending the national: unfinished agenda for international schools *International Schools Journal* European Council of International Schools: Petersfield, England **10**, 7–16

Hill, Ian (1990) IB development in Australia *International Schools Journal* European Council of International Schools: Petersfield, England **19**, 26–34

Jacobson, Gilbert (1986) International schools foster world-wide education *School Business Affairs* **52** (10), 56–59

Khalid, Mansour (1989) The greatest challenge, the greatest opportunity: preparing our children for

a common future *The International Schools Journal* European Council of International Schools: Petersfield, England **17**, 18–26
Knight, Michael and Leach, Robert (1964) International schools and courses *The Yearbook of Education 1964* Evans Brothers Limited: London, England
Liss, Kathryn (1984) A course in international communication in a multicultural classroom *International Schools Journal* Number Eight European Council of International Schools: Petersfield, England, 33–38
Lunn, R M C (1988) Problems and challenges in international schools *ECHA News* **3**(2/3), 9–10
Malpass, Derek (1987) ECIS accreditation: what it is and what it is not *International Schools Journal* European Council of International Schools: Petersfield, England **14**, 16–20
Mattern, Gray (1988) Meteorology and the international school: unsettled days ahead followed by brighter days – maybe *International Schools Journal* European Council of International Schools: Petersfield, England **16**, 7–14
Mathews, M (1979) The scale of international education: part one *International Schools Journal* European Council of International Schools: Petersfield, England **17**
Monn, Christine (Ed.) (1989) *Insights* International Schools Association: Geneva, Switzerland
Obura, Anna P (1985) The needs of Third World children in international schools away from home *The International Schools Journal* European Council of International Schools: Petersfield, England **9**, 17–30
Orr, Paul G and Conland, Amy L (1985) Overseas schools and international relations: perceptions of governance and leadership *The International Schools Journal* European Council of International Schools: Petersfield, England **9**, 55–60
Paterson, John (1984) Student teaching in international schools *International School Journal* European Council of International Schools: Petersfield, England **8**, 63–67
Ronsheim, Sally B (1970) Are International Schools Really International? *Phi Delta Kappan* **7** (2), 43–46
Sanderson, Joyce (1981) *International Schooling: The "Mobile" Pupil and His Educational Needs* MSc, Oxford University
Soedjatmoko (1984) Global crossroads: which way to the 21st century *International Schools Journal* European Council of International Schools: Petersfield, England **8**, 7–12
Steele, Rosalind (1984) Project to create a centre for international curriculum development *International Schools Journal* European Council of International Schools: Petersfield, England **8**, 23–32
Stobart, Maitland (1989) A new programme for a time of change *Forum* The Council of Europe: Strasbourg, France **38**
Terwilliger, Ronald I (1972) International schools cultural crossroads *The Educational Forum* West Lafayette, Indiana **36** (3), 359–363
Thomas, George H (1983) Here's a world class curriculum *The Executive Educator* **5** (12), 17
Wilcox, Alan (1989) An international school system? practising what we preach *International Schools Journal* European Council of International Schools: Petersfield, England **17**, 35–40
Williams, Shirley (1981) Education for international understanding *International Schools Journal* European Council of International Schools: Petersfield, England **1**, 7–14
Willis, David B (1984) A select bibliography on international schools *The International Schools Journal* The European Council of International Schools: Petersfield, England **7**, 59–67

Books and pamphlets

Beck, Robert Holmes (1971) *Change and Harmonization in European Education* University of Minnesota Press: Minneapolis, Minnesota
Bereday, George Z F and Lauwerys, Joseph A (eds) (1964) *The Year Book of Education 1964* Evans Brothers Limited: London, England
Deutsch, Steven E (1970) *International education and exchange: a sociological analysis* The Press of Case Western Reserve University: Cleveland, Ohio
Gordon, Enid and Jones, Morwenna (1988) *Portable Roots* Preses Interuniversitaires Europeennes: Maastricht, Holland
Henderson, James Lewis (1968) *Education for World Understanding* Pergamon Press Ltd: Oxford, England
Husten, Torsten and Postelthwaite, T Neville (Eds) (1985) *The International Encyclopedia of Education* Pergamon Press Ltd: Oxford, England

Knowles, ASA S (Ed) (1977) *The International Encyclopedia of Higher Education* Jossey-Bass Limited: London, England
Leach, Robert (1969) *International Schools and Their Role in the Field of International Education* Pergamon Press: Oxford, England
Mallinson, Vernon (1980) *The Western European Idea in Education* Pergamon Press Ltd: Oxford, England
Neave, Guy (1984) *The EEC and Education* Trentham Books: Stoke-on-Trent, England
Newcombe, Norman (1977) *Europe at School* Methuen and Co Ltd: London, England
Peterson, A D C (1972) *The International Baccalaureate: an experiment in international education* George C Harrup & Co Ltd: London, England
Peterson, A D C (1987) *Schools Across Frontiers* Open Court: LaSalle, Illinois
Scanlon, David G (Ed) (1960) *International Education* Teacher's College Columbia University: New York, New York
Schultze, Walter (1970) *Schools In Europe Volume III Part A* Verlag Julius Beltz: Federal Republic of Germany
Sharpes, Donald K (1988) *International Perspectives On Teacher Education* Routledge: London, England
Tysse, Agnes N (1974) *International Education: The American Experience, A Bibliography Volume I Dissertations and Theses* The Scarecrow Press Inc: Metuchen, New Jersey
Walker, David A (1976) *The IEA Six Subject Survey: an empirical study of education in twenty-one countries, International Studies in Evaluation IX* Almqvist and Wiskell International: Stockholm, Sweden.

Official and corporate publications

Banks, J A G (1977) *European Schools – The European Baccalaureate* Department of Education and Science: London, England
Belcher, John (1989) *Higher Education Market Survey: International Schools* Educational Counselling Service: The British Council: London, England
DES (1987) *Statistics of Education – Schools* London
Faure, Edgar (1972) *Learning To Be: The World of Education Today and Tomorrow* United Nations Education, Scientific, and Cultural Organization-Harrup: Paris, France
—— (1983) *A Nation of Risk: The Imperative for Educational Reform* Washington DC: The US Government Printing Office
—— (1987) *Guide to School Evaluation and Accreditation* The European Council of International Schools: Petersfield, England
—— (1989) *The International Schools Directory* European Council of International Schools: Petersfield, England
—— (1987) *A Short Guide to the International Baccalaureate* International Baccalaureate Office: Geneva, Switzerland
—— (1988) *United World Colleges Annual Report 1987/1988* L & T Press Ltd: London, England
HMSO (1987) *Scottish Statistics in Education* London
Wood, Richard, J (1989) The Earlham President's Report 1988–1989 *Earlham: To Fashion the Future* Earlham College, Richmond, Indiana

Related organizations

These organizations and institutions supply information, activities, and course work related to international living, international education, and international studies.

BRUSH
BRUSH UP
P J Arthern, Editor
Chemin du Panorama 3
B-5890 Bonlez, Belgium

Centre for Global Education
University of York
Heslington
York YO1 5DD
UK
Tel: (0904) 433444

Centre for International Studies
Meadowlea House
Litleham Road
Exmouth
Devon EX8 2QT, UK
Tel: (0395) 264902
Fax: (0395) 268031
Secretariat for: Council for International Education, European Development Education Curriculum Network; International Network on Global Education

Council of Europe
BP 431 R6
F-67006
Strasbourg, France
Tel: (33) 61 49 61
Telex: EUR 870 943F

East Midlands Regional Examination Board
Robins Wood House
Robins Wood Road
Aspley
Nottingham NG8 3NR, UK
Tel: (0602) 296021

European Council on High Ability (ECHA)
21 Montagu Square
London W1H 1RE, UK
Tel: (071) 486 2604

European Council of International Schools, Inc (ECIS)
21B Lavant Street
Petersfield
Hampshire GU32 3EL, UK
Tel: 44 (0) 730 68244/63131
Fax: 44 (0) 730 67914
Telex: 9312102171EC G
E-mail: 87: ECL001

European Journal of Special Needs Education
NFER-NELSON
Darville House
2 Oxford Road East
Windsor
Berkshire SL4 1DF
Tel: (0753) 858961
Fax: (0753) 856830

Global Education Network
6 Endsleigh Street
London WC1H 0DX, UK
Tel: (071) 3830693

Global Futures Project
Institute of Education
University of London
10 Woburn Square
London WC1H 0NS, UK
Tel: (071) 636 1500 ext 385

Initiative for Peace Studies in the University of London (IPSUL)
University of London
Institute of Education
28 Woburn Square
London WC1H 0AA, UK
Tel: (071) 636 8000 ext 4310
Fax: (071) 436 2186

International Baccalaureate Office (IBO)
15 route des Morillons
CH 1218 Grand Saconnex/Geneva
Switzerland
Tel: (41 22) 791 02 74
Fax: (41 22) 791 02 77

International Schools Association (ISA)
CIC CASE 20
CH 1211 Geneva 20
Switzerland
Tel: (41 22) 733 6717

Jordanhill College of Education
Overseas Programming Unit
Southbrae Drive
Glasgow G13 1PP, UK
Tel: (041) 959 1232
Fax: (041) 950 3268

Mark Goldstein Memorial Trust
University of London
Institute of Education
10 Woburn Square
London WC1H 0NS, UK
Tel: (071) 636 1500
Fax: (071) 436 2186

Surrey Library of Teaching Resources
6 Phoenice Cottages
Dorking Road
Bookham
Surrey KT23 4QG, UK
Tel: (0372) 56421

University of Cambridge Local Examination Syndicate (UCLES)
Publications Department
1 Hills Road
Cambridge CB1 2EU, UK
Tel: (44) 223 61111
Fax: (0223) 460278
Telex: 94012736 =SYND G

UNESCO Press
Commercial Services Division of the UNESCO Press
7 place de Fontenoy
75700 Paris
France
Tel: (1) 45 68 10 00
Telex: 034461 PARIS

United Nations Publications
Sales Section
Room DC2-853
New York, New York 10017
Tel: (212) 9638302

United World Colleges (UWC)
London House
Mecklenburgh Square
London WC1N 2AB, UK
Tel: (071) 833 2626
Fax: (071) 837 3102
Telex: 296459 UWCLON G

World Wide Fund for Nature International
CH 1196 Gland
Switzerland
Tel: (022) 64 91 11
Fax: (022) 64 42 38
Telex: 419 618 wwf ch

Index